MW01166874

THE COMPLETE IDIOT'S GUIDE TO

Budgeting for Your Wedding

by Sue Winner

alpha books

Macmillan USA, Inc.
201 West 103rd Street
Indianapolis, IN 46290

A Pearson Education Company

To Michael, David, Jeffrey, Amy, and Matthew, who make me want to be able to do it all! And to my wonderful Jonathan, who has helped me believe that I can!

Copyright © 2000 by Sue Winner

All rights reserved. No part of this book shall be reproduced, stored in a retrieval system, or transmitted by any means, electronic, mechanical, photocopying, recording, or otherwise, without written permission from the publisher. No patent liability is assumed with respect to the use of the information contained herein. Although every precaution has been taken in the preparation of this book, the publisher and author assume no responsibility for errors or omissions. Neither is any liability assumed for damages resulting from the use of information contained herein. For information, address Alpha Books, 201 West 103rd Street, Indianapolis, IN 46290.

THE COMPLETE IDIOT'S GUIDE TO and Design are registered trademarks of Macmillan USA, Inc.

International Standard Book Number: 0-02-863366-0
Library of Congress Catalog Card Number: A catalog record is available from the Library of Congress.

02 01 00 8 7 6 5 4 3 2 1

Interpretation of the printing code: The rightmost number of the first series of numbers is the year of the book's printing; the rightmost number of the second series of numbers is the number of the book's printing. For example, a printing code of 00-1 shows that the first printing occurred in 2000.

Printed in the United States of America

Note: This publication contains the opinions and ideas of its author. It is intended to provide helpful and informative material on the subject matter covered. It is sold with the understanding that the author and publisher are not engaged in rendering professional services in the book. If the reader requires personal assistance or advice, a competent professional should be consulted.

The author and publisher specifically disclaim any responsibility for any liability, loss or risk, personal or otherwise, which is incurred as a consequence, directly or indirectly, of the use and application of any of the contents of this book.

The authors and publisher specifically disclaim any responsibility for any liability, loss or risk, personal or otherwise, which is incurred as a consequence, directly or indirectly, of the use and application of any of the contents of this book.

Publisher
Marie Butler-Knight

Editorial Director
Gary M. Krebs

Product Manager
Phil Kitchel

Associate Managing Editor
Cari Luna

Acquisitions Editor
Randy Ladenheim-Gil

Development Editor
Lynn Northrup

Production Editor
Mike Thomas

Copy Editor
Susan Aufheimer

Illustrator
Brian Mac Moyer

Cover Designers
Mike Freeland
Kevin Spear

Book Designers
Scott Cook and Amy Adams of DesignLab

Indexer
Lisa Lawrence

Layout/Proofreading
Darin Crone
Terri Edwards
Mary Hunt
Donna Martin
Mike Poor

Contents at a Glance

Contents

Foreword

This book begins with a simple statement: "Weddings today aren't exactly what they used to be." That has been true for almost every generation in recent memory.

Despite this, two things remain constant.

First, all you need to get married are the two of you—and a witness (it helps if the witness has the legal or religious authority to be one, rather than just one of your buddies).

The second thing is much more important and goes to the heart of this guide. We often hear it hyped that your wedding day is "the most important day of your life." If that were true, *everything* that follows (including your wedding night and the birth of your first child) is less important. Let's get a grip on reality.

Your wedding *is* important and a very special day. But what is truly important is your commitment to each other—and that is free. All the rest, all the fun, music, favors, photos, food, dancing, clothes, all the decisions that seem so important when you are planning the event—they are of little importance compared with your public declaration of your love for and commitment to each other.

This is an outstanding book that puts it all in perspective. You can have a grand time on your wedding day without putting yourself in debt for the first ten years of your marriage. Your dad doesn't have to mortgage the house. Your little brother doesn't have to eat peanut butter sandwiches for a year to help the family save.

It's your special day. Don't think you have to do what all your friends did or what the bridal magazines say you should do. Do what is important to you.

It's all a matter of priorities. Keep that in mind as you let Sue Winner help you turn your dreams into reality within the reality of a budget.

Sue has been a member of the Association of Bridal Consultants since 1986 and frequently participates in and presents at conferences. She has served as the Association's Georgia state coordinator since 1994. And she is a Master Bridal Consultant, one of 16 in the world.

Sue knows what she is writing about. Pay attention. Keep your priorities straight and have a blast planning the wedding.

Gerard J. Monaghan
President
Association of Bridal Consultants
New Milford, Connecticut

Introduction

For over 15 years, my goal as a bridal consultant has been to help hundreds of brides and grooms enjoy the wedding of their dreams, regardless of their budget. "Is this possible?" you ask. You bet it is! Managing your dollars and "sense" abilities throughout this process is both achievable and fun.

I wrote *The Complete Idiot's Guide to Budgeting for Your Wedding* to help you through the complicated maze of orchestrating your own wedding. With the helpful information in this book, you can take charge of your imagination and plan a wedding that everyone, including you and your mate, will be delighted to attend. It will be beautiful and meaningful—a real celebration.

How do you accomplish all this on a budget? How can you afford to make your dreams come true without going broke? How do you plan one of the most memorable days in your life while holding down a full time job? How can you avoid the stress most brides complain about? These questions and many you have not even thought to ask will be answered in the pages of this book.

Why is planning a wedding so difficult? It's not! Some brides think it is only because they neglect the basics—diving into the process without doing the simplest research; signing contracts without reading them; and making emotional decisions before considering their options. It doesn't take long before the bride feels overwhelmed, exhausted, and stressed. The fun is gone, and both she and the groom wish they had eloped! But this can be the *happiest* time of your life! Planning a beautiful, romantic celebration and knowing that you can truly afford it is a perfect way to start your life together. I know you will find the suggestions and tips in this book helpful. You'll have to do your part, too, but together we can create your dreams—and you'll still have money in your pocket the morning after.

As you go through the planning process you'll see many beautiful things, and, if you're like most brides, you'll want them *all*. While it won't be possible for you to purchase everything you see and still stay on your budget, by using the principles in this book you should be able to create a beautiful wedding on your realistic budget. Wedding budgets are like household or corporation budgets: They list all the expected expenses and allow you to plan for them in advance. However, they're *unlike* other budgets, because the goal is *not to exceed* your budget, not come in *under budget*. In other words, you're not trying to *save* money—you're trying to spend it wisely.

How to Use This Book

Before you start spending money, read this book all the way through and highlight those items that you will want to refer to. You'll begin to understand the wedding industry, and this understanding will help you determine the kind of wedding you really want. If you know what's most important to you, you'll also find out what you *don't* want, what you *might* want to include, and what you don't *have* to include. Since the whole point is saving money, the more you know, the more you will be able to save.

Part 1, "Budgeting Basics," gives you an overview of wedding budgeting and the things you will need to consider as you begin creating a budget you can live with for your wedding.

Part 2, "Creating a Budget," talks about *everything* you could possibly spend money on for your wedding and how to create a budget. Here you'll find the ultimate budget worksheet.

Part 3, "Sticking to Your Budget," brings you help in deciding how to spend your money. Planning a wedding is like standing in a candy store with a nickel in your hand while all the candy seems to cost a dime. You want it all, but need some help getting it with the money you have.

Part 4, "Reception Details," helps you look at all the details of your reception and decide where you can most easily control the money you spend.

Part 5, "The Honeymoon," looks at this romantic getaway and how you can plan a trip as short as two nights or as long as two months and make sure your memories will last a lifetime.

In addition, you'll find five appendixes with helpful information ranging from a glossary of wedding attire terms, to a discussion of Weddinginsurance, a list of more resources for budget and wedding planning, an example of a complete wedding budget, and finally a list of Master bridal consultants.

Extra Features

Throughout this book you'll find special information boxes to help you. These boxes explain unfamiliar terms, give you tips and money-saving ideas, share interesting stories and historical information, and alert you to any pitfalls as you make your wedding plans.

Wedding Blues

Check these boxes for warnings and explanations of things that might create problems for you.

Sue's Suggestions

In these boxes you'll find tips and ideas that will help you save time and money.

Language of Love

These boxes clue you in to the lingo of the wedding industry. When you can speak your vendor's language, you'll have a much easier time communicating!

Tantalizing Trivia

These boxes share enjoyable stories and historical information about weddings.

Acknowledgments

Special thanks to these members to the Association of Bridal Consultants: Lois Pearce, Master Bridal Consultant, Connecticut State Coordinator, Beautiful Occasions, Hamden, Connecticut (203-248-2661); Mimi Doke, Master Bridal Consultant, Arizona State Coordinator, The Wedding Specialist, Lake Havasu City, Arizona (520-453-6000); Frank Andonoplas, Illinois State Coordinator, Bridal Consulting & Event Planning by Frank, Chicago, Illinois (773-275-6804); and Jean Picard, Accredited Bridal Consultant, California State Coordinator, Jean Picard Wedding Consulting, Santa Barbara and Ventura, California (803-642-3201).

Special Thanks to the Technical Reviewer

The Complete Idiot's Guide to Budgeting for Your Wedding was reviewed by an expert who double-checked the accuracy of what you'll learn here, to help us ensure that this book gives you everything you need to know about planning for the most important day of your life—without going broke in the process. Special thanks are extended to Mary Kelley.

Mary Kelley has been working in the wedding and special events industry since 1974. She is author of *The Resource Directory*, a directory of wedding suppliers to the trade; and *The Bridal Show—A Planner's Guide*, a guide to planning, producing, and participating as a vendor in bridal trade shows. Ms. Kelley is Director of Retail Services for the Association of Bridal Consultants, the only international trade organization devoted solely to the wedding industry.

Ms. Kelley holds the titles of Certified Special Event Professional (one of approximately 80 in the world) through the International Special Events Society, and Master Bridal Consultant (one of approximately 50 in the world) through the Association of Bridal Consultants. She is currently Special Events Manager at High Prairie Farms Equestrian Events Center in Parker, Colorado.

Trademarks

All terms mentioned in this book that are known to be or are suspected of being trademarks or service marks have been appropriately capitalized. Alpha Books and Macmillan USA, Inc. cannot attest to the accuracy of this information. Use of a term in this book should not be regarded as affecting the validity of any trademark or service mark.

Part 1
Budgeting Basics

Weddings today aren't exactly what they used to be. A generation ago weddings were hosted by the bride's family, and as hosts, they made all the decisions about what form this celebration would take and how much it would cost. Increasingly brides and grooms are planning and paying for their weddings themselves. If you are one of these couples and want to have a wonderful wedding but don't want to spend your entire savings on it, this book is for you! A realistic and carefully planned budget is the road map of your wedding. It will help you stay on course and prevent you from making any wrong turns and getting lost in costly mistakes along the way.

Chapter 1

The Changing Face of Marriage

> **In This Chapter**
>
> ➤ Marriage the way it used to be
>
> ➤ How weddings have changed over the years
>
> ➤ Who pays for what: a checklist
>
> ➤ How much money do you want to spend?

Weddings today aren't exactly what they used to be. A generation ago weddings were hosted by the bride's family, and as hosts, they made all the decisions about what form this celebration would take and how much it would cost. Increasingly, the bride and groom are planning and paying for their wedding themselves. If you're one of these couples and want to have a wonderful wedding but don't want to spend your entire savings on it, this book is for you! A realistic and carefully planned budget is the road map of your wedding. It will help you stay on course and prevent you from making any wrong turns and getting lost in costly mistakes along the way.

Planning a wedding really requires the careful use of two budgets. Your first budget is the written plan listing everything you'll need and the approximate amount each item will cost. As you work through your wedding plans, you'll probably adjust this budget, spending slightly more on one item and less on another, so that the bottom line—the total—remains relatively the same.

The second budget concerns your time. Whether you're a full-time student or a career woman, it's a pretty safe bet your days and nights are already full. Finding a way to interview vendors, choose the clothes, flowers, music, and maintain a loving relationship with your Prince Charming will require some fancy footwork and careful scheduling. With a little planning and the tips in this book, you can have the wedding of your dreams and not come up broke in the process. So let's get started!

Marriage in the Old Days

In today's society we no longer think of women as commodities or acknowledge that fathers have to pay young men to marry their daughters. However, in the nineteenth century in a society where women could not own property, fathers provided the best *dowry* they could afford in hopes of attracting the best possible mate for their daughters. The dowry was intended to give the couple a start in their lives, and fathers saw it not so much as buying mates for their daughters but as protecting her future.

In those days when most people lived on farms and worked the land to survive, the dowry might have included a few acres of land, perhaps a few chickens and a cow. In that way the father made sure his daughter and her new husband would be able to support themselves. He provided them with land on which to plant some vegetables and gave them eggs, poultry, and milk—things they could both use themselves or trade for items they could not produce. Sometimes the family even helped the groom build a house on the property.

Language of Love

A **dowry** was the money, goods, or estate that a woman brought to her husband in marriage.

The preparation for a young girl's marriage often began very early in her life. Her mother would collect feathers from the chickens and geese on the farm to make a featherbed in anticipation of her daughter's eventual marriage. Very young women learned to cook and practiced their sewing skills by making linens to be used in their future homes. Even into the middle of the twentieth century it was not uncommon for young women to have hope chests in which they stored the items they had made in preparation for their married life.

From the middle ages until modern times, young men were often shepherds and moved from place to place as they tended their flocks. When the time came for a young man to take a wife he would go into the nearest village and ask which of the families had eligible daughters. Negotiations then began between the young man and the girl's father until an equitable settlement was reached and a date for the wedding was set. The couple did not meet until the wedding, and love as we know it today did not figure into the equation.

Tantalizing Trivia

Superstition tells us that it's bad luck for the groom to see the bride before the ceremony but what is the bad luck and where does this belief come from? In very ancient days, young men wandered the countryside tending their flocks. When the time came for a young man to marry he would enter the nearest village and ask which of the families had daughters of marrying age. The young men would strike a deal with the girl's father—so many sheep for his daughter's hand in marriage. If the future groom saw the bride before the wedding day and found her unattractive, he would leave town, taking his sheep with him.

Times Change and So Does Marriage

Nearly every wedding planning book you open today gives you a list of the items traditionally paid for by the bride and her family, the groom and his family, the bridesmaids, and the groomsmen. These lists vary slightly from book to book, but most of them follow the scenario that has been accepted behavior for generations. Usually the bride's family paid for most of the wedding, just as in most cultures the bride's family provided the dowry. As times changed and the world became more industrialized, families moved into the city and fathers no longer owned property that they could give to their future son-in-laws to help provide for their daughters.

Just how has the institution of marriage changed over the years? Let's take a look.

The Roaring Twenties

Early in the twentieth century around the time of the World War I, men and women began to work together and date; slowly the concept of marriage for love began to emerge. Young people began to select their own mates and no longer wanted their parents to arrange their marriages. When the bride's family was pleased with her choice of a mate, they wanted to celebrate her marriage and began paying for this celebration rather than providing the dowry common in the previous century. The country was prosperous and big city weddings became elaborate affairs with long gowns, seated dinners, and magnificent floral arrangements. They didn't serve champagne since prohibition was in effect, but "bathtub gin" was probably readily available.

The crash of the stock market in the fall of 1929 did not immediately affect the average family since they were not heavily involved in stocks. However, by the early 1930s they were seeing the effects on their daily lives, and weddings changed to reflect the limited funds available. Brides wore borrowed gowns and if there was a wedding ceremony at all, the guest list was usually limited to the couple's immediate family. The most elaborate weddings might have served cake and punch but seldom much else.

This was a very formal wedding in 1923—notice the bride's headpiece and very long veil. Notice also the elaborate floral bouquet that must have weighed a ton! The groom is wearing a tuxedo and white gloves for the ceremony.
(Photo from the author's collection)

The Depression and War Years

Couples continued to marry even as the Depression continued, but ceremonies were very simple. The couple would go into the clergyman's study or the magistrate's office to exchange vows, and only their witnesses would be present. The bride might have worn her favorite dress or suit, but she seldom purchased something new for the occasion. After the wedding the newlyweds moved in with one set of parents until they could afford their own apartment. At a time when a man considered himself lucky to earn $18 a week, moving into their own apartment was simply not an option for most couples.

In this photo from 1930, the Depression had just begun but people were attempting to celebrate weddings anyway. This bride and groom both wore borrowed clothing and were photographed in the photographer's studio. There was no bridal party. (Photo from the author's collection)

This pre-World War II couple was married at home in 1938. She wore a new dress and a small corsage, with no head-piece at all. He's wearing his newest suit, but no flowers. Immediate family only attended this wedding.
(Photo from the author's collection)

During World War II as young men went off to fight, many got married before they left. These marriages took place in the office of the justice of the peace and frequently his secretary was the witness and the only other person there. In the summer of 1940 so many young couples applied for marriage licenses that there was talk of closing the license bureau in some cities. Some larger weddings did take place, but since so many young men were in the service and not able to get home to attend the celebration, bridal parties consisted of bridesmaids but no groomsmen or ushers.

The effects of the depression had reached Charleston, South Carolina, when Sylvia and Louie decided to marry in late 1933. The ceremony was held in Sylvia's parent's living room and she wore a blue dress. The couple honeymooned in New York City, where they saw a sign advertising wedding photos. The photographer loaned them wedding attire and handed Sylvia a bouquet of paper flowers. (Photo from the collection of Eileen Wolper Joseph. Reprinted with permission)

Many marriages also took place after the war ended and the soldiers came home. There was little thought to flowers, gowns, or music. Couples simply wanted to be together after their long separation. Some couples were married in their clergymen's office; others went to the courthouse and were married by a justice of the peace or a magistrate. Everyone was eager to get to work rebuilding America. America entered a period of prosperity. Suburbia and suburban living was born and so were many, many babies!

In this 1940 photo of the author's parents, the Depression is over and elaborate flowers are back. This bride borrowed her gown and headpiece, but the groom rented his tuxedo. The wedding was held in a restaurant and dinner was served to the guests.
(Photo from the author's collection)

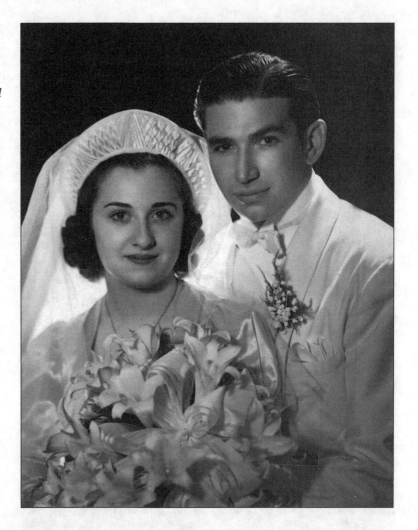

The Fabulous Fifties

Prosperity and growth continued during the fifties. Weddings reflected this feeling of well-being and began to be quite elaborate again. Brides began choosing new gowns and several of the gown manufacturers that we know of today opened their doors during this time. Bridal parties included groomsmen and ushers as well as bridesmaids. Wedding celebrations often included a dinner dance and it was not uncommon to have elaborate floral arrangements for centerpieces or dance bands to entertain the guests. Weddings were planned and paid for by the bride's family; the groom's family hosted a dinner after the rehearsal the night before the wedding. Couples frequently came from the same community and the majority of their guests lived close by, so little thought was given to special entertainment for the limited number of out-of-town guests.

Tantalizing Trivia

During the Depression, most couples married after high school graduation since few went on to college. Brides were generally 17 years old and grooms were 18. During the '60s as more young people began going away to college and meeting their partners on campus, the average age of brides jumped to 22 and grooms to 24, allowing the bride to complete her education and the groom to get started in his career before getting married. As women began concentrating on creating their own careers before marrying, the average age of the bride rose to 27.3 years old and the average age of the groom to 29 years old.

By 1950, big weddings were back! (Photo from the author's collection)

The '60s, '70s, and '80s

In the last part of the twentieth century, weddings began to change again. In the sixties many couples graduated from college, got jobs, and got married. They were so busy graduating and getting started in their jobs that they had no time to plan the wedding. They never questioned the fact that the bride's mother planned the wedding and her father paid for it. During this period, it became more and more common to marry someone you had met while away at school, so the couple's parents didn't know one another and no one even considered that they would share the expenses of the wedding. The oil embargo of the seventies and the inflation of the eighties created an economic downturn. Jobs were difficult to get and sometimes even harder to keep and many couples did not feel financially secure enough to consider getting married.

At the same time, there was another major change in American society. Unmarried couples began living together. The sexual revolution took the urgency out of the rush to get married. A couple could live together until they felt financially secure enough to start a family and then get married. Some couples even decided to have a family without getting married!

Toward the New Millennium

Today, couples have become secure in their careers. They have their own incomes and want their weddings to reflect their lifestyles. Often they've been living independently for several years and are earning salaries far beyond their expectations. Since couples are marrying later, they may have already established sizable savings accounts and may even own their homes or be in the process of buying homes as part of planning their weddings. Their ideas of a perfect wedding may, in fact, be quite different from their parents and couples may want to assume a major role in planning and paying for their celebration.

One thing has not changed from the very beginning: The bride and groom still have no real experience hosting a major event, and they have limited experience creating and following a budget. And that's exactly why I wrote this book!

Language of Love

A **trousseau** refers to the clothes and general outfitting of a bride prepared at her own or her family's expense. A **paper trousseau** refers to the different types of stationery considered proper for a woman's social correspondence.

Who Pays for What?

In the middle of the twentieth century, as wedding celebrations became more elaborate, the bride's parents continued to assume the role of host and hostess and provide those things that would start their daughter off in her new married life. This included providing her with a *trousseau*, a wardrobe of clothing for the wedding itself, and the proper attire for her new life and position as a married woman in the community.

There are still a few things that are universal. It really doesn't matter how long the couple has been dating or how long they've been talking about getting married; as soon as the engagement becomes official, every mother starts a diet and every father begins staring at his checkbook as if the figures are written in some foreign language!

The bride's parents were responsible for providing the services of the bridal consultant. (See Chapter 4, "Getting Ready for the Big Day: Wedding Essentials.") Her parents purchased the invitations, announcements, and postage for the wedding, and provided the stationery necessary to complete the bride's *paper trousseau*. This included the informal notes on which the bride would write her thank-you notes with either her new name or monogram engraved on them; calling cards; and stationery in her new name. In the late nineteenth and early twentieth century it was very important to use the correct stationery for all your correspondence, and people paid particular attention to selecting what was fashionable and expected by others.

Sue's Suggestions

Weddings are supposed to be fun, and planning them should be the most fun of all. Keep smiling and you can enjoy this process!

The bride's parents also paid for the photography and videography, the music for both the ceremony and the reception, and transportation from the ceremony to the reception for the bride and groom and the entire bridal party. They were responsible for all the expenses of the reception: food, beverages, rental fees, custodial charges, cake, favors, and flowers. Naturally, they were responsible for their own clothing, transportation, and lodging as well.

The bride provided gifts for her own attendants and a wedding gift for the groom. She was responsible for paying for her own blood test, if one was required in her state to obtain a marriage license. If the couple had decided to each wear a ring, she paid for the ring she would give to the groom during the double-ring wedding ceremony.

Sue's Suggestions

Every bride knows what she wants to do to personalize her wedding celebration, so plan for it. If there's something you want to include in your wedding that is "over the top," be prepared to pick up the tab yourself.

The groom's family was responsible for their own transportation to the city where the wedding was being held and for the expenses connected with their stay, which might include their accommodations and car rental. They were responsible for the expenses related to their own clothing for the ceremony. Customarily they were the host and hostess of the rehearsal or prenuptial dinner and assumed all the expenses related to that event, from invitations to transportation of the guests. Traditionally, either the groom or his parents paid the clergyman's fee. While the bride's family selected and paid for flowers for the ceremony and the reception, the groom or his family was responsible for certain floral items. These included the bride's bouquet, the mothers' and grandmothers' corsages, and the fathers' and groomsmen's boutonnieres. (I'll tell you all about budgeting for flowers in Chapter 7, "A Rose By Any Other Name.")

Sue's Suggestions

In a time when women have great careers, it's no longer true that the groom is responsible for the honeymoon and all the expenses thereafter. Marriage today is more of a partnership than ever before, both during and after the wedding.

Wedding Blues

No one should be expected to spend more money on a wedding than they can comfortably afford. If the bride's parents can't pay for everything the couple wants, the couple should be willing to either pay for some items themselves or adjust their plans accordingly.

The groom was responsible for the bride's engagement ring and for her wedding band. He paid for his own blood tests, if they were necessary to obtain a marriage license in the state, and he was responsible for the fees associated with obtaining that license. He also purchased a gift for the bride and gifts for all his attendants. The groom was also traditionally responsible for the expenses of the honeymoon … and for all the couple's expenses thereafter!

While being invited to be a bridesmaid or groomsman in a wedding is a wonderful honor, it does carry with it some financial responsibilities. Bridesmaids are responsible for purchasing the dress and shoes the bride selects for them to wear for the ceremony. They provide their own transportation to and from the city of the wedding and, if necessary, their own hotel accommodations. Bridesmaids often host a party in honor of the bride and usually cohost the bachelorette party with the bride as their guest. In addition, each bridesmaid gives a wedding gift to the couple. It can be very expensive to be a bridesmaid in a friend's wedding. Groomsmen have the same financial responsibilities except that they do not have to purchase their clothing, but merely rent it. Because of these financial obligations, bridesmaids and groomsmen should be made to feel comfortable telling the bride and groom if they aren't financially able to be part of the wedding.

Most wedding planning books list the financial responsibilities of the people involved in the wedding as a starting point, understanding that this scenario is not appropriate for all families or all weddings. The following checklist is a common breakdown and a good one—if it works for your situation.

The Bride's Parents:

- ❏ Ceremony site rental
- ❏ Reception site rental
- ❏ All food and beverages served at the reception
- ❏ Flowers (except for those assigned to the groom or his family)
- ❏ Bridesmaids' bouquets, aisle runner, decorations (including a chuppah, if necessary)

- ❏ Both wedding cake and groom's cake (if one is used)
- ❏ Photography (including an album for the bride and groom and for themselves)
- ❏ Videography (including a tape for the bride and groom and for themselves)
- ❏ Bride's wedding day attire and trousseau (including her paper trousseau)
- ❏ Music for the ceremony and reception
- ❏ Wedding invitations and announcements, including postage
- ❏ Taxes and tips on the items they're responsible for
- ❏ Transportation of the bridal party from the ceremony to the reception
- ❏ Their own clothing (and lodging, if necessary)
- ❏ Their own transportation (if the wedding will not be in their home town)
- ❏ Gift to the bride and groom

The Bride:

- ❏ Her blood test
- ❏ The groom's wedding band
- ❏ Bridesmaids' gifts
- ❏ Bridesmaids' luncheon (optional)

At one time, the bride or her family was responsible for the accommodations of the out-of-town bridesmaids. This is no longer considered necessary. However, if one or more of the bridesmaids will have difficulty affording hotel accommodations, it's appropriate for the bride or her family to arrange for them to stay with a local friend.

The Groom's Parents:

- ❏ Host the rehearsal/prenuptial/groom's dinner the night before the wedding
- ❏ Transportation to the rehearsal dinner for out-of-town guests if deemed necessary
- ❏ Flowers (unless paid for by the groom; for a list of flowers, see *The Groom* following)
- ❏ Their transportation to the city where the wedding will be held
- ❏ Their lodging if the wedding is not in their home town
- ❏ Their own wedding clothing
- ❏ Gift to the bride and groom

The Groom:

- ❏ The engagement ring and wedding band for the bride
- ❏ His blood test

❑ The marriage license

❑ Flowers (including the bride's bouquet; corsages for the mothers and grand-mothers; boutonnieres for all male members of the bridal party)

❑ Gifts for his attendants

❑ Fee for the ceremony officiant

At one time, the groom or his family was responsible for the accommodations of out-of-town groomsmen and/or ushers. This is no longer considered their responsibility; however, if this will create a hardship for a member of the wedding party, it's appropriate for the groom to arrange for this groomsman to stay with local friends or family.)

The Bridesmaids and Groomsmen:

❑ Their wedding gifts to the bride and groom

❑ Their own clothing for the ceremony

❑ Their own transportation to the city of the wedding

❑ The bachelor party (usually hosted jointly by the groomsman, with the groom as their guest) or the bachelorette party (usually hosted jointly by the brides-maids with the bride as their guest)

Determining How Much Money to Spend

Before even beginning to organize the budget, it's helpful if the couple determines how much money they have to spend on the wedding and reception. In addition to determining how much of their savings account they want to invest, they need to have a conversation with their parents to find out what role their parents would like to play. It's possible that one or both sets of parents have been planning to pay for the whole event and will be willing to assist the couple with the finances or do some of the work. Planning a wedding is a big job so the couple will probably want to accept whatever assistance is offered to them.

If their parents are no longer married to each other it may be necessary to have a conversation with their parents separately. The couple may discover that everyone wants to make a contribution to this celebration. Perhaps the bride's father wants to be responsible for the open bar and her grandmother wants to purchase the wedding gown while her mother wants to accept responsibility for the invitations and flowers. Whatever portions of the wedding they accept responsibility for will free the couple's funds for other expenditures—and will give them more time to plan the other elements of the wedding.

Whether their parents are contributing financially to the wedding or not, the couple can assume that their parents may have some very good ideas about what works well and what doesn't. There are brides who want their weddings to be different from their friends' weddings just for the sake of being different. This is not usually the best plan. People do things a certain way because it works—because guests are comfortable and the event runs smoothly. Your wedding day is not the best time to try to re-invent the wheel; so while it can be fun to be creative and put your own stamp on the celebration, be careful not to get carried away.

Sometimes the groom's family wants to contribute to the financial end of the wedding. Whether the couple knows this or not, they should include the groom's family in these early conversations for several reasons. The groom may be the only son in a large family and his parents may want to do the same things for their son that they've done for their daughters. They may want to pay for a part of their son's wedding, just as they paid for their daughters' weddings. If this is their motivation, they may be willing to give the host and hostess of the wedding a sum of money to represent their participation in the event. This no-strings-attached contribution would certainly be appreciated by the bride's parents, if they're hosting, or by the couple themselves, if they're giving the wedding. Perhaps the parents of the groom want to make a more specific contribution; for instance, they may wish to pay for the band or the bar or both.

It's appropriate for the groom's family to make the first overture if they wish to participate financially in the wedding. According to etiquette experts, the groom's family should offer financial help to the host (whether this is the bride's family or the couple themselves). If this offer is rejected, the groom's family should not mention it again, nor should the hosts change their minds and ask for help. For this reason, the best answer for the host to give is one that leaves the door open to financial participation, such as, "Thank you for your offer. We'll get back to you when we've done some research and know what things will cost, and you can tell us specifically how you would like to be involved."

These contributions, while welcome, carry a different kind of message and have to be viewed in light

Sue's Suggestions

Be sensitive to what your parents say when you discuss your wedding plans with them. You might have known all along that you met Mr. Right and your relationship was moving toward wedding bells, but this news may come as a surprise to your parents. Let them get used to the idea before they start writing any checks!

Sue's Suggestions

When many people contribute to the wedding financially, it's easier if the couple opens a separate wedding checking account into which all the money is deposited. All payments of wedding expenses can be made from this account so there is a clear record of expenses.

of this message. For instance, if the groom's parents are paying for the band, they get to select the band. Hopefully they will make their selection in consultation with the bride and groom and the host and hostess of the event so the band's style will fit in with the overall feeling of the wedding. Hopefully, by giving the funds for the band directly to the host and hostess, the groom's parents will allow the hosts to actually write the check that pays the band. This helps the band become a part of the wedding team and doesn't confuse them with too many masters to please.

Tantalizing Trivia

Vendors find it impossible to please everyone at a wedding, so they concentrate on pleasing their client, the person who signs their check. This presented a problem for one family, where the groom's parents paid the band. The father of the groom was invited by the band to make a toast and the mother of the groom read a poem. The father of the bride, however, was not invited to the microphone to welcome the guests or toast his daughter's marriage. He was not even invited to dance with his daughter for the traditional father-daughter dance and he was the host of the event!

Who pays for the various parts of the wedding can vary from region to region. In some communities, it's expected that the groom's family will play certain roles in the funding of the wedding. In one community, for instance, the groom's family is responsible for FLOP:

➤ Flowers

➤ Liquor

➤ Orchestra

➤ Pearls

Naturally, they should be allowed to select the things that they pay for. While this can certainly ease the difficulty of paying for the wedding, it does take control of the wedding out of the hands of the host and hostess and puts it into the hands of a larger group of people. While this can be a good idea, the result can also have an uncoordinated effect on the wedding day.

In another region of the country, the groom's parents are expected to pay for the band and the bar. As couples meet and marry people from different areas of the country, these regional customs can sometimes create confusion. The groom's family coming from one location may think they're expected to provide certain items and may be planning to do so, only to discover that the bride's family, coming from a different region, are expecting something else entirely.

Good, open communication is always the best way to deal with financial matters, though some people are not comfortable doing so. If the bride and groom can help create an atmosphere where each set of parents feels comfortable contributing whatever they feel they can afford, without feeling that they're not measuring up to the couple's expectations, the total budget can be determined more quickly and with less hard feelings.

One mother of the groom got herself into some real trouble in this area. The bride and groom planned to use their entire savings account of $5,000 to finance their wedding. They were concerned that this amount would not cover the number of guests they hoped to include in their celebration and shared this information with the groom's mother. She was concerned that depleting their savings in this way would leave them unable to handle the other costs of starting their marriage, but instead of saying that, she offered to pay for half the wedding. The bride and groom misinterpreted her offer and assumed they now had enough money for a $10,000 wedding, instead of $5,000 for the wedding and $2,500 to remain in their savings account. Had the mother offered $2,500 instead of half the wedding, everything would have been much clearer.

Then there is the issue of the guest list. Once the host and hostess of the wedding have done enough research to have an idea what the event will cost per person, they will determine how many guests each family can invite to the wedding. It may work out that of the total 200 guests invited, 60 would be guests of the bride's family; 60 would be guests of the groom's family; and 80 would be guests of the bride and groom. One family may need to invite more people than they're allocated. If, for instance, the bride and groom are paying for the wedding and her parents want to invite more than the 60 people they've been allot-

Wedding Blues

When it comes to weddings, expect the golden rule: The guy with the gold will rule. But to avoid any hard feelings, whoever is paying for the event should consult the bride and groom before final decisions are made.

ted, they can offer to pay for the additional guests. However, if the couple has settled on a certain number of guests because they want to host an intimate wedding, they have the right to refuse this offer and ask her parents to cut their list to the 60 people they've been assigned.

The same thing would be true if the couple selected a facility that can accommodate only the number of people the couple wanted. However, if they selected this number simply on the basis of their budget, they may be willing to accept the additional guest list with the additional funds coming from the bride's parents. When the bride's family is permitted to invite the additional guests, they should be prepared to write a

Wedding Blues

No one has the right to make the host and hostess, whoever they are, spend more money on an event than they're comfortable with, so it's important to be honest with one another when planning the guest list.

check to the groom covering the total expenses for each guest, above the 60 originally assigned. This check should be given to the host at least a week before the wedding so he or she will not be without the funds to pay for the event as bills become due.

There may be some very lucky couples out there who have other family members or friends who want to help sponsor the wedding or parts of it. The bride's grandmother may want to buy her wedding gown. Either the bride or groom may have a family member or friend who would like to provide services for the wedding at greatly reduced fees, or even for free. Perhaps there is an uncle who is a bandleader and will ask his band to play the event at a reduced fee or as a wedding gift. Whatever offers you receive will certainly affect your bottom line.

The Least You Need to Know

➤ Years ago, fathers provided the best dowry they could afford to attract the best possible mate for their daughters.

➤ The giving of dowries eventually evolved into the bride's family paying for all aspects of the wedding.

➤ Weddings have changed throughout this past century.

➤ Some weddings are still paid for by the bride's family, but often with the help of the groom's family or other family members.

➤ Increasingly, brides and grooms are contributing to their own weddings, sometimes completely on their own, sometimes with additional help from family members.

Is Doing It Yourself an Option?

Once you begin planning your wedding, everyone you meet will step forward to give you advice. Since one of the major challenges of planning a wedding is keeping it within your budget, you may find that most of the advice is in the area of saving money. That doesn't mean that it's *good* advice! Listen, certainly, but educate yourself. Will that idea really work? What might happen? Is there a way to take this suggestion, and with a little thought and planning on your part, head off the disaster that seems to be lurking just around the bend?

In this chapter I'll share some of those *good* ideas, along with the problems that they brought some brides. I'll also give you suggestions for avoiding those problems, so you can do it yourself without doing yourself in.

Preparing Your Own Food for the Reception

Since food costs are usually the largest part of the reception expenses, many people believe that if you provide your own food, you will be saving a lot of money. Those same people don't consider the additional expenses related to the cost of the food.

There is much more involved than just preparing your own food. The chef needs the space and the cooking utensils to prepare food for a large number of people. There needs to be storage space—both refrigerator and freezer space—to keep the food until it's ready to be served. Then there needs to be a crew of people who will be responsible for putting the food on the trays and then on the table. Keeping the food hot or cold and the trays full and attractive is quite a lot to think about if you also happen to be the bride!

Cooking for a Crowd

If you love to cook and can plan a menu that can be made ahead, preparing the food yourself really isn't a bad idea. Just keep in mind it may not be as inexpensive as you think. Most caterers know how much food to prepare for the number of people you will be hosting, and because they do this all the time and work with food wholesalers they can probably purchase the food at discounted or bulk rates. You'll have to pay for your food in the grocery store at its retail price, so you'll probably not get any bargains there. You will be able to save some money by purchasing some items at your local warehouse store such as Sam's Club, Price Club, Costco, or Nobel Sybco. While these stores may offer lower food prices, they don't necessarily stock the same food items each week. Be sure to speak to the food manager well in advance to find out if you'll be able to order the specific fresh item you'll need.

Sue's Suggestions

Traditionally, your wedding reception needs to serve only cake and champagne. If you can keep it simple, it will be lovely and come in on budget!

In addition, think about just how much food you'll need for the number of guests you're expecting, and what you'll serve it in. Most people don't own enough serving pieces to host easily an event the size of your wedding reception and will have to borrow—and return—countless items from family and friends.

Food Prep

Naturally, you will begin preparing the food well in advance of the wedding weekend, which means freezing and storing the food where? Then, the day of the wedding, you'll have to get the food transported to the reception hall without the help of your groom, because you don't want to see him before the ceremony. Remember, you may be having your hair, make-up, and nails done that day and will be taking pictures about two hours before the ceremony, so when do you plan to get all this done? The biggest problem will be warming the food and then serving it while you pose for the rest of your pictures, greet your guests, and dance with your groom.

Enroll some help here. If you plan to tackle this, get over to your local library or log on to the Internet and find out how much food to prepare for this number of people. You may be able to take a short course at a community college or technical school that will help you in this area.

You may be fortunate enough to have friends and family who don't mind helping in the kitchen even though they are guests at your wedding. Discuss this with them in advance so they can be prepared with aprons to protect their clothing and comfortable shoes that won't slip if the floor gets wet. Remember to plan for several people to clean up after the reception and to bring enough plastic wrap and foil to package up the leftover food you'll want to send home with some of your helpers. Most facilities operators expect you to leave the kitchen spotless when your event is over—and I can promise you won't feel like cleaning up in your wedding gown even if you haven't left on your honeymoon yet! When cleaning up, be careful with the food on your buffet table. If it has been sitting out for any length of time, you'd be wise to throw it away. This may sound wasteful, but botulism is neither fun nor free!

Wedding Blues

The amount of money you save by doing the work yourself won't amount to much if you make too much food. On the other hand, any cost savings will become meaningless if you run out of food and leave some guests with nothing. Plan carefully!

When to Call in the Pros

There may be some foods that are really best prepared at the last minute. If you would like to contact a caterer to prepare just that one dish, perhaps the server will come along with it. Whatever you do, if you are preparing your own food, keep the menu simple. Another option is to contact a staffing company to hire someone just for the day. If you plan enough ahead, you may be able to get this person to stop by your home and pick up some of the food and take it to the reception facility while you are getting ready for the wedding. This same person can arrange the trays of food, keep them refilled, and clean up along the way. There will be a charge for these services; but you may find that it's well worth the money not to have to worry about these details, so you can enjoy your wedding reception.

Is Doing It Yourself Really Cheaper?

Here's one story where doing it themselves *didn't* pay off. One mother prepared all the food for her daughter's wedding reception of 200 guests. It took her four months to prepare everything and she had to borrow freezer space from everyone in her neighborhood. Her two sisters agreed to help her set up the trays and chafing dishes to get the food heated. Of course, they had to leave the church before the ceremony

Wedding Blues

Don't try to cut costs by serving an inappropriate menu, such as hors d'oeuvres, at a 6 P.M. reception when people will be hungry for dinner. Be sure to serve food that is appropriate for the time of the reception. For example, serve a dessert buffet at a reception after 7 or 8 P.M..

was over in order to have everything ready when the guests arrived. When the wedding was over and the mom totaled up what she had spent, she discovered that the food, rental items, and paper supplies had come to a whopping $11,421.00! Why so much? She had prepared about 30 different dishes for the buffet—way too much food!

The caterer she had originally contacted had wanted to charge her $32.60 per person, including food, linens, dishes, silverware, tax, and tip. That would have come to a total of $6,520.00. Of course, the caterer was not planning to serve as many different kinds of foods as the mother prepared, but there would have been enough food for everyone just the same. In addition, the bride will remember the sight of her favorite aunt cleaning the reception hall floor in her new silk dress for the rest of her life!

Just Desserts

Probably the easiest reception to prepare yourself is a dessert reception. After all, everyone loves desserts! You can bake a wide variety of cakes and cookies in advance. You can rent beautiful crystal and silver platters to display them on and have quite an elegant reception for very little money. Be sure to assign a trusted friend to return all the rented items the next business day, so you're not charged overtime because your items were returned late.

Bring a Dish

In some communities, the bride and groom's family and friends each prepare a portion of the reception food in a small to medium quantity and bring it on the wedding

Sue's Suggestions

Rent a beautiful punch bowl and serve a colorful and delicious non-alcoholic party punch at your dessert reception. This saves you money on alcohol as well.

day. This "covered dish" reception can be very charming, and it's certainly less expensive. Naturally, if you decide to have this kind of reception, you'll need to hold it in a facility, such as a church hall or clubhouse at an apartment complex, that will allow you to bring in your own food.

There are several ways to organize this kind of reception, and organization is critical. The bride or her mother may assume the responsibility for assigning a course to each person who is planning to cook. This is important because you want to be sure that you end up with enough variety to create a meal, instead of having 11 Jell-O molds, 6 cakes, and only 10 pieces of fried chicken. Keep the menu simple. It's better to have 6 people prepare chicken in similar ways—say, all fried—than to have 6 different kinds of chicken. If the food is similar, it can all be put together on the same platter. But if everyone cooks a different kind of dish, you could end up using 50 platters to serve 100 guests.

If someone wants to participate but doesn't enjoy cooking (or isn't a very good cook), you can ask that person to be responsible for the soft drinks and ice. You can either assign someone to bring the paper plates and plastic utensils, or if you want to be in charge of the decor, you can supply those items yourself.

Dividing up the reception responsibilities this way puts only a minimal financial burden on any one person. But better than that, when this is the standard in a community, everyone takes part in the celebration, which makes everyone feel important.

Language of Love

An **open bar** (also called a hosted bar) is one where the guests' drinks are paid for by the host.

Providing Your Own Beverages

A good way to cut the total cost of your reception is to arrange to provide your own beverages. This is not possible in every reception facility, so if it's something that you would like to do, be sure to discuss the plan with the reception facility before actually deciding to hold your reception there. Many facilities insist on providing the beverages because most money is spent in the bar—but that's exactly why you might like to handle it yourself.

Once you've found a facility that will allow you to provide your own beverages, you'll need to decide what you would like to serve. Think about what your friends have offered at their receptions. A colorful punch can add such a festive feeling to the event, unless all your guests are expecting an *open bar*. If your reception will be held in the summer or will include children and teens, a punch—which is usually nonalcoholic—is almost a must! You can make it well in

Sue's Suggestions

When you make your punch at home, take some of the mixture and freeze it in a ring-shaped gelatin mold. This frozen ring keeps the punch cold without watering down the taste of your punch. You can add whole strawberries, sliced kiwi, or star fruit to the ring mold to decorate it. If you decide to freeze all your punch, allow plenty of time for it to defrost!

advance of the event, and bring it to the reception site in gallon milk jugs. It's very easy to just pour the punch into the punch bowl and keep refilling it as needed from additional jugs of punch.

If you've decided to offer your guests alcoholic beverages in addition to punch and soft drinks, the question of how much to purchase always comes up. As a basic rule of thumb, you will want to provide approximately 8 ounces of liquid refreshment for each guest for each hour of the reception. Naturally, if you expect it to be a warm day, you'll want to have additional soft drinks on hand, because people tend to drink more soft drinks when they're hot. You can estimate the quantities you will need, but you should certainly review your thoughts with someone at the liquor store who may be more knowledgeable. There are a number of factors that affect the amount your guests will drink; the salesperson will ask you several questions before making suggestions.

Tantalizing Trivia

A 26-ounce bottle of champagne or wine will yield 6 drinks; a keg of beer is 15 gallons, or about 520 8-ounce servings. Be sure to purchase 8-ounce cups for your beer to yield this count. A gallon of hard liquor makes about 32 mixed drinks. Mixed drinks are usually three parts mix to one part liquor. Plan 2 to 3 mixed drinks per adult for the first hour of your reception, and one to two mixed drinks for each adult for each hour after that. Plan three soft drinks per person throughout the reception for adults and children who will not drink alcohol.

Liquor laws vary from state to state, and the facility's liquor license spells out how and what can be served there. Different facilities may have slightly different regulations if your state offers more than one type of liquor license. For example, one facility may by able to serve only beer and wine, while a facility just down the street may be able to serve a full bar, including all kinds of *hard liquor.*

Language of Love

Whiskey, vodka, scotch, bourbon, gin, and rum are considered **hard liquor**, as opposed to beer and wine.

If you are obligated to serve the house liquor (liquor provided by the facility), you can expect to pay a specific fee for every bottle that is opened. If so, you won't want to have four bars when two would do, since four bars could have four bottles of each liquor opened, even if only one drink was consumed out of each bottle. If you are bringing your own beverages, but using the bartender staff hired by the facility, you might be expected to pay a cork fee or a set-up fee for either each bottle opened or each guest at the reception. This fee is usually nominal, but you should be sure to ask about it if it's not in your written contract.

If you are allowed to bring in your own bartender, be sure to do thorough reference checks on him or her. You'll want to be sure that this professional bartender knows the state laws regarding serving guests who have obviously had too much to drink, since you may be legally responsible for any accidents your guests may become involved in after leaving your event. You will also want to know that this bartender uses a light hand when pouring drinks, so the amount of alcohol you have purchased will last throughout the evening.

Wedding Blues

Please do not consider a cash bar (also called a no-host bar), where guests pay for their own drinks, at your wedding. If you can't afford to offer an open bar, select either beer and wine or just punch, but a cash bar has no place at a wedding.

Whether you're providing the alcohol or it's one of the reception facility's responsibilities, be sure to review how you want the evening to flow. Do you want the bar to be open all evening, or would you prefer that it close during the seated dinner? At a seated dinner, where wine is served, the bar is usually closed during that time and reopened after the meal has been cleared. Offering after-dinner drinks to your guests is an elegant yet inexpensive option to end your wedding reception. Guests generally consume very little of these very sweet beverages, but appreciate being offered them.

Using Recorded Music for Your Ceremony

While hiring a disc jockey can be a terrific choice for your reception, and perhaps even for your ceremony, trying to record music for your wedding ceremony yourself probably will not give you the smooth feeling you want and may distract from, rather than complement, the ceremony.

Generally there are four different kinds of music played as part of a wedding ceremony, in the order that they're presented:

1. The *prenuptial concert* is played as the guests arrive and are seated. It can be anything that you like from classical music to show tunes, unless your church requires sacred music.

2. The *processional music* is what the bridal party will walk down the aisle to, so it should have enough of a beat to make it possible for the bridal party to hear and walk to.

3. The *bride's music* announces the entrance of the bride. Again, it should have a consistent beat, but be regal enough to announce the bride's arrival.

4. The *recessional* is played as everyone leaves the ceremony. This music is usually upbeat and somewhat faster than the previous music.

Since there is such a regular pattern to these types of music, brides often think that they can save money on ceremony musicians by recording this music themselves and just turning it on at the ceremony and letting it play. The problem is that as many times as you may practice it and actually time it, you can't be certain that your bridal party will take a specific amount of time to get down the aisle. If they take longer than you expected, there will either be silence for the last members of the bridal party, or the maid of honor will walk down the aisle to the bride's music—making the bride walk in silence! If they walk more quickly than you expected, there will be long portions of music during which no one comes down the aisle, and your guests will be wondering what is happening next.

When you have a live, professional musician at the ceremony, the musician watches the bridal party carefully. Usually this musician has worked with the bride and encouraged her to select a piece of music that can either be played over and over again or can be stopped at several points without the guests really noticing. As the bridal party enters, the professional either repeats the music or brings it to a close as the last members of the bridal party begin down the aisle. There may be a moment of silence as the musician moves from one piece of music to the next, but more often, the musician can run the pieces together without a noticeable break.

Here's one bride's story that shows how quickly things can go wrong with even the best-laid plans. Leslie was determined to record her own music for the ceremony. The wedding was going to be held in a garden, and she was pretty sure that electricity would be a problem, so she planned to use a battery-operated boom box to provide the music. She realized that the prenuptial concert would need to be about 30 minutes long, so she recorded that much music. She agonized over how to determine how long it would take for the bridal party to walk down the aisle. Finally Leslie decided to ask three of her bridesmaids to practice walking down the aisle enough times to equal the number of people in the bridal party while she timed them. She then recorded that amount of music for the processional.

On the wedding day, Gus, the best man, started the tape as the first guests arrived and everyone lined up to walk down the aisle. The groomsmen and the bridesmaids were nervous and walked much more quickly than Leslie had expected. The bridal party finished about four minutes ahead of the music. Four minutes doesn't sound like a long time, but at that point in the ceremony, it sounds like an eternity!

Leslie really wanted to walk to her own music, so she waited those four minutes until her music began before she and her dad started down the aisle. The guests had no way to know she was waiting for her music and began whispering that she had changed her mind! Leslie discovered that excitement made her walk faster than she had expected as well, and the minister had to wait for the music to end before he could begin the ceremony, creating another delay.

Leslie had timed the minister when he performed her maid of honor's wedding ceremony two months earlier, and knew he had taken 17 minutes between "Dearly beloved ..." and "I present to you Mr. and Mrs. ..." So she left the tape running without music for exactly 17 minutes. She didn't notice that the phone rang during that time, so she was very surprised during the ceremony when she heard the phone ring, but she ignored it, and everyone else was polite enough not to mention it. The problem was that her minister got a little long-winded, and the recessional music began before he even pronounced the couple "husband and wife"! He finished quickly—and loudly—so he was heard over the jubilant music. The bride and groom kissed and hurried up the aisle, more quickly than most couples depart. Leslie was mortified! She had wanted everything to be so perfect!

If you really want to record your own music for the ceremony, a better way to do it is to assign a friend to operate the recorder, controlling the fast forward and volume dials as needed to make the music appropriate for whatever is happening in the ceremony. Doing it yourself will save you money, but if you don't arrange for the help, you may have memories of the mishaps, only, and suddenly the money seems insignificant!

Sue's Suggestions

If you have a friend who plays a musical instrument well and has some experience performing in front of a crowd, ask him or her to play for your ceremony. The personal connection will make a great memory and your friend will be able to change music as necessary by watching what is happening.

Using Flowers from Your Garden for the Bouquets

If you have a very large garden and a flair for arranging, you may be able to use the flowers in your own garden for your bouquet and even for the bridesmaids' bouquets. The problem here is time. Because you want the flowers to be fresh, you won't be able to do this even the day before the ceremony.

Perhaps a better plan might be to purchase your flowers from a wholesale flower market on the morning of the wedding and ask one or two of your bridesmaids to assist you in making hand-tied bouquets. It will be more costly than growing your own, but the bouquets will have a slightly more consistent appearance since you can be sure that each girl gets the same number of the same flower in her bouquet.

Wedding Blues

There's always the possibility that the night before your wedding there will be a storm and your garden flowers will not look as you expected!

The biggest problem here remains *time*. On your wedding day there are simply not enough hours to accomplish everything you want to do, so deciding to do your own bouquets is probably one job too many! Ask a friend to do your bouquets, and then be willing to make hers when she gets married. You'll have all the fun and none of the stress!

If you're determined to arrange the flowers yourself, the best option is to use silk flowers. They will last forever and look beautiful even when prepared and arranged weeks in advance. The biggest drawback seems to be that they really aren't any less expensive than fresh flowers. If you would like to use this option, watch for sales at your local craft shop, and buy all the flowers you need when they go on sale. Speak to the store manager about a quantity discount. If you can negotiate such a discount, do your homework! Determine exactly how many flowers of each type you will need in advance so you will be able to purchase them all at the same time. Fortunately, you can do this well in advance of the wedding, so while the cost of the flowers will be a wedding expense, it won't be a wedding *day* expense. You might even consider taking a floral arranging class along the way.

Having a Friend or Relative Take the Pictures

Having a friend or relative take photographs of the wedding may sound like a good idea, but the end product is usually not what you expected it to be. Let's say you ask your favorite uncle to be the photographer because he enjoys taking pictures. He knows the members of your family well, but doesn't know the groom's family at all. You might get lots of pictures of your family (especially the photographer's wife and grandchild) but few photographs of the groom's relatives and even fewer of your friends.

Sue's Suggestions

If a friend will be taking pictures, he or she probably won't absorb the costs, so be sure to compute the cost of purchasing and developing the film. When everything is totaled, will you have saved enough money to make it worth the effort to use a nonprofessional photographer—especially if you end up with less than wonderful pictures?

One bride gave one of her friends several rolls of film so she could take candid shots of the guests and some of the action of the wedding. The friend took lots of pictures, but she drank a great deal, and to this day she can't remember what she did with the film—or the camera! This is your special day, one that will live in your memory for years to come, and if the record of that memory is less than you hoped, you'll certainly remember any disasters for a long time.

Another option is to hire a professional photographer to shoot your formal portraits before the wedding and take photos at the ceremony, itself. Then, to save money, you can place single-use cameras on tables around the reception room for your guests to take photos of your reception. This can be a great alternative since your guests will tend to photograph each other enjoying the reception, and you will receive a candid record of your celebration instead of formally posed pictures. Be sure to buy disposable cameras that have a built-in flash attachment (a must if your reception is indoors).

If you decide to use a friend or family member as your photographer, do so with a little planning. Invite your photographing friend or relative to go through some of your other friends' wedding albums. Determine what kind of pictures you definitely want to have, and discuss where the completed rolls of film will be deposited, since you will be having them developed yourself.

Since you'll be purchasing the film yourself, watch for sales or use coupons to buy the film at a discount. You'll want to think about the lighting in the room where your reception is being held, and be sure to purchase the correct speed of film. If most of the pictures will be taken with a flash, be sure your film is fast enough to properly light the scene.

It's also a good idea to make a list of all the pictures you know you want and who should be in them. This will be especially helpful if you list each person in the groom's family that should be in a particular group shot and ask a member of the groom's family to assist your photographer in collecting these people. This advance planning will let your photographer check off the pictures as he or she completes them.

Photographing a wedding is hard work. Your amateur photographer will be working at your reception instead of enjoying it. You can avoid this problem by asking several people to take photographs, each for a short period of time. Your pictures may have a different style to them, but the sheer number of photographs may allow you to select enough to put together a great album. This may mean that you have more rolls of film, so processing may be slightly more expensive, but probably not significantly so.

The Least You Need to Know

➤ In the long run, it's unlikely that preparing the food for your reception will actually cost less than having it catered, but you still have options.

➤ Be sure to make yourself familiar with your state liquor laws if you plan on providing your own beverages for your reception.

➤ If you decide to tape your own ceremony music, ask a friend to control the tape recorder so the music will match what's happening in the ceremony.

➤ Planning to use the flowers from your garden is risky since Mother Nature doesn't know it's your wedding day!

➤ Your photos are the only things remaining after the day is over. Consider carefully before trusting an amateur.

FLOWERS, CAKE, DRESS, CATERING...

Chapter 3

Getting Organized

In This Chapter

➤ Keeping track of all the details

➤ Counting down to the big day

➤ Asking vendors the right questions

➤ The value of a payment calendar

➤ Information at a glance: the all-important address book

Have you ever watched a friend plan her wedding and seen the stress take over her life? Stress comes from many directions during the planning of a wedding, but it can be easily relieved if you carefully organize your wedding planning tasks. The more organized you are, the more focused you will be on what needs to be accomplished.

In this chapter we'll talk about some of the tools you'll need to become organized and focused. These tools will guide you and your fiancé to a beautiful and stress-free wedding. Most important, by being organized, you'll stay on track, avoid false starts, and you'll save money.

Organizing Your Records

It's time to get organized—to assemble those things that you really need to begin planning your wedding. First you'll need something in which to file information. My favorite type of organizer for a wedding is a notebook with a different divider for each vendor/category and a series of plastic presentation sleeves to hold original documents like contracts. You can select any type of filing system you prefer, as long as it holds papers securely, and it's easy to take with you to various appointments. You should have a calculator, since you'll want to keep close tabs on your financial totals as they change. You'll also need to have a hole punch so you can add brochures and business cards to your notebook as needed.

Sue's Suggestions

Use carbon paper when you take notes during meetings with any of your vendors. At the end of the meeting, ask the vendor to initial the notes and give the original copy to the vendor, keeping the carbon for your file. This gives you a record of everything that was discussed.

Sue's Suggestions

Include another divider labeled "*Good Ideas*" or "*Recommendations.*" When your friends make suggestions or recommend specific vendors, write down their ideas and file them in this section so you can review them later. If you write down recommended vendors here, you'll know exactly where to find them when you're ready to research that category. You can also add magazine pictures and photographs to refer to later.

Some brides choose an accordion file to hold their information and leave it either on the front seat of their car or at home, referring to it as needed but not attempting to carry it around. This works well, so long as you carry a tablet with you for notes that can be added to the file after the appointment. Other brides purchase wedding planners with pockets in them to hold these brochures and extra pages. You'll find many options at your local discount office supply store or stationery store. Don't worry about choosing the "right" system; choose whatever works for you.

Once you've decided which method you will use to organize your event and purchase your supplies, it's time to set up your system and begin using it. I recommend you begin by labeling your dividers as follows:

➤ *Ceremony*

➤ *Reception*

➤ *Music*

➤ *Photography*

➤ *Caterer*

➤ *Florist*

➤ *Guest list*

➤ *Invitations*

➤ *Contracts*

➤ *Budget*

As you move through the planning process, you may add additional categories and label additional dividers as needed. Remember, the most important reason to create a method of organization is so you can retrieve your information as quickly as possible when you need it.

Countdown to a Wedding

Near the front of your file, keep a record of your progress. Laying out a *timeline* is an effective way to keep you on target and record your progress on the tasks that you have left to accomplish. Timelines can be created for however long your engagement will last. This following sample spreads the planning of a wedding over a full year, but if you don't have a year, you can condense the activities into a much shorter period of time. As each task is completed, check it off your timeline and move on. Remember that every wedding will not need every task listed.

Language of Love

A **timeline** is list of jobs and the dates on which they must be completed. If you construct a timeline for your wedding planning, you'll be able to keep track of the decisions you must make and actions you have to take.

One year (or more) before the wedding …

- ❏ Make general wedding decisions (date, style, size).
- ❏ Set a preliminary budget.
- ❏ Choose the location for the ceremony and the officiant.
- ❏ Reserve the reception site.
- ❏ Select and hire your bridal consultant.
- ❏ Begin researching caterers (unless one is included with the reception site), musicians, photographers, and videographers.
- ❏ Begin compiling your guest list.

Nine months before the wedding …

- ❏ Select your bridal party.
- ❏ Have your engagement photos taken.

Eight months before the wedding …

- ❏ Select and order your dress and headpiece.
- ❏ Begin researching your bridesmaid dresses.
- ❏ Make sure contracts have been signed and deposits paid to the reception site, reception musicians, photographer, videographer, and caterer (if separate from the reception site).
- ❏ Begin researching florists.
- ❏ Begin making honeymoon plans. If you plan to leave the country, apply for passports or whatever visas are required, and research any immunizations necessary.
- ❏ Continue working on your guest list, making sure addresses are current. Encourage families to work on their guest lists.

Language of Love

A **bridal shower** is a party given in honor of the bride to which each guest brings a gift to "shower" the couple as they start their married life together. A **bridal luncheon** is a party given in honor of the bride to which the guests do not bring gifts.

Six months before the wedding …

❏ Order the bridesmaid dresses.

❏ Announce your engagement in the newspaper.

❏ Make sure both mothers have ordered their dresses.

❏ Groom should select his tuxedo and send cards to all groomsmen and/or ushers requesting their measurements.

❏ Help your shower hostesses select a date for your *bridal shower,* prepare the guest list, and get it to the hostesses.

❏ Help your luncheon hostesses select a date for a *bridal luncheon,* prepare the guest list, and get it to the hostesses.

❏ Reserve limousine transportation for the wedding day.

❏ Make arrangements for the rehearsal dinner.

❏ Schedule cake tastings to decide on flavors and style.

❏ Register at a bridal gift registry.

Language of Love

Announcements are printed cards that are mailed to people who were not invited to the wedding informing them that it has taken place. Wedding announcements, like birth announcements, are strictly informational and do not require any response or a gift.

Four months before the wedding …

❏ Order invitations, *announcements,* and personal stationery.

❏ Purchase stamps for invitations—outer envelopes, response envelopes, and thank-you notes.

❏ Visit your physician or a health center for medical blood tests, if required in your state.

❏ Shop for gifts for your bridal party.

❏ Get your marriage license.

❏ Research guest transportation for the weekend.

❏ Make sure the contract with your florist is finalized and signed.

❏ Research make-up artists, if you plan to use one.

❏ Begin visiting hairdressers to determine how you will wear your hair.

❏ Speak to hotels about a block of rooms for your guests and have reservation cards printed.

Three months before the wedding ...

❏ Get the invitations and guest list to the calligrapher.

❏ Choose and order your wedding bands.

❏ Order your wedding cake.

❏ Schedule hairdresser and make-up appointments for your wedding day.

Two months before the wedding ...

❏ Shop for your gift for the groom.

❏ Follow up on your bridal attire and make sure that everything is on schedule.

❏ Pick up invitations from the calligrapher and assemble them. If you have any guests living out of the United States, mail their invitations at this time.

❏ Confirm that all groomsmen have returned their cards and tuxedos have been ordered.

❏ Complete your honeymoon plans.

❏ Shop for any missing accessories: bra, shoes, hosiery, guest book, cake knife, garter.

❏ Schedule the rehearsal.

> **Wedding Blues**
>
> Mailing your invitations more than six weeks before your wedding will not get your responses earlier; in fact, most responses are returned later when the invitations are mailed too soon.

Six weeks before the wedding ...

❏ Mail invitations to your out-of-town guests.

❏ Make final menu selections.

❏ Attend your bridal shower and bridal luncheon.

❏ Write thank-you notes for shower gifts.

❏ Confirm transportation arrangements for the wedding weekend.

❏ Have your bridal portrait taken. (If your dress is too big, use clothespins on the back to make it fit; don't alter it yet.)

❏ Send a letter to everyone in your bridal party reviewing all the details of the weekend and making sure everyone has directions to every event.

Five weeks before the wedding ...

❏ Mail the weekend program to all your out-of-town guests.

❏ Record the responses from the out-of-town guests as they arrive.

❏ Hire security for your wedding ceremony and reception, if necessary.

Wedding Blues

Some shops are so busy with alterations, they schedule fittings several weeks before the wedding. While this is fine, many brides lose weight in the two weeks before their weddings and need to go back again for alterations—at an additional charge. Find out the shop's policy on this issue.

❑ Meet with your seamstress to determine necessary alterations on your gown. If you're having your gown altered by the bridal shop, tell the seamstress there to start alterations now. If you're using a private seamstress, let her schedule your appointments based on her schedule.

❑ Write thank-you notes for all gifts that have arrived.

Four weeks before the wedding …

❑ Meet with your bridal consultant for a detailed planning meeting to make sure you're on track and nothing has fallen through the cracks.

❑ Mail invitations to your local guests. (You may be able to add guests if some of your out-of-town guests are not able to attend.)

❑ Pick up all your travel documents for your honeymoon.

❑ Continue writing thank-you notes.

Three weeks before the wedding …

❑ All responses should be in; if there are any guests you haven't yet heard from, call them.

❑ Check your clothing for the other events of your wedding weekend and begin packing for your honeymoon.

❑ Begin writing thank-you notes for any wedding gifts you've received; address them, stamp them, and put them in a box to be mailed after the wedding. You'll still need to write thanks yous to the guests who bring their gifts to your wedding, but you'll be caught up in no time.

❑ Make sure bridesmaids have purchased their shoes and are having them dyed.

Two weeks before the wedding …

❑ Verify any security arrangements for your wedding.

❑ Confirm the selection of your music.

❑ Prepare your wedding announcement for the newspapers.

❑ Address your wedding announcements and put them in the box with your thank-you notes to be mailed after the wedding.

❑ Contact the hotel and make sure all your out-of-town guests have reservations.

Ten days before the wedding …

- ❏ Call your florist with a table count so flowers can be ordered.
- ❏ Get guests' names to the calligrapher so table cards can be written.
- ❏ Designate one shopping bag as a ceremony bag and fill it with everything you will need for the ceremony: wedding bands and marriage license, for example.
- ❏ Designate one shopping bag as a reception bag and fill it with everything you will need for the reception: cocktail napkins, guest book and pen, toasting goblets, table cards, and cake knife, for example.

One week before the wedding …

- ❏ Pick up your wedding bands.
- ❏ Give a guest count to your caterer.
- ❏ Make sure all your bridesmaids have their dresses back from the seamstress.
- ❏ Verify that all attendants have shoes, hosiery, and so forth.
- ❏ Verify the ceremony reserved-seating chart, and make sure the bridal consultant has a copy of it.
- ❏ Assign reception seating for your guests.
- ❏ Review all your vendor contracts and make sure checks are written for all vendors who will need checks at the wedding.
- ❏ Review any household bills that will be due during your honeymoon; write and mail the checks in advance.
- ❏ Review the list of guests attending your wedding, and make a list of any special pictures you want taken during your reception.

Three days before the wedding …

- ❏ Remind the groom and other male party members to pick up their tuxedos and try them on.
- ❏ Make sure the ceremony and reception bags are complete and near the door, where they can't be forgotten.
- ❏ If the ceremony and reception are in two different locations, deliver the reception bag to your catering manager at the reception site.

Two days before the wedding …

- ❏ Attend your bridal luncheon or your bachelorette party.
- ❏ Groom attends his bachelor party.

Wedding Blues

Be sure to schedule your bachelor and bachelorette parties two or more days before the wedding (*not* the night before). Feeling hung over or tired can ruin your wedding!

One day before the wedding ...

❑ Make sure all cars have been washed and have full tanks of gas.

❑ Have your nails done for your rehearsal dinner.

❑ Attend the rehearsal and arrive on time.

❑ Attend the rehearsal dinner.

❑ Write table numbers on the inside of the table cards for the reception. (Wait until all guests from out of town have arrived, in case you have to change some tables.)

❑ Give table cards to the caterer to set out for the guests to pick up.

❑ Give your groom his gift.

❑ Get a good night's sleep.

On the wedding day ...

❑ Give the best man your suitcase so he can check you into the bridal suite.

❑ Get your hair and make-up done.

❑ Give your announcements and stamped thank-you notes to a friend to mail tomorrow.

❑ Remember to eat something.

❑ Arrive at the wedding site *on time* or a few minutes early.

❑ Take several deep breaths to help you relax.

❑ Have a terrific time!

After the wedding ...

❑ Enjoy your honeymoon.

❑ Finish your thank-you notes.

❑ Have a happy life!

Questions You'll Want to Ask

Create a list of questions to ask each of the vendors you want to interview, and file the list in your vendor category divider. When you get the answers to the same questions from each of the vendors, you can get a picture of the kind of job that each vendor will be doing at your wedding. Some brides create a chart of these questions.

Most of the charts list the questions down the left edge of the paper, and the name, address, and phone number of the vendor across the top edge of the paper. The answers the vendor gives to each question are placed in the box below that vendor's name and next to the question. If the bride is interviewing three vendors, she can see each one's answers by just reading across the page.

Here are some general questions you should ask every vendor:

➤ How long have you been in business?

➤ How many events do you handle each day?

➤ Can you provide a minimum of three references?

➤ What can you tell me about your services?

➤ Are taxes and gratuities usually included in your quote? If not, what percentage is charged for tax and what for gratuities?

➤ How many staff people will you be bringing to the wedding?

➤ What do you charge to work my wedding and how it is paid? Is a deposit required? If so, how much is it and when is it due?

➤ Is my deposit refundable if the event is canceled? If not, will you apply that money to another event I might host?

➤ Do you accept credit cards? Which ones?

Sue's Suggestions

Once you start a list of questions for your vendors, you'll think of more questions throughout the day. Keep index cards in your purse, and write down your questions right away so you won't forget them. You can add them to your list later.

In addition to these general vendor questions, there are specific questions that you'll want to ask the caterer:

➤ Can you show me pictures of your presentation? (Most caterers have photos of various parties that they've worked, and these can help you assess the creativity of their setup as well as the appearance of the food.)

Sue's Suggestions

If any of your guests will need special meals—vegetarian, kosher, low-salt, or diabetic, for instance—ask if the caterer can either prepare what's needed or secure it for you.

➤ Will I be allowed to have a tasting of the menu that I select or of the two menus I'm choosing between? (The caterer you select should be willing to offer you this tasting, but don't expect a tasting from each caterer that you interview.)

➤ What beverages are included with the meal? Are any available at an additional charge?

➤ Do you have a liquor license? Will you be providing liquor for the party, or will I be able to provide my own liquor? If I supply it, will you provide a bartender for the event? Exactly what's included in any setup charge (glassware, stirrers, lemons, olives, cherries)?

➤ Will you provide table linens, napkins, china, glassware, and flatware in the per-person price? If these things are additional, will I have a choice of these items?

➤ Will you provide some kind of table decoration?

➤ What's the difference in price between a sit-down and buffet dinner? (Generally they cost about the same, but you will want to be very clear on each caterer's charges and presentation. If you decide on a buffet dinner, or even a cocktail buffet reception, ask what will happen to the extra food. Some caterers will provide take-home containers; others will make sure it's packaged and delivered to homeless shelters.)

Tantalizing Trivia

If your reception buffet is held in a hotel or restaurant, there may not be any leftover food—even though there is plenty of food remaining on the buffet at the end of your event. That's because the facility might use the remaining chicken in tomorrow's chicken salad that's on the restaurant menu, for instance. As long as all your guests were fed, this is not a problem.

➤ Is a wedding cake available, either included in the price or at an additional fee? (If this caterer does not bake wedding cakes, be sure to ask if there is a charge if the caterer's staff serves the wedding cake you purchase from another vendor.)

All these questions are just a start to show you how to begin thinking about all the issues surrounding your wedding planning and how to start organizing the information you gather. We'll be talking more about vendors and what you need to discuss with each of them in later chapters. But first let's talk about tracking how you spend your money.

Creating Your Payment Calendar

One of the dividers in your notebook will have your written budget (I devote all of Chapter 13, "Money, Money, Money!" to this topic). Another divider should be your payment calendar. The payment calendar is an accurate listing of what you have spent, what you owe, and when it's due. If you think of your budget as the *plan* of your wedding expenses, then the payment calendar represents the *actual* expenditures.

There are two ways to create this payment calendar. One is to use an ordinary wall calendar that starts with the day you get engaged and continues until about two months after your wedding date. Each time you make a payment to a vendor, you record the person paid, the amount paid, and your check number on the calendar date. Then move ahead to the date that the next payment is due to this vendor and record how much is due to whom on that date. If your vendor requires multiple payments before the wedding, with the final payment on the wedding date, record all of the payments due on the calendar. In this way, as you continue to sign contracts and make payments, your calendar will be filled up, and each day you'll know exactly what you have spent and what you still owe.

Many brides find themselves recording appointments on this same calendar so it becomes a record of the weeks and months before the wedding. If this works for you, that's fine.

If you have a personal computer, you may find that it offers you an even more effective way of creating a payment calendar. Using just about any word processing program, you can list every day and date between your engagement and two months after the wedding, and then record every deposit paid, to whom, and the check number on these dates, just as we did on the wall calendar

When I work with a bride and she sends me her contracts for review, I always ask if she has created a payment calendar. I'm constantly surprised when I learn that she is not working with this wonderful tool. A payment calendar virtually puts your wedding finances together in one place. Just as a budget will keep your planning on track, a payment calendar will tell you where you are at any given moment. If you can do this on a computer, it's easily updated on a daily basis.

Your Address Book

One of your dividers should be an address book, which includes the name, address, and phone number of all your vendors (and those recommended by

Wedding Blues

I'm always surprised at the number of brides who can't remember who their appointments are with on a specific day, and don't seem to have any way of retracing their records. Since your address book page will probably be in front of you when you make the appointment, it's a good place to note the appointment, and it gives you a backup record.

your friends). Initially you may think that these names and addresses will be important to you only until you actually sign contracts, and that is mostly true. But sometimes situations arise that make it necessary to contact someone again, even after you've decided not to work with that vendor. Keep all your notes until well after the wedding. You may even find that you'll want to share what you've learned with friends who marry after you.

When you record names and addresses, include as much information as you can about each vendor. The more you put into this record, the more valuable it will be when you begin calling vendors and actually planning your wedding. Your notes may look like this:

Videographer:

Videotimes—Tracy Misner—404-555-TAPE

333 Sandy Springs Circle, #208, Atlanta 30328

Records wedding on video, can do 1, 2, or 3 camera jobs; recaps available.

Montage of baby pictures. B&W segments used.

Tracy is booked on 4/29/00 but associate (David) is available.

8/16/99 at 11:30 A.M.—meet with David.

The Least You Need to Know

➤ Select a type of file or notebook to keep all your wedding information together.

➤ Label your dividers with every aspect of your wedding plans.

➤ Make sure that you include a timeline so you can check off items as you complete them.

➤ To keep track of all of the financial details of your wedding, create and use a payment calendar.

➤ Create a section for addresses, and record as much information as possible about the vendors you plan to contact.

Part 2
Creating a Budget

Creating a budget for your wedding should not be intimidating. After all, you've created budgets before. Every year when you make out your Christmas shopping list you're making a budget. You decide whom you want to buy gifts for and how much money you have to spend for each person on your list. There will always be some special people on your list that you will spend more money on and some people you will spend less money on. In other words, you will prioritize—set priorities. This is exactly what you'll be doing with your wedding budget.

Chapter 4

Getting Ready for the Big Day: Wedding Essentials

In This Chapter

➤ The lowdown on wedding consultants, wedding guilds, and bridal consultants

➤ Love hurts: getting the blood test

➤ Finding out what your state requires for the marriage license

➤ Hassle-free reception rentals

➤ Officiants and their fees

There are a variety of things that you must do before your wedding day comes around, and even the most organized of brides may feel overwhelmed with all the details. That's where wedding consultants, wedding guilds, and bridal consultants can help. In this chapter, I'll tell you who those people are and what they can do for you, so you can decide whether to include them in your budget.

I'll also give you the lowdown on such nonromantic but necessary details as blood tests, marriage license requirements, reception rental fees, and officiants' fees. All of the topics covered in this chapter are wedding essentials; and like everything related to wedding planning, the more you know about them, the more easily you can plan to save money.

Weddings "R" Us: Calling in the Pros

Planning a wedding raises a lot of questions: What is a wedding director? What is a wedding guild and who serves on it? What is a bridal consultant? What is the difference between a bridal consultant and a wedding consultant?

With the entrepreneurial spirit alive and well in the wedding industry, many professionals might call themselves by names that differ from the terms for professionals that I use in this book. I know that makes it tough on the consumer (you), but the terms in this book should help you understand who you're talking to and what that person does—after all, a rose by any other name is still a professional!

Wedding Directors

Wedding directors are hired to generally assist the bride and groom at the rehearsal and the day of the ceremony. The wedding director usually meets with the bride and groom to get their input on where the members of the bridal party will stand. The wedding director will also need information about their families so he or she can be prepared to pin the corsages and boutonnieres on the appropriate people. The wedding director may also assist the photographer by getting family members lined up for their pictures after the ceremony. Most wedding directors don't get involved in planning the reception, though there may be exceptions to this.

Language of Love

A **wedding director**'s primary responsibility on the wedding day is to provide flowers, food, music, or photography.

Wedding Guilds

Many churches have *wedding guilds* (also called wedding committees) that brides getting married in that church are required to work with. These guilds or committees are usually made up of volunteers who are primarily responsible for the church and making sure the rules of the church are adhered to. They know where the unity candle and kneeling bench are stored and how much to pay the altar boys. Usually these volunteers organize the rehearsal since they are knowledgeable about the clergy's way of doing things and know what to have ready for the ceremony.

Language of Love

A **wedding guild** is a committee of volunteers within a church. One member of the guild is assigned to work with the bride, assist the minister with the rehearsal, and make sure the church is prepared properly for the wedding day.

Depending on the particular church, the wedding guild member that is assigned to a particular bride and groom will meet with them prior to the rehearsal and determine how many people are in the bridal party. The member will ask questions about the family dynamics so guild members can pin on corsages and help the photographer with group pictures after the ceremony. In some congregations it is customary to compensate the wedding guild members that work on a wedding. In other congregations the couple is charged a specific amount for the use of the wedding guild, but the money actually goes to the guild and not to the specific person who was present. If your church has a wedding guild, you will not need a wedding director, since they do exactly the same thing.

Bridal Consultants

Bridal consultants meet with the bride and groom to understand the couple's dreams and wishes for their wedding celebration. The bridal consultant will help the couple determine their budget and recommend vendors that can create the wedding the couple wants on the budget they have in mind. He or she then sets out to turn those plans into reality, helping organize the vendors the bride and groom have hired into a cohesive team whose combined goal is to produce a perfect wedding and reception for this couple. An independent bridal consultant is in business for him- or herself and does not have a financial relationship with any other vendor. The bridal consultant is employed by the couple and is their advocate, helping them interpret their wishes to the vendors and making sure that their wedding is everything the couple wants it to be.

Language of Love

A **bridal consultant** is the bride's advocate, hired to represent the bride, and is responsible for coordinating all the other services into a team to make the wedding happen.

Members of the Association of Bridal Consultants (ABC), a professional organization serving members of the wedding industry worldwide, who have successfully completed the professional development courses may be designated Professional Bridal Consultant, Accredited Bridal Consultant, or Master Bridal Consultant, depending on the level of education they completed.

The designation Professional Bridal Consultant is granted when the original correspondence course work is successfully completed and is valid for three years. When this designation expires, the bridal consultant is allowed to apply for the designation of Accredited Bridal Consultant. To achieve this, the consultant must complete a written examination and supply letters of recommendation from both former clients and vendors. This designation is also valid for three years and when it expires, the consultant must successfully complete a series of requirements indicating his or her skill and experience level.

The next level is Master Bridal Consultant. This designation does not expire and generally identifies men and women who are viewed as experts in the field. To date there

Sue's Suggestions

It's important to check references on any vendor you consider hiring, including a bridal consultant. Ask brides who have used a particular bridal consultant, "If you were planning your wedding today, would you hire this professional again?"

are just 16 Master Bridal Consultants in the world. In addition to offering the professional development courses, the ABC offers educational seminars in different communities around the country each year and an annual conference. All of these seminars and courses lead to an educated professional group ready to assist brides and grooms with the details of their weddings.

Even with the large number of professional organizations available to members of the wedding industry, membership in a professional organization is not required to work in the industry. Brides and grooms are free to hire whomever they choose to assist them with their wedding plans. However, when you are paying a fee for their services, it is reasonable to inquire about the level of education and experience you are receiving for your money.

How can a bridal consultant help you plan your wedding? The bridal consultant ...

➤ Can recommend vendors such as caterers and photographers.

➤ Can read the contracts the vendor has given you and call your attention to anything that might need further investigation or clarification by you before the contract is signed.

➤ Can attend your gown fittings and will organize the wedding rehearsal (if the church does not require you work with their wedding guild or wedding committee).

➤ Will arrive at the wedding site on the day of the wedding early enough to steam your gown and sand the soles of your shoes (so you won't slip on the carpeting).

➤ Will be on hand to answer your questions and make sure you have the wedding of your dreams!

Bridal consultants also know how to prepare for the unexpected. On more than one occasion, I have had to move an outdoor wedding inside at the last minute because the heavens suddenly opened and the wedding site was underwater. This has happened so often that it is now my policy to ask the florists of my outdoor weddings to add additional ficus trees and potted plants to their delivery truck when loading up to deliver flowers for an outdoor wedding. That way, if we have to move the ceremony inside at the last moment, we have decorations handy to turn a less than beautiful room into something quite lovely. Most florists own these items and don't worry about being paid for them unless they're actually needed. There usually isn't time to return to the studio/warehouse for a second shipment of decorations when they're needed, so it's the quick thinking of your professionals that will prevent unexpected disasters.

Tantalizing Trivia

Bridal consultants must be prepared for just about anything and they can be very resourceful. At a recent wedding, just as Grandma Sarah took the first step down the aisle, the heel came off her shoe! This could have been a disaster, and everyone looked shocked—except for the quick-thinking bridal consultant who didn't miss a beat. Because she carried a hammer and nails in her emergency kit, she repaired the heel right on the spot! (This probably wasn't the first time someone lost a heel at one of her weddings.) Grandma Sarah proudly started the processional just a few moments later.

Many brides believe that hiring a bridal consultant is just an extra line on their budgets and an expense that they could eliminate if they did the work themselves. In fact, this is not correct. If the bride and groom let the bridal consultant guide them, the bridal consultant could actually *save* the couple money on their wedding. The bridal consultant will do this by listening carefully to the couple's ideas about their wedding and then recommending vendors who can provide the service the bride and groom are looking for on the budget that the couple has established.

There are also many brides and grooms today whose jobs require them to be out of the city several days a month. The bridal consultant can follow up with the arrangements while the bride is out of town. This gives the bride someone to turn to who can troubleshoot on her behalf. It may be a cliché, but time *is* money. The time that your consultant saves you can translate to earnings if it is time you do not have to take off work to do this research or to follow up with your vendors.

But in some situations, bridal consultants can do more than refer you to vendors. Suzie Weiss, owner of Wonderful Weddings in Winter Park, Florida, shared a potential nightmare with me. She was sending the bridal party down the aisle at the church when her beeper began to vibrate. The number was unfamiliar, so she continued what she was doing. She opened the doors to the sanctuary and sent the bride and her father down the aisle and then stepped outside the church and returned the call. It was from the disc jockey hired to provide music for the reception, which was scheduled to begin in about an hour. He was calling from an ambulance on his way to the emergency room, where he was certain he would learn that he had a broken leg. It seems that as he traveled to the reception site to begin setting up his equipment, someone had run a red light and hit his car. He called Suzie to give her as much notice as possible that he would not make it to the reception tonight.

Suzie knew what to do. In her car was her vendor address book. She began calling disc jockeys, finally reaching a young man she had not worked with in several months. He agreed to get to the reception site immediately and start setting up.

Suzie didn't have a chance to tell the bride or groom about the situation before they got to the reception site; in fact, it was just before the couple's first dance that Suzie took them aside and explained what had happened. The rest of the reception was a terrific success, and none of the guests had any idea what had nearly gone so wrong.

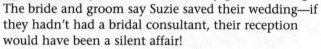

The bride and groom say Suzie saved their wedding—if they hadn't had a bridal consultant, their reception would have been a silent affair!

A bridal consultant does weddings every weekend, so she will have the experience to know where to cut corners and get the look the bride and groom are trying to achieve without spending the whole budget in one area. While the bride and groom will be paying the consultant a fee, most bridal consultants are able to save the bride and groom an amount at least equal to the fee for service.

Sue's Suggestions

Be sure to discuss fees when hiring any professional for your wedding. You need to find out whether your bridal consultant charges a flat fee, a percentage, or an hourly rate. Also find out if the consultant pays referral fees to vendors for sending the couple to him or her. If so, how is the fee used?

Let's say, for instance, that your consultant is charging you only a nominal amount of money as a flat fee for his or her services, but is receiving a referral fee from each vendor he or she refers you to. You should expect that these referral fees become a part of the consultant's total compensation for his or her services on your wedding. If, however, the consultant is charging you a larger fee for services *and* receiving a referral fee, the consultant may be refunding those referral fees to you in the form of "discounts" from the various vendors.

Wedding Blues

Florists, like caterers and hotels, have minimums below which they cannot afford to do business. If a vendor's proposal is higher than you believe is necessary for your particular event, even after you have eliminated all the expensive items, find out if the vendor is charging a minimum fee.

Some bridal consultants work with a "stable" of vendors. When you hire this bridal consultant, you automatically are working with the specific band, photographer, videographer, and caterer with whom the bridal consultant regularly works. In this situation, he or she may even sign the contract with the vendor and be responsible for paying that vendor for you. You would simply pay the bridal consultant. While the bridal consultant may be very familiar with his or her vendors' services, he or she may not be taking into consideration *your* particular tastes and uniqueness. While your wedding may fit perfectly into your stated budget in this situation, it may not reflect your taste and may feel like all the other weddings you have attended.

You will be better served by those bridal consultants who recommend four or five vendors in each category, allowing you to meet each and make a decision about who can create the wedding of *your* dreams. Your consultant will still have guided you and narrowed down the number of people that you have to speak to in making your decision; but remember, chances are that your consultant is just getting to know you and may not exactly understand your taste and expectations when he or she makes his or her earliest recommendations. Keep the lines of communication open. If your consultant recommends a vendor who doesn't meet your expectations, tell the consultant what you don't like about that vendor.

Brides who don't work with consultants and jump right in to finding their own ceremony and reception sites often feel an overwhelming frustration that there is nothing out there that is right for them. This comes from having to see so many sites because there is no way to eliminate anything without seeing it. Until you've seen the facility for yourself, you really can't tell if the person who wrote the advertisement is purposely making the site sound wonderful to every bride, or if the facility really *is* wonderful. You won't know if you can afford to rent it, or even if it will accommodate the number of guests you are expecting, until you call! Sometimes just getting the right person on the phone can take several calls, usually during business hours when your boss is expecting you to be doing other things.

Perhaps the greatest service that the bridal consultant provides to the bride is an assurance of quality service from his or her vendors. That's because the consultant represents repeat business to each vendor—if the vendor does a good job, the bridal consultant will continue to bring business to that vendor. It's this promise of future weddings that keeps the vendor striving to please the couple.

> ### Sue's Suggestions
>
> If hiring a bridal consultant doesn't fit into your budget, consider hiring a consultant just for the Big Day. For a reasonable fee, the consultant will steam-clean your gown, calm your bridesmaids, and make sure the ceremony and reception sites are ready for your arrival. Be sure to meet with the consultant beforehand to discuss exactly what you want.

Getting the Blood Test

There was a time when every state required a blood test in order for a couple to be married in that state. Today, however, many states do not require this test. The following states still require a blood test before a marriage license can be obtained:

- ➤ Connecticut
- ➤ Georgia
- ➤ Hawaii
- ➤ Massachusetts
- ➤ Michigan
- ➤ Mississippi
- ➤ Montana
- ➤ New Mexico

- ➤ New York
- ➤ Oklahoma
- ➤ Rhode Island
- ➤ Washington
- ➤ West Virginia
- ➤ Wisconsin
- ➤ Washington, D.C.

Most of these states require testing for venereal disease, but New York, Rhode Island, and Washington require additional testing.

In states where blood tests are required, you have several choices of places to have the blood drawn. You can have your blood drawn at your personal physician's office (which will be the most expensive) and have your own doctor complete the state forms. Or you can go to your county health department (which will be the least expensive), which routinely draws blood for these tests and processes the results for brides and grooms. In many communities there are also free-standing laboratories that are licensed to perform premarital blood tests. The charges at these facilities should be less than your personal physician's, but more than the charges at the county health department. Be sure that you completely understand the requirements of your state and the way the forms must be filled out before leaving the doctor's office. This varies by state and rules change from time to time, so please contact your individual marriage license bureau for the current requirements in your state.

Wedding Blues

Don't wait until you're off work on a holiday to apply for your marriage license. Most marriage license bureaus are closed on holidays! Also, secure your blood test and license well ahead of your wedding date, preferably early in the week. Marriage license bureaus are busiest on Fridays, since most weddings are held on weekends and many couples wait until the last minute to apply for a license.

A License to Be Married

Most states have similar requirements for marriage. For instance, couples can marry when they're 18 years old without parental consent in most states; however, Utah requires couples under the age of 19 to receive premarital counseling. Nebraska requires both bride and groom to be at least 19 years old, and Mississippi and Puerto Rico both require the couple to be 21 years old to marry without their parents' consent. Under those ages, marriage may be permitted with the consent of parents or guardians.

Several states still require a waiting period between the time application is made for the license and the time the license is actually granted. You'll need to know if your state requires you to wait, and how long, so you can be married exactly on the day you planned. Both the bride and groom need to appear in person for the license to be issued. In most states this is strictly a cash transaction. Call in advance and make sure you have sufficient cash to pay for the license since most states will not accept personal checks or credit cards. The days of the two-dollar marriage license are long gone, and you can expect to pay between $20 and $50 for your license.

If you or your groom don't currently live in the city where you plan to be married, be sure to contact the marriage license bureau in the state where the wedding will take place and determine what their regulations are. If you plan to be married in a state that requires blood tests, make sure the state will allow you to get your tests where you're currently living. Request that the proper state forms be mailed to you. There also may be regulations as to where in the state you can secure your license. You may be required to secure the license in the county where the wedding will take place. But if one of you or a member of your family is a state resident, you may be able to secure the license in the county where you or your family reside, *or* in the county where the ceremony will be performed. (Nevada doesn't require blood tests or waiting periods—in fact, everyone knows you can go to Las Vegas and be married in a drive-thru ceremony!)

Tantalizing Trivia

On the first Fourth of July wedding I ever consulted, the couple had stored their wedding license in their safe deposit box and had completely forgotten about retrieving it before the ceremony. The minister went ahead with the ceremony but could not pronounce the couple husband and wife! The couple was married later in the minister's office. The moral to this story is: Once you get your marriage license, store it in a safe place until the wedding, but not some place you can't get to on the day of your wedding! You can't be married without a license and the officiant needs to sign it when the marriage takes place.

While marriage licenses are valid indefinitely in Georgia, Hawaii, Idaho, Iowa, Mississippi, New Mexico, Puerto Rico, Rhode Island, South Carolina, and Wyoming, they expire in nearly every other state. South Dakota's license is valid for only 20 days. You will want to contact your state early in your planning and work out the specific details that apply so you get your license properly.

If you've decided that you would really like to be married in a foreign country, you will need to contact that country's tourist information office or consulate (most have offices in New York, Los Angeles, or Chicago). You will need information about residency requirements, waiting periods, ages, blood tests, and fees. The good news is, if your marriage is valid in that country, it is valid in the United States with no further paperwork.

Reception Rental Fees

I'll talk much more about receptions in Part 4, "Reception Details," but let's touch on fees here. When you begin to look for a reception location, you'll discover that nearly every place you're considering comes with a rental fee. This really isn't a problem. Things are generally worth about what you pay for them, and since you are planning to hold your wedding reception in this location, you will want to know that it's being maintained. The rental fees will vary from place to place, just as what is included in the fee varies. Be sure to ask if the following are included in the fee:

➤ Tables and chairs

➤ A caterer's kitchen

➤ Parking

➤ A full-time maintenance person (someone who can find the fuse box if the power goes out)

Language of Love

The **minimum revenue requirement** is the minimum amount of money a facility needs to earn during any specific time frame in order to turn a profit on an event.

Some other questions to ask are: Does the facility have an on-site caterer or can you bring your own? How many amps of power will the electrical outlets handle? Will your band or disc jockey have any difficulty with the power available? Does the facility have a liquor license and will it provide alcohol, or can you bring that in yourself? Is there a dance floor and staging available for the band or DJ?

Most hotels also charge a room rental fee, but many wave it for wedding receptions when they have a *minimum revenue requirement*. This amount of money identifies the minimum you must spend on food and beverage in their facility in order for them to be willing to rent you the room for that time period. In most cases, Saturday evening events have the highest minimum revenue requirements, but each time slot will have a different amount. A facility will be reluctant to rent a room to you for an event that they deem to be too small to cover this requirement. Exceptions to this may occur if the event date is drawing near and they suspect they won't be able to find another client to fill the room on that date.

Tantalizing Trivia

Julie and Ted wanted to host their wedding reception in the ballroom of a five-star hotel, but when they called the hotel 15 months in advance, they were told that while the room was not booked, it was also not available to their reception of 75 people. With further investigation, the couple learned that the hotel could not afford to reserve the ballroom so far in advance to a small reception at which no alcoholic beverages would be served. This would take the hotel out of consideration for larger events that might want to book reservations later in the year. Julie and Ted were instead offered another room in the same hotel that was lovely and within their budget.

While we generally think of room rental fees as relating to *rooms,* there are rental fees that relate to other wedding sites as well. If you want to hold your ceremony or reception in a public park, for example, you need approval from your county or state and you can expect to pay a fee for the privilege. This fee might cover the cleanup after the event. If you want to host your reception in a museum, you would also be expected to pay a rental fee. Be sure to ask what is included in your rental fee, and what each place requires. Some museums will require you to purchase all your alcoholic beverages from them, but may not provide tables, chairs, or a dance floor as part of your rental fee.

The Officiant's Fee

If you've decided to host your ceremony outside of a religious setting, you may find that you'll need to locate someone to perform the ceremony. It's possible that your minister or rabbi will perform the ceremony wherever it is. But let's say you don't have a minister or rabbi—then what do you do?

It always struck me as incredibly romantic to be married by a ship's captain, like weddings we used to see on the television show *The Love Boat*. But ship captains are not authorized to perform marriages. Most states determine who can legally perform ceremonies, and you actually have a lot of options. There are judges, justices of the peace, or magistrates; there are also a number of nondenominational clergymen available in most communities. You will be able to find some of these advertising in the local magazines. In some states, it's not necessary for a person to have any religious affiliation to perform a marriage, and sometimes a psychologist, social worker, or a marriage and family counselor is authorized to do so. You will want to be sure that the person you choose is authorized to perform marriages in your state.

Tantalizing Trivia

Utah allows anyone, not just the clergy or government officials, to perform marriages within the state. Recently I consulted on a wedding in Utah where the officiant became ill the day before the wedding. He was sick enough for the couple to begin searching for someone to replace him—a very difficult task on such short notice. The bride asked *me* to be prepared to step in if necessary! Fortunately for the officiant, the couple, and me, the officiant was fine by ceremony time.

When you speak to the person you are considering to perform your ceremony, the most important question is, will that person be available? Only when everything finally comes together—the officiant, the location, and your schedule—can you believe that your wedding date is set!

If "Are you available on my date?" is the *most* important question, then "What do you charge?" must be the next most important question. Couples are often uncomfortable asking members of the clergy and even judges what their fees are. Traditionally, the groom or his family is responsible for paying the officiant at the ceremony. When the bride and groom or either of their families is a member of the officiant's congregation, there is usually no fee for the wedding ceremony—this fee is covered by the membership dues. When this is the case, it is appropriate for the groom or his family to make a contribution either to the officiant's discretionary fund or to the church or synagogue. If you're not sure how much this contribution should be, or who it's payable to, ask the officiant or his or her secretary.

The Least You Need to Know

➤ Hiring a wedding guild member, or a professional wedding director, bridal consultant, wedding consultant, or wedding coordinator will say you time and money.

➤ Contact the local marriage license bureau well in advance to find out if blood tests are required in the state where you'll be married.

➤ Some states have no laws governing who is permitted to perform a marriage, so be sure to consider your options.

➤ Most facilities have some kind of rental fee, but some have a minimum revenue requirement.

Dressing the Bride

Most girls have fantasized about their wedding gowns since they were little girls. You might have even played with a bride doll. You have your magazines and you've poured over the pictures and think you know exactly what you're looking for. You might even be a little nervous about this—you've probably never spent so much money for one dress before in your life, certainly not one you already know you'll never wear again!

When you put on the right dress, you'll know it immediately. The right dress is the one that makes you feel like a princess and fulfills all your dreams. Brides have said that putting on the right dress makes them feel slimmer, taller, and more beautiful than any other dress they've ever put on. So how do you find this magical creation? More important, how can you afford it? There are lots of options and lots of wonderful dresses. There are even ways to save money on the most magical of designer gowns. Shopping for your wedding gown can be so much fun—so let's get started!

Buying a Dress Fit for a Princess

It's probably a good idea to do some preparation before actually trying on wedding gowns. Look through bridal magazines to get an idea of what you like and what you don't like. When you're ready to make your appointments to try on gowns, take along a pair of shoes with heels the height you think you'll be wearing. Most traditional bridal shops will let you borrow undergarments (strapless bras and slips) from them while you try on the gowns.

Language of Love

Custom made means made especially for you, to your measurements, and sometimes with your own design elements. **Made-to-order** means there is no hanging stock in this design. The dress is made in the exact size and color that you order from the sample you saw in the store. Wedding gowns are usually made to order.

Language of Love

The **interior measurement** of the gown is the finished measurement of the inside of the gown. This is important because if, for instance, the bride measures 32-24-35, she won't be able to get into a gown that measures 32-24-35 from the outside. (Try inserting two envelopes of the same size inside on another.)

Traditional Bridal Shops

Buying a wedding gown is a unique experience. First of all, in most bridal shops, you'll need an appointment just to try on a dress, especially on the weekend. Then you'll discover that all the dresses are the same size—either an 8 or a 10! You've been reading the bridal magazines and think you know exactly which manufacturer you'll look great in; but all the labels have been removed from the gowns and you have no idea what you're looking at. Finally you learn that even if you love the dress and want to buy it, you can't take it home with you—it has to be ordered and it might not be in for several weeks or even months! What is all this about?

Buying a bridal gown is not like buying any other article of clothing, and running a bridal shop is not like running any other type of retail business. The shop is often very elegant, with upholstered sofas and full-length mirrors. It has samples of gowns, all shipped from the manufacturer in size 8 or size 10, white or ivory—whatever the manufacturer believed was appropriate. These gowns sometimes are not for sale; instead, they are intended to be used as samples, for the brides to try on. The gowns are then made to order. Traditional bridal shops will be able to show you dresses ranging from about $350 to over $5,000, though not every store will offer this broad price range.

Made-to-order is not *custom made*, because the dress is not made to the measurements of the bride, but rather to a size on the manufacturer's size chart that is closest to the bride's measurements. Manufacturers provide the stores with measurement charts in one of two versions:

➤ A body chart, which shows the body measurement of the bride who can wear a size XYZ from this company

➤ A garment chart, which tells the salesperson the *interior measurement* of the gown in each size

Naturally, if the bride's measurements are the same as the garment's interior measurements of a particular size, she won't be able to wear that size and should select one size larger or smaller. You might wear a size 6 in most dresses at the mall, but when you get to the bridal shop you could discover that you're a size 4 in one manufacturer and a size 8 in another! It's important to understand these charts, so you'll know what size to select. A bride should always ask to see the measurement chart for the company she's ordering from so she can decide, with the help of the salesperson, what size to order. She should understand that the sample she is trying on has probably been tried on by hundreds of other brides, and may be stretched as much as two sizes.

In a community that has several bridal shops, you can expect the price ranges of the dresses in a particular store to be appropriate for the neighborhood in which the store is located. Mall bridal shops tend to have the widest range of prices because they serve the widest range of brides. In general, the buyer for a bridal shop would rather not purchase the same gowns that other stores in his or her community carry. Bridal shop owners usually stock a variety of dresses in a variety of prices ranges. They know that brides will shop the competition, so shop owners want to give a bride plenty of options.

You may have seen your dream dress at the first shop, but decided that it was more than you wanted to spend. You decided to do a little research to see if you could find the same dress for less money. Perhaps you even asked for the manufacturer's name, or looked for it on a label in the dress and found the label missing. That's when you learned that this information is a closely guarded secret! Bridal shops don't want you to price-shop this dress.

Wedding Blues

Every manufacturer uses its own size chart to determine the dress size a bride (or bridesmaid) should order. Be sure to look at the size chart and follow the manufacturer's recommendations. All dresses can be made smaller, but very few can be made larger.

Wedding Blues

Bridal shops usually tell brides their dresses will arrive in 12 weeks, but each manufacturer quotes a different delivery time for their gowns. While 12 weeks is the average delivery time, there are several designers who take much longer. Ask the bridal shop how long it takes for you to get your gown and what the shop can do for you if your gown does not arrive when promised.

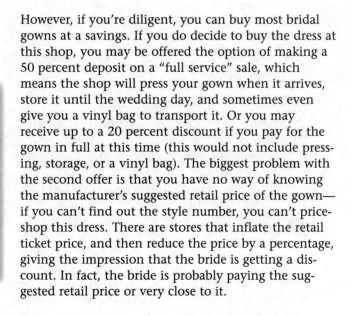

However, if you're diligent, you can buy most bridal gowns at a savings. If you do decide to buy the dress at this shop, you may be offered the option of making a 50 percent deposit on a "full service" sale, which means the shop will press your gown when it arrives, store it until the wedding day, and sometimes even give you a vinyl bag to transport it. Or you may receive up to a 20 percent discount if you pay for the gown in full at this time (this would not include pressing, storage, or a vinyl bag). The biggest problem with the second offer is that you have no way of knowing the manufacturer's suggested retail price of the gown—if you can't find out the style number, you can't price-shop this dress. There are stores that inflate the retail ticket price, and then reduce the price by a percentage, giving the impression that the bride is getting a discount. In fact, the bride is probably paying the suggested retail price or very close to it.

What Is a Bridal Warehouse?

Most communities have a variety of places to purchase wedding gowns at greatly reduced prices. There may be bridal warehouses in your community, or you may see bridal gowns offered at greatly reduced prices in a one-day hotel sale. You can expect to find dresses from $75 to $499. Usually these warehouses and hotel sales carry discontinued gowns or gowns purchased from stores that have gone out of business. Sizes are generally limited, and when you purchase a dress from them it's usually an "as is," "cash and carry" situation. Warehouse stores will frequently take checks and credit cards, while the one-day hotel sales may take only cash and credit cards.

Sue's Suggestions

Some large department store catalogs offer bridal and bridesmaid dresses at greatly reduced prices. Often these are dresses a designer has made specially for the store to sell at a reduced price. The dresses are probably designer copies made in different fabrics. Check these out!

Wedding Blues

If you buy your gown at a bridal warehouse or one-day sale, you won't be able to return it or get any adjustments once you leave the store, so be very sure you examine your dress carefully before you pay for it.

David's Bridal

David's Bridal, a manufacturer and a warehouse store rolled into one, is available to brides in many communities. David's Bridal manufactures all the dresses that are sold in its stores. Prices range from $99 to $899, you can often find dresses on sale for $150. These dresses look like designer dresses, and carry manufacturer names that sound like the names you see in national bridal magazines. A bride should be able to find a style to her liking at a price considerably below those she finds in the typical bridal shops. David's Bridal accepts cash, personal checks, and credit cards for your purchases. You can reach the company toll free at 1-800-399-2743.

Personal Buying Service for Brides

Another option, Discount Bridal Service, Inc. (DBS), may be the budget-minded bride's best friend. This company offers most national brands at a 20 to 40 percent discount off the suggested retail price. The bride is responsible for doing all her own research to find the bridal gown, veil, bridesmaid dress, mothers' or flower girl dress she wants. Then the bride need only call her local DBS representative, give her the manufacturer's name and style number or the page number of the magazine where the gown is pictured. The DBS representative will give the bride a price over the phone. If the bride likes this particular price, she can make an appointment to meet the representative, be measured, and place her order for the gown. When she places the order, the bride will pay for the gown in full, including any necessary taxes and a small shipping fee, and the dress will arrive at the bride's door. The DBS representative charges no fee to the bride.

Most DBS dealers accept credit cards, all accept checks, and all can recommend seamstresses if the gown needs alterations when it arrives. This company is committed to the bride receiving perfect merchandise, so all gowns are inspected before being shipped to the bride. In addition, most DBS dealers can assist brides with discounts on invitations, bridesmaids' gifts and a variety of accessories as well. Discount Bridal Service has dealers all over the United States. To find the dealer closest to you, call 1-800-874-8794.

Tantalizing Trivia

Years ago women married in their best dresses, not necessarily white, but whatever color they chose. Red was popular in the middle ages in Europe, while black silk was often worn in France and England during the nineteenth century. Green was the color choice of Norwegian brides, and royal English brides traditionally wore dresses made of silver-colored cloth. Queen Victoria advocated a return to simplicity, and throughout the Victorian era and into the twentieth century, brides imitated her by wearing white. Although the white dress came to symbolize purity, today white symbolizes the wedding itself and can be wore by anyone.

Rent a Gown?

Renting a wedding gown can also be a good way to save money; but this option can be tricky, and the bride needs to know what questions to ask. You may be able to rent a designer gown, which would sell for several thousand dollars, for only a small percentage of that cost, between $250 and $1,000. Unfortunately, in many cases, even this small percentage may be more than you would expect, and possibly more than you would have to pay for a new wedding gown. Also, if you own the gown, you can make whatever alterations are necessary, whereas alternations may be limited on rental gowns.

If you don't want to buy a wedding gown, rent one from a company that can tell you how many times they intend to rent the gown to other people before your wedding day. Wedding gowns can certainly be dry cleaned, and most will still look great after two or three cleanings; but some fabrics will begin to look limp, and heavily beaded gowns may lose some of their sparkle after repeated dry cleaning.

Resale Shops

Resale or consignment shops have become popular ways to save money on your wedding gown. There may be shops in your community that specialize in bridal attire and they may even be able to help you with bridesmaids' dresses. You can find them in your local yellow pages. Even if you decide not to purchase your wedding gown at a resale shop, you may want to sell your wedding gown to the shop after the wedding, if you decide not to keep it. Just keep in mind that you won't be able to sell the gown for what you paid for it, and there may be "rules" to consider. For instance, some shops will accept only gowns that have been dry-cleaned and are less than five years old. Some shops require an original receipt, some impose a time limit for how long they'll keep the dress in the store, and some also want the authority to reduce the selling price if they deem it necessary.

Sue's Suggestions

Sometimes you can find a truly elegant headpiece in a consignment shop. Don't worry if the illusion veiling is crushed or dirty looking; you can replace it for pennies at your fabric store.

Something Borrowed

Before you think about borrowing a gown, consider what it takes to keep a gown as beautiful today as it was the day the bride got married. Many brides have their gowns preserved so their daughters and even their grandchildren have the option of wearing these beautiful dresses. Dry cleaners preserve gowns but the process involves much more than dry-cleaning, and there are many companies that specialize in preserving wedding gowns.

I spoke to David Galusha, an archival hand cleaner, to understand the process. David explained that the gown is first dry-cleaned to remove all the soil possible. The fabric is then purified, which means that all chemicals from the dry-cleaning and manufacturing processes are removed. The gown is then pressed, folded, and stuffed with acid-free tissue paper and placed in an acid-free box.

The entire process can take about three months to complete and will keep your gown as beautiful as the day you wore it for generations to come. You can expect to pay anywhere from $139 to $400 for this service. For additional information you can find David Galusha on the Internet at www.professionalcleaners.com, or you can call toll free 1-800-690-2146.

If you have a friend who was married in a gown you loved, ask her if she will allow you to borrow it. But if her gown has been preserved, you may have to have it re-preserved after you try it on, and certainly after you wear it. Be sure to ask, because trying it on could cost you hundreds of dollars just to try on your friend's gown!

Even if you plan to borrow a gown, it is a good idea to try on some dresses to see which styles of gowns really look the best on you. We all know what we *think* we look good in, but sometimes when we try it on, we discover it doesn't flatter us at all. By trying on various styles of new wedding gowns you'll have an idea of what looks best on you, so when you see your friend's gown in her pictures, you'll have an idea of how it might really look on you. This research will save you money on re-preserving your friend's gown if you choose not to try on gowns you know will not be complimentary to you.

Sue's Suggestions

Look through your mother's (sister's, cousin's, aunt's) wedding album. Is her dress wonderful? Have you considered borrowing it for your wedding?

The Perfect Fit

Even as you order your gown, give some thought to altering it to fit you perfectly. No seamstress can predict exactly how much it will cost to alter your gown until she sees it on your body. It simply doesn't work to look at the sample gown and quote you a price for alterations. Most seamstresses charge an hourly rate for their work and they base these charges on how many hours it will take them to take the dress apart, make the alteration, and put the garment back together again.

When your dress arrives, the seamstress will look at you in the gown and determine how she will custom fit the gown to you. She will study the way the dress is constructed and determine if she will have to remove beading or separate the lining and how much time this will take her. Only then can she quote you an estimate for alterations. This may sound like a complicated process, but actually alterations can be done quite quickly—most seamstresses tell me they can complete even a complicated alteration in just a day or two. The issue is the number of dresses they have waiting to be altered ahead of any particular bride.

Don't be too concerned about the beading on your dress; most beaded dresses are actually beaded on to a piece of lace and the lace is then attached to the dress. So to alter it, the whole piece of lace is removed, the dress altered, and then the lace and beading are re-attached. You'll want to take note of how the dress is made for alteration purposes, however.

When we talk about hemming a wedding gown, we're talking about shortening the skirt only between the two side seams across the front of the gown. The sides and back of the gown remain long because they will naturally trail behind you as you walk forward. If the front of the gown is too long, however, there is danger that you'll step on it as you move quickly up the aisle after your ceremony. If you step on the front, you'll fall forward. Ideally, when you're wearing your shoes, your dress and slip should measure a generous one and one-half inches off the floor at the toe. Don't be concerned that it doesn't touch the floor—wedding gowns aren't intended to.

If you order your dress from a shop that offers alterations you should start your search for a seamstress right there. But don't feel you *must* have your gown altered there. Get a price and a timetable, and if these do not meet your expectations, you can certainly take your gown to a seamstress of your own choosing. If your dress comes months before the wedding, don't rush to have it altered at this time, but do ask the seamstress what her time schedule indicates. Sometimes, if she's not busy at the moment, a seamstress will recommend that you come in right away and have your long sleeves shortened and perhaps have the gown hemmed and bustled. Then you can go back two weeks before the wedding to have the body of the gown altered. Many brides lose weight as their weddings approach, causing them to have their gowns altered again. While excitement and nervousness can cause some weight loss, nothing I know of will make you get any taller as your wedding approaches.

Wedding Blues

Order your wedding dress based on your measurements *today,* not on what you hope they will be on your wedding day. Wedding gowns are designed to be taken apart and altered. It's much easier to take in a dress if you lose weight than it is to let the dress out if you don't!

Seamstresses who work out of their homes charge between $8 and $10 per hour for their work. Bridal shops hire these same seamstresses to do alterations for the their clients. You can expect to pay slightly more for alternations done at a bridal shop, because, after all, the shop needs to make some money, too.

Trains

Many, but not all, wedding gowns come with trains. A train is a length of fabric that trails behind the bride as she enters the ceremony. Trains come in different lengths depending on the formality of the gown—the longest trains are the most formal. In fact, "the whole nine yards" is an expression that comes from a time when brides at very formal weddings had 27-foot trains on their wedding gowns! The expression came to mean a formal wedding that included everything.

These are the names and sizes of trains you'll encounter in your research:

➤ A *royal train* extends more than three yards from the waist.

➤ A *cathedral train* extends three yards from the waist.

➤ A *chapel train* extends one and one-half yards from the waist.

➤ A *court train* extends one yard from the waist.

➤ A *brush train* is the shortest train and simply brushes the floor.

➤ A *sweep train* is a short train, just slightly longer than a brush train.

Bustles

Your seamstress will also devise and install a *bustle* for your dress, unless you have a gown with a detachable train. The bustle can be done a variety of ways to get the train of the gown up so you can move comfortably during your reception. The seamstress will probably make suggestions for the appropriate bustle for your particular gown style. If you're not working with a bridal consultant, be sure that your maid or matron of honor goes with you to your final fitting so she will know how to bustle the gown. Even if you understand the bustle, you will not be able to do it for yourself while you're in the dress!

Once your dress is bustled, it should be one and one-half inches off the floor all the way around. Many seamstresses like to leave a short (8 inches) train lying on the floor because they think the train makes you look "bridal." The only problem with this is that when you're dancing on a crowded dance floor, if one of your guests' heel lands on that train, your bustle will come down and there is a chance the dress will tear. Besides, dancing is much easier if you do not have to deal with the train on your gown. Nicely, but firmly, indicate that you want your dress bustled completely off the ground for the reception. You'll be so glad that you did!

Language of Love

A **bustle** is a gathering of fabric caught up with a detail at the back of a gown. When a seamstress creates a bustle for your gown, she collects the fabric of the train and gathers it up to the waist of the gown so it will not drag during the reception.

Your Headpiece and Veil

Your bridal gown is just a fancy white or ivory dress until you put on your headpiece and veil—then suddenly you're a Bride! Since this bit of tulle and lace is so important in creating the bridal look, it surprises me that so many brides wait to select theirs. This is an important accessory and it will be in many pictures, so be sure you really like how it looks on you. Try on lots of styles with your hair down and up to see what look you like the best.

Sue's Suggestions

You can easily make your headpiece yourself. Many craft stores carry all the materials, including a variety of how-to books.

Tantalizing Trivia

Rebecca, the first bride mentioned in the Old Testament, is said to have covered herself with a veil as a sign of modesty when her groom Isaac approached her. She is credited with wearing the first bridal veil. The bridal veil was eventually introduced into Europe by returning crusaders. At that time in history, the bride was swathed in a veil, and revealed to her mate only after the ceremony. In Anglo-Saxon times, the bride wore her hair hanging loose as a part of her wedding ritual.

Headpieces do not go with the dress, as evidenced by the fact that only a few gown manufacturers even manufacture headpieces. Instead, veils go with heads and especially with your hair type and style. For instance, a bride with thick curly hair would select a very different headpiece than someone whose hair is fine and straight and will be worn up. If your headpiece is the same color as your gown and has the same kind of beading (pearls with pearls, or rhinestones with rhinestones) they will match perfectly!

It's interesting that headpieces, not gowns, represent the largest profit for most bridal shops. In order to assure this, many shops buy one-of-a-kind headpieces and veils from women who make them in their homes and sell them to the shops, usually for very little money. The shops will triple and sometimes even quadruple whatever price they paid for the veil. Frequently they do this when they sell veils they've purchased from national companies as well. It is very difficult for the customer to price-shop a veil since names and style numbers are usually removed and the differences between styles can be very slight. And every first-time bride needs a veil! (Traditionally, second-time brides skip the veil.)

If you're handy, you can make your own headpiece and veil for approximately $25 with supplies you purchase at most fabric stores. If you decide to purchase your veil from a traditional bridal shop, you can expect to pay between $60 and $350. Veils and headpieces are also available at reduced prices from all the places that sell gowns at discount listed earlier in this chapter.

Brides tend to use the terms *headpiece* and *veil* interchangeably, but in fact they describe two different and separate items. The headpiece is that bit of lace and beading that actually sits on the bride's head. It could be anything from a headband to a decorated barrette. The veil is the "illusion" fabric that attaches to the headpiece and trails down the back. Some brides also select a *blusher* or face veil which is a smaller piece of illusion that can be attached to the front of the headpiece and covers the bride's face as she comes down the aisle.

Other types of veils include

> ➤ A *Madonna* or *flyaway veil* is shoulder length, between 18 to 27 inches long.
>
> ➤ An *elbow-length veil* is between from 28 to 36 inches long.
>
> ➤ A *fingertip veil* is usually 48 inches long, to graze your fingertips when your fingers are extended.
>
> ➤ A *waltz* or *ballerina veil* should end 8 to 12 inches above the floor.
>
> ➤ A *chapel veil* should just skim the floor with nothing trailing behind, but its standard length is quoted as 90 inches, which would certainly make it trail on most brides!
>
> ➤ A *cathedral-length veil* has a very long train, usually longer than the gown itself, generally 108 to 180 inches long.

The headpiece and veil add to the allure of the bride, but can be hard to wear all evening. Many brides find that when they're dancing, their partners may accidentally pull on the veil, which in turn pulls their head back. A way around this is to have the veil attached to the headpiece with Velcro so it can be easily removed after the ceremony. Sometimes brides attach the much shorter blusher to the back of the headpiece after the ceremony so they still have the look of the veil at the reception without having to deal with its length.

The Secrets Underneath It All

Every bride thinks about her gown and her headpiece, but that does not complete her attire for her wedding day. Wearing the proper undergarments not only makes her dress fit properly, but can make a major difference in her own enjoyment of the day.

If your gown has a scoop neck front and back, you may be able to wear the same bra that you wear every day and be wonderfully comfortable as you walk down the aisle, pose for photographs, or boogie 'til dawn. But what if your gown is strapless or backless?

In the best scenario, you'll be able to try on a variety of undergarments when you're trying on your dress. That way you can be sure that the undergarment is low enough in the back and that it complements the bust line of the dress. There are a variety of strapless bras on the market, both the short variety and the longer type, sometimes called a merry widow. Both will work with your gown and are good choices if you find them comfortable.

Comfort is key in this issue. You might choose the longer garment to get the benefit of the waist-cinching effect, but be sure to pay close attention to where the garment ends on your body and whether or not it will rub or dig into you when you sit or dance. Move around in it when you try the garment on, so you can see what it will feel like. The longer variety usually comes with detachable garters that attach to your stockings. You can remove these, or leave them attached and use them. Some brides respond initially to the sexiness of this garter look without realizing the garters actually do the job of holding the long-line garment securely in place.

Sue's Suggestions

Put your panties *over* your stockings and the bottom of your long-line undergarment so you'll be able to use the bathroom once you're in your wedding gown. If you put your panties on underneath, you'll not be able to get to them to remove them.

If your dress has a halter-type top, you'll have choices here, too. There are bras on the market that have criss-cross straps, straps that wrap around your waist, and halter tops. Try on several with your gown and remember to move in as many ways as you think you'll be moving on your wedding day. You won't just be walking down the aisle.

Another option many girls choose is to have cups sewn into their dresses so they will not need to wear a bra at all. This can be a terrific solution and certainly will be comfortable. While this solution sounds simple, it does need to be considered from another angle as well. Wedding gowns are designed with their weight in mind. You probably haven't thought much about it, but all that satin, tulle, lace, and beading will weigh more than your average outfit. The designer considered all this and placed the straps strategically to keep the dress on you for the evening.

By adding cups to the gown, you're adding weight to the top front of the gown without adding a balance. In most gowns, this will not create any problem at all, but if your gown is totally strapless and has no *stays* or *bones* in the midriff portion, but beading in the skirt, adding weight to the top of the gown will increase the pull of gravity as you dance. When you get your video back, you may see that you spent your whole evening grabbing the top of your dress and lifting it back up!

In this case there are two better ideas. You can have your seamstress add cups, and also add hidden spaghetti straps that are tucked inside the top edge of your gown. During the reception if you begin to feel that your dress is slipping, you just slip into the ladies room with your maid of honor and pull the spaghetti straps out and put them on. The spaghetti straps will not detract from the overall beauty of your gown. Besides, by the time you get to the reception, your pictures will be mostly over and you'll be much more interested in simply having a great time.

The other option is to wear a strapless bra and have your seamstress add a modified bone to the inside of the gown to keep it in place. That means that she'll remove the bone from its fabric covering, cut about a two-inch piece off the top of the bone and then insert both pieces back into the fabric covering, leaving a small space between the two pieces. The bottom or longer piece of bone is stitched to the center front lining of your gown, leaving the smaller top piece of bone free so it can move almost like a knuckle on your index finger. You put on your strapless or long-line bra and tuck the top piece of bone into your bra. The dress is now "attached" to your bra and won't move, whatever gravity's pull. Since the bone is covered in its original soft fabric sleeve it will not dig into you.

Some seamstresses have sewn "industrial weight" snaps into the front lining of strapless gowns with the other part of the snap sewn to the bra. This option works on some gowns but will show on others, so follow your seamstress's advice.

Most bridal shops have a selection of undergarments that work with wedding gowns, specifically bras and slips. Or, you may decide to purchase your wedding garments at Victoria's Secret, which has stores in major malls all across the country and offers many styles through their catalogs. If you'd like a slightly sexier look, be sure to check out the Frederick's of Hollywood stores and catalogs. In recent years Frederick's has begun carrying a wide variety of undergarments that work well under bridal attire both for you and for your bridesmaids, and they can be so much fun to shop for!

Language of Love

Stays or **bones** refer to the flat pieces of plastic, roughly $\frac{3}{8}$ inch wide, covered in a soft fabric, that are attached to the lining fabric of strapless gowns to create the support that holds the fabric smooth and the gown in place.

Wedding Blues

You might be tempted to save money by passing up fancy undergarments for your wedding gown—after all, you're going to wear this dress only once. But this is not a place to scrimp; you want your dress to fit you well and this means wearing the correct undergarments.

I hope you'll agree that selecting your wedding gown, headpiece, veil, and all your accessories can be one of the most exciting parts of your wedding planning—and one of the most intriguing. For additional help, please check out Appendix A, "Glossary of Wedding Attire," where I define all the terms you'll find in this chapter and throughout the rest of the book.

The Least You Need to Know

➤ There are many ways to save money when buying your wedding gown.

➤ Planning the alterations of your dress will save you time and money.

➤ Take your undergarments and shoes to every fitting for the very best alteration job.

➤ The train and bustle of your gown, as well as your headpiece and veil, complete your bridal outfit.

➤ Wearing comfortable undergarments will help your dress fit well.

Chapter 6

Your Prince Charming

In This Chapter

➤ What kind of tuxedo should you wear?

➤ Renting a tux

➤ Should you buy a tuxedo?

➤ Other dress options for more informal weddings

➤ Getting the groom involved

Here's a chapter just for all you grooms out there. The men have it easy. The groom simply goes into a tuxedo rental store, selects the style of tuxedo that he'd like to wear, and gets measured. The store then orders this tuxedo from its warehouse and has it ready when the groom comes to pick it up. The groom also selects the tuxedo style that his groomsmen will wear. This can be the same as the groom's, or slightly different.

In this chapter, I'll give you some insights on your wedding attire and try to cut through the confusion surrounding men's formal wear.

Tuxedo Etiquette

It's commonly believed that tuxedos shouldn't be worn until after 6 P.M., but this isn't true. The belief comes from the fact that a major tuxedo company is named "After Six." In fact, tuxedos are appropriate for formal weddings at all times of the day, but the *style* of tuxedo may vary depending on the time of day.

The classic *tuxedo* is a black double- or single-breasted jacket with matching trousers. The tuxedo is available in a variety of fabrics and the groom may select a lighter-weight version for the hot summer months or in warmer climates. It's always worn with a dress shirt, cuff links and studs, a bow tie, and vest or cummerbund. At a formal morning or noon wedding, where guests wear tuxedos, you can expect to see to them in the classic tuxedo. This is because it's the style of tuxedo that most men decide to own, and it's acceptable around the clock.

Wedding Blues

Some tuxedo shops recommend the groom wear an ivory shirt if the bride is wearing an ivory gown. This is usually not a good idea, because the difference in the texture of the fabrics will make them accept the dye differently and when they are next to each other one may make the other appear dirty.

Language of Love

White tie and tails refer to the white piqué tie and tail coat that are worn to very formal affairs.

If the wedding is scheduled between 11 A.M. and 4 P.M., the groom would select the *cutaway/morning coat*. This jacket tapers from the front waist button to a long, wide back tail and is worn with a wing collar shirt, an ascot, and a coordinating vest. His attendants would wear the *stroller/walking coat* version. This jacket is slightly longer than a suit jacket and is worn with a spread collar shirt and a four-in-hand tie (a necktie knotted so the ends hang vertically). Both jackets are available in black or gray and are worn with matching pinstriped trousers.

In an ultra-formal morning wedding, the groom and his attendants may all wear the cutaway/morning coat. For the slightly less formal morning wedding, they may all choose to wear the stroller/walking coat. If the ceremony begins after four o'clock, the groom can choose a white or ivory dinner jacket with black formal trousers for his formal or semiformal wedding, or he can wear a classic all-black tuxedo.

The ultra-formal evening wedding calls for *white tie and tails*. The tail coat jacket is short in the front with two long black tails. It is worn with a white, pique-front, wing-collar shirt, a white tie, and a vest. A tail coat can be worn for a formal daytime or evening wedding in white, gray, or navy with matching ties and cummerbunds.

Tuxedo jackets come with three basic lapel types. Some are more flattering to certain body types than others:

➤ The *wide peak lapel* looks very nice on a short, slender man.

➤ The *slim shawl collar* looks great on a short, muscular, or athletic body, but also looks terrific on a tall, husky man.

➤ The *notched collar* is similar to suit-jacket lapels and looks good on many body types.

Tantalizing Trivia

The tuxedo is said to have gotten its name from the coat that Griswold Lorillard, a tobacco heir, wore to the annual autumn ball at the Tuxedo Park Country Club in 1866. It is reported that guests were shocked when he arrived in a tailless black dinner coat. Mr. Lorillard explained that his coat was fashioned after one worn by the Prince of Wales, and soon after this new style caught on. Prior to this time men's formal attire consisted primarily of tailcoats. Today, tailcoats are included in the general term "tuxedos."

A groom should try on tuxedos with each of the lapel styles to determine which is most flattering.

Selecting the right pant style is also critical, so be sure to try on several different styles of trousers before making your decision. The length of the pant is important to your overall appearance. It's important to understand that tuxedo pants are worn on the waist, while most men usually wear their pants below their waist. If you're measured for a tuxedo from the wrong point, the pants will not be the right length. The perfect pant leg should break slightly at the top of the shoe and angle a bit downward in the back.

The major difference in shirt styles is in the collar. Generally you can find shirts in many different colors, with or without ruffles, pleats, or stripes, in every different collar type:

➤ The *band collar* stands up around the neck above the buttons. It's a very contemporary style and can be worn with either a bow tie or a large button cover at the neck. You'll see band collar shirts with buttonholes for studs or with hidden buttonholes where no studs are worn.

➤ The *traditional* formal shirt is white with buttons or stud closures. Usually the shirt has pleats on either side of the buttons and French cuffs.

Sue's Suggestions

Encourage your groomsmen to return their measurement cards as soon as possible so all the tuxedos for your wedding can be pulled from the newest tuxedos in stock at the warehouse. This way your whole bridal party will look their best, since all the tuxedos will fit well.

➤ The *spread collar* shirt is very similar to a man's dress shirt. The button front shirt can be worn with or without studs.

➤ The *wing collar* is similar to the band collar but with two turned down points in the front. The "wings" can be worn either over the bow tie or just behind it.

Shirt sleeves should extend approximately one-half inch below the jacket sleeves. This is true for all jackets, whether they're tuxedos or every-day suits.

If clothes make the man, accessories definitely make the tuxedo! This is probably the only outfit a man ever wears where the accessories require so much attention. Most tuxedos require the bow tie, *cummerbund*, studs, and cuff links. Occasionally a groom will select a Euro-tie, which is a long, knotted square-bottom necktie worn with a wing or spread collar. Suspenders are generally included with a rented tuxedo but it's not mandatory for the groom to wear them. But keep in mind that tuxedo trousers do not have belt loops and the cummerbund may not be sufficient to hold up trousers on some body types, so suspenders may be necessary.

Grooms can select vests instead of cummerbunds if they decide to wear a single-breasted tuxedo. When the vest is worn, it should be long enough to cover the waistband of the trousers, and the bottom button is left unbuttoned. When they make that decision, they often choose a tie that matches the vest. An *ascot* is worn with the daytime cutaway jacket and a wing-collar shirt. It's similar to a wide necktie, almost like a scarf, that is held in place with a tie tack or stickpin.

Tuxedo jackets are worn buttoned over a vest but unbuttoned over a cummerbund. Single-breasted tuxedo jackets may be worn either buttoned or unbuttoned but double-breasted jackets are always worn buttoned. For this reason, it is unnecessary to wear a cummerbund with a double-breasted jacket.

The groom's outfit is not complete until he selects his shoes. Black plain-toed shoes and dress socks are appropriate with black tuxedos. The groom may select either a laced shoe or a loafer style, often in shiny patent leather or in a highly buffed plain leather. Tuxedo shops usually do not include shoes in the rental price but offer them for a small additional fee. Unfortunately, rented shoes can be quite uncomfortable, often because they're vinyl instead of leather. If

Language of Love

A **cummerbund** is a satin sash with pleats that face up. It's wider in the front than it is in the back where it attaches. It's worn instead of a vest and should match the bow tie.

Sue's Suggestions

If you will be taking a cruise for your honeymoon, ask the tuxedo shop if it offers a cruise package. Cruises generally include one or more formal nights. This package extends the rental period to include your honeymoon and can include an extra jacket and an additional shirt for a small additional fee.

the groom owns his own plain-toed black dress shoe (wing tips are *not* appropriate) he might be wise to consider wearing his own shoes. Naturally, if the groom selects a white tuxedo he will wear white shoes and white *dress* socks—no tube or athletic socks on your wedding day!

Once the groom has made his decision and selected the tuxedo he wants to wear for the wedding, he will then select either the same tuxedo style for his groomsmen and ushers, or something that is complementary.

It may be hard to believe, but the same tuxedo can rent for $45 in one store and $145 in another just across town. This difference in pricing can be caused by many factors, not the least of which is whether or not the warehouse owns its own dry cleaning machines. Be diligent enough to price-shop the tuxedos for your wedding just as you would any other item that you are selecting.

Once the decision has been made, the tuxedo store will provide a set of postcards for the groom to mail to each out-of-town member of his bridal party, including both fathers, so they can go into a tuxedo shop or store that sells quality men's clothing in their town and get measured. The postcard will ask for a specific set of measurements such as waist, out seam, sleeve length, neck, and usually the man's height and normal suit size. These measurements will allow the tuxedo store to have the proper size on hand when the groomsman, usher, or father arrives.

The person who measures the groomsmen will write those measurements on the card and mail it to the tuxedo store that the groom has selected, and the groomsmen's tuxedos will be ordered from there. While stores all over the country are happy to measure groomsmen for weddings that will take place somewhere else, each store has its own sizing guidelines. That's why the tuxedos sometimes don't fit even when the measurements are accurate. A good way to minimize this problem is to have your local groomsmen all measured by the same store.

Sue's Suggestions

Some tuxedo rental companies offer the groom a free tuxedo if a minimal number of tuxedos are ordered for the wedding. Remember to count both the bride and groom's fathers to take advantage of this special deal.

Wedding Blues

Matthew's two cousins from Australia, who were groomsmen, submitted their measurements in centimeters instead of inches and feet! The tuxedo shop did its best to convert the measurement, but when the cousins arrived, their tuxedos did need some additional alternations.

Where Do Tuxedos Come From?

Have you ever wondered where the tuxedos for your wedding actually come from? The store has only a few styles to show you and not every style is available in every size, so how does it supply tuxedos for all your groomsmen in all their varied sizes and shapes? The answer is quite simple, the stores are supplied by a large tuxedo warehouse. This warehouse has the styles of tuxedo the store has shown you in every imaginable size, with several in the most common sizes.

Typically, tuxedo orders must be received by the warehouse no later than ten days before the wedding. This is the date that the items needed to fill your order will actually be pulled from stock. If alterations are necessary on a tuxedo in your order, they will be done at this time, and then all the pieces will be assembled. The next day, your order will be checked again and loaded on to a truck to be delivered to the store where you'll be picking up the tuxedo either on Thursday evening or Friday.

Sue's Suggestions

If most of your groomsmen are in town on Thursday, it's a good idea to arrange to pick up the tuxedos as early in the day as possible. Tuxedo stores can be very busy on Friday and if someone needs repairs you will be picking up the corrected suit on the Saturday morning of the wedding.

When the groom and his groomsmen arrive at the tuxedo shop, they should allow plenty of time to try on their tuxedos to see if everything fits and all the parts showed up. Many tuxedo shops have tailors available to make whatever adjustments may be necessary to assure a most acceptable fit. If the groom or groomsmen wait until the day of the wedding to try their tuxedos on, they might have a problem!

Most tuxedo rental stores request that the tuxedo be returned on the first business day after the wedding, usually a Monday. The store counts the tuxedo parts to make sure everything has been returned, and then the warehouse picks them up. Tuesday is usually dry-cleaning day at the warehouse where all parts of the tuxedo are dry cleaned and made ready for the process to repeat itself the next week.

Rent or Buy?

If your lifestyle is such that you'll wear a tuxedo two more times this year, you'd probably be wise to purchase your tuxedo. Depending on the cost of the tuxedo, the rental fee could be more than one third of the purchase price. When you own it, you can alter it to fit you exactly, and you'll be much more comfortable in it than you could possibly be in a rented suit.

You may find that several members of your bridal party also own their own tuxedos. If this is the case, you can certainly suggest that they wear their own tuxedos and you can all rent matching vests and bow ties to coordinate the look. If your tuxedo is single-breasted, but two of your groomsmen own double-breasted tuxedos, consider asking them to rent single-breasted jackets to create a more uniform look. If the only difference is in the lapels, take a look at the peak, shawl, and notched tuxedo lapels in the tuxedo store and see if you notice the differences between them when they're all lined up. If you notice the difference and it bothers you, you'll probably want to be sure that the guys in your wedding all have the same lapel and may find yourself right back renting tuxedos. If you don't find the differences objectionable, then don't worry about it; let your groomsmen wear their own tuxedos—one lapel will be covered with a boutonniere anyway!

Do I *Have* to Be Married in a Tuxedo?

Of course not! If you and your bride are planning an informal wedding, you can be married in a dark suit, a navy blazer and white slacks, or if it's very warm, just an oxford shirt, pretty tie, and khaki slacks. You'll want to coordinate your outfit to the formality of the bride's wedding gown (even though she won't let you see it) and the feeling of the event. Whatever you choose, your attendants should be similarly dressed and you will still want to honor them with boutonnieres. (See Chapter 7, "A Rose By Any Other Name.")

Sometimes tuxedos are selected because the members of the bridal party don't all own dark blue or charcoal gray suits. Chances are it would be much more costly for everyone to buy the same color suits than it would be for them to rent tuxedos. One groom explained his reason for wearing a tuxedo, even though his wedding was quite informal: He didn't want to make this lifestyle change while wearing the same suit he had worn to negotiate a business deal last week. He really wanted his wedding attire to be special even if it didn't *belong* to him!

"Just tell me when to show up!"

Many grooms tell their brides they are happy to leave the planning to her since they completely trust her opinions and taste. They probably assume the bride really doesn't want them to be involved and would prefer to do this on her own. Besides, many grooms feel completely out of their element in the world of flowers, music, and cakes. Brides often interpret this as a lack of interest, not just in the wedding plans, but in the new life that they are beginning together. Unless this is handled carefully, the whole issue of the groom's involvement in the wedding plans can become a major problem with communication between them.

One good way to avoid this problem is for the groom to volunteer to take care of certain parts of the wedding himself. He can do all the research and then present the options to the bride so the couple can make the final decision together, just as the bride has been doing. By doing this, he will experience some of the excitement his bride is talking about and be saving her time so she will not feel overwhelmed with so many details to accomplish.

Ring My Chimes

For example, the groom may be the perfect person to research the purchase of the wedding bands. He has already worked with a jeweler when he selected the engagement ring, so he has some experience in this area. The place to start is with the original jeweler, especially if he would like to present his bride with a wedding band that matches the engagement ring. The original jeweler will have the companion band, or will be able to make one to accompany the engagement ring simply by taking an impression of it. This does sometimes mean the engagement ring has to be returned to the original jeweler for a short time.

Some couples prefer a plain gold wedding band. If that's the case, the groom might not want to go back to the original jeweler, but instead to any one of several independent jewelry or even discount stores. He can do the legwork, comparing the weight, width, and prices on the bands he most admires. If he is planning to wear a wedding band, he can select the one he would like to wear and bring his bride back to that location so she can purchase it. He may select a band just like his to present to his bride so they will have matching bands. Usually a woman's band is a different width than the man's, but that is simply a matter of taste. Once the wedding bands are purchased and sized, the groom should be responsible for picking them up and putting them in a safe place until the wedding day.

Wedding Blues

When Jim picked up the wedding bands three weeks before the wedding, he took them directly to the safe deposit box at the bank for safe keeping. The problem was, he forgot to pick them up before the bank closed on the Friday before his wedding. Jim and Katy borrowed her parents' bands for the ceremony, but didn't get to wear their real wedding bands until they returned from their honeymoon!

The Paper Chase

Researching the marriage documents and making all the necessary appointments is another good place for the groom to get involved. If your state requires blood tests, the groom can make the arrangements to have these done at the proper time. (See Chapter 4, "Getting Ready for the Big Day: Wedding Essentials.") If proof of identification is required, he can set about locating the couples' birth certificates or passports so they will be ready when the time comes to get the license. If either the bride or groom is underage and needs parental consent for the license to be issued, he can secure the letter of consent from the parents or coordinate the plans to get the license so that a parent can accompany the couple to the license bureau. About the only thing he can't do is secure a copy of the bride's divorce decree, if she has been married previously. She probably has documentation of this decree in her safe deposit box, but if not, she will have to apply for it in person.

Get Up and Go

Wedding day transportation can be a major issue and this is another area in wh
the groom can lend a hand. You may need a limousine to pick up the bride, her p
ents, and the bridesmaids and take them to the church for the ceremony. A second
limousine may be necessary to pick up the groom and his parents. After the ceremony, the bride and groom will ride in one limousine to the reception site; the parents may all ride together in the second limousine; but then, how do the bridesmaids
and groomsmen get to the reception? After the reception, how do the bride and
groom get to their wedding night hotel? How do the parents get back home, or back
to their hotel? Friends can come in handy here—the bridal party's dates and/or
spouses can take them home. Parents can ride with friends if they choose not to leave
a car at the reception site earlier in the day. And sometimes a hotel will send its own
car to pick up people.

It's a good idea for the groom to drive the various
routes and write out clear directions to the bride's
parents home and from there to the church.
Another set of directions will be needed to wherever the groom and his parents will be picked up
and from there to the church. A third set of directions will be needed from the church to the reception site. If these directions are sent to the
limousine company in advance, you can feel secure
that the transportation will be waiting for you at
the appropriate time and no one will get lost.

Be sure to work out costs and payment before the
wedding weekend. Very few people carry money or
credit cards to weddings, so you will want to have
everything handled on your credit card before the
event, including the tip.

Sue's Suggestions

When making reservations with the
limousine company, ask for the
name and car phone number of
your driver. This way you can contact him directly if your plans
change or if the car does not arrive
when you are expecting it.

Pick Up the Loose Ends

Selecting gifts for your groomsmen and ushers should be accomplished well in
advance of the wedding weekend. If the gifts are to have a monogram, be sure you
label each as you wrap it so each groomsmen receives the correct gift. It is customary
for the groom to present his bride with a wedding gift. Select this well in advance,
too, and have it wrapped and ready to present when you present the gifts to your
attendants.

Begin speaking to your travel agent about the honeymoon early in your engagement
and be careful that all your plans are completed and you have your tickets at least a
week before the wedding. The bride will have participated in much of the decision
making and certainly will have done her own packing for the honeymoon, but the
groom can be responsible for picking up the tickets and final travel documents.

Tantalizing Trivia

...ne Anglo-Saxon groom often had to defend his bride from kidnappers, so she stood to his left, allowing him to have his right hand free to wield his sword. The best man, who traditionally was the best swordsman in the village, stood to his right, ever ready to assist him in his defense of the bride should it become necessary.

Most grooms get themselves organized so that everything they need for the rehearsal dinner (place cards, name tags, attendant gifts, bride's gift) is in one bag labeled "Rehearsal Dinner." Things needed for the ceremony, such as rings and the marriage license, are in a bag labeled "Ceremony"; and things needed for the honeymoon, such as tickets, passports, traveler's checks, and money (including several dollar bills for tips), are in a third bag labeled "Honeymoon." If these bags are lined up near the door, the groom knows he won't forget to take something with him to the appropriate place. If the best man is actually checking the bride and groom into their wedding night hotel before he arrives at the church, he will be able to collect the bag of honeymoon documents when he picks up the groom's suitcase early in the wedding day.

A groom can be a big help to his bride simply by expressing interest in the planning she's doing and by accomplishing in a timely manner the tasks he agrees to perform. This will help her stay stress free and will keep her the lovely woman he wants to spend the rest of his life with.

Sue's Suggestions

It's not necessary for you to have champagne poured for the toast unless you like champagne and believe your guests do as well. Any sparkling wine (or nonalcoholic sparkling grape juice) will work, so if champagne is very costly, or you have guests who don't drink alcohol, select something else.

Toasts

Toasts are an important part of the rehearsal dinner and wedding reception, but if they are not well planned, they can feel like they are going on forever and yet going nowhere! Every member of your bridal party is not required to make a toast—in fact, only the best man has the privilege (and requirement) of the first toast at the wedding reception. During the rest of the wedding reception the groom may toast his bride, the bride's father may toast the couple, and the bride and groom should toast their parents. Other guests may toast the couple simply by tapping their glasses to get everyone's attention.

Generally the host of the wedding welcomes the guests imm￼
dance. If the bride and groom are paying for the event, the
the welcome. If the bride's parents are the hosts, the brid￼
welcome. It is very nice if the bride and groom and her mot￼
him, so it appears that he speaks for all of them as he welcomes
wonderful celebration. A welcome is *not* a toast! So the father shoul￼
couple at this time. The best man will either toast the couple immediat￼
the welcome, or he may wait to offer his toast when the cake is cut later i￼
evening.

If you know that you have several uncles or very close friends who will want to oft￼
toasts at your wedding reception, it is probably a good idea to assign them a time to
do this. By doing this your other guests will not have to sit through five toasts all at
one time. Ask two of your uncles to toast between appetizer and salad; two to toast
between salad and entrée and one to toast between entrée and dessert. This not only
spreads the good wishes throughout the evening but keeps you from breaking the
action on the dance floor for endless toasts.

Wedding toasts may be amusing, sentimental, loving, clever or serious, but they *must* be tasteful!
This is not the time for off-color jokes or for relating stories that have meaning only to a small number of the guests. No one in the room should be
made uncomfortable by the content of any of the
toasts. The toasts should be brief, usually not
longer than two minutes, and it's probably a good
idea for the person offering the toast to make some
brief notes so he or she will remember what to say.

Sue's Suggestions

The person(s) receiving the toast should never drink at the end of the toast, but should remain seated and smile.

Tantalizing Trivia

David was dressing for his brother's wedding when he decided to begin his toast with the words "As I was getting ready this morning and putting on my panty hose ..." He was sure everyone would laugh, so he planned to pause for their laughter before continuing with his toast. Instead, the guests all looked at each other in bewilderment and whispered to one another "I didn't know he wore panty hose!" David was so embarrassed he rushed through the important part of his toast and couldn't wait to get rid of the microphone!

The rehearsal or prenuptial dinner follows a slightly different set of rules when it comes to toasting. This group is usually smaller and more intimate, so the toasts can be slightly more personal but they also need to be in good taste. It is not necessary for each member of the bridal party to toast at the rehearsal dinner, but several members may create one toast, skit, or song together. If there is any question about the appropriateness of your toast, run it by a close family friend before offering it.

The Least You Need to Know

➤ Part of renting a tuxedo is being professionally measured to ensure the best fit possible.

➤ Tuxedos are appropriate for all hours of the day and evening. The cutaway and stroller versions are most appropriate for morning weddings.

➤ Accessories are an important part of wearing a tuxedo and care should be used in selecting the perfect accessories to complement your look.

➤ If your lifestyle merits it, buying a tuxedo may be more cost-effective than renting one.

➤ For a less formal ceremony, you and your groomsmen may wear dark suits or other more casual options instead of tuxedos.

Chapter 7

A Rose By Any Other Name

In This Chapter

➤ Why bigger is not always better when it comes to bridal bouquets

➤ Following your florist's advice on flower selection

➤ Two weddings, one set of flowers?

➤ Low-cost corsages, boutonnieres, and throwaway bouquets

➤ Do-it-yourself ideas that look great and save you money

➤ Understanding the florist's contract

Because most florists can work more than one wedding into a day, you'll have more time to research your florist than you will for your disc jockey, bandleader, or photographer. Slow down here and really do some research. Flowers create the image of your wedding—they set the scene, so you'll want to give some careful thought to what you choose.

Floral charges can be a little confusing, however, because they include the cost of both the blossoms and the labor charges for making up the arrangements, personal bouquets, boutonnieres, and corsages. For centerpieces, you usually need to add the cost of renting the base or container, too. There's usually a delivery fee or service charge, and you'll be charged tax on the cost of your total order.

In this chapter I'll guide you through working with your florist to get the most for your money.

Bigger Is Not Always Better

Don't get carried away with the size of your bridal bouquet. It should complement you and your gown, not overpower you. You can save money on your bouquet by choosing an open, airy bouquet with fewer, perhaps larger flowers, and some ivy or baby's breath to fill it out. Nosegay bouquets (small round bouquets) tend to be less expensive than large cascading bouquets. If you love an exotic or expensive kind of flower, such as gardenias or orchids, select one for the center of your bouquet instead of using it for the whole bouquet. You'll get the effect with a much lower price tag.

Tantalizing Trivia

Small round bouquets called "nosegays" are very popular today. These bouquets got their name in the early 1800s, before plumbing was available. Most people used chamber pots that were emptied on the street each morning. When ladies walked down the street, they carried small round bouquets of fresh flowers to "keep their noses gay"—hence the name, nosegays! This bouquet style is very popular at the present time and works well with hand-tied bouquets.

Another benefit to carrying smaller bouquets is their lighter weight. You'll be holding your bouquet for the pictures, and then for the ceremony, and maybe for pictures after the ceremony as well. Most brides never think about the weight of their bouquets, which can be heavy. If your bouquet is created in a plastic holder, which helps keep the flowers fresh, the bouquet will be not only heavy, but awkward and difficult to hold. When a bouquet is heavy and awkward, it will tend to make you feel tired and sluggish—not how you want to feel on your wedding day!

Let Your Florist Guide You

For many brides, flowers represent a "blind item." Few brides have enough experience to know if $100 is too little money to spend on flowers or if $5,000 is too much. It's usually easier to look at each item individually and determine what the bride is comfortable spending on each one—her bouquet, her bridesmaids' bouquets, centerpieces, and decorations. This way she can deal with the cost in parts instead of the whole, which is much less intimidating.

In addition, most brides don't really know which flowers are in season and reasonable and which are exotics and very expensive and fragile. For this reason the bride should get to know her florist well and be comfortable explaining her ideas for the wedding first, before discussing the kind of flowers she wants. In most cases, the florist will guide you to the flowers that will work best for your ideas, for your colors, and on your budget. As a professional, a florist can be expected to know flowers and what they will and won't do. We can get into trouble if we insist on the florist producing something he or she doesn't have faith in. If you don't feel that you can trust this florist's suggestions, then he or she is the wrong florist for you.

One bride, who loved tulips, decided that she wanted each of her four bridesmaids to carry a different color bouquet of hand-tied tulips. The florist explained that tulips were not a good choice for bridal bouquets, and would be better suited in the centerpieces where they could have a constant water supply and where their hollow stems could be maintained at a more constant temperature. But the bride insisted, so the florist created four hand-tied tulip bouquets for her client.

Sue's Suggestions

Select the most popular and inexpensive flowers for bouquets and centerpieces. If you love a certain flower but it's expensive, ask to have one blossom surrounded by less expensive flowers in your bouquet.

The bride and her bridesmaids took nearly an hour and a half's worth of pictures in the garden before the ceremony. It was a very warm spring day and the bridesmaids held their bouquets throughout the picture-taking process. By the time the ceremony began, the tulips had opened so far that most of the petals had simply fallen off and the bridesmaids walked down the aisle carrying stems with only a few peach-colored petals. Angry as she was, the bride had only herself to blame. The florist had explained that the tulip stems would absorb the bridesmaids' body heat and open very quickly. The bride had just refused to listen!

Selecting a single flower tied with a pretty ribbon for your bridesmaids saves the costly labor charges. Or you could select just a few blossoms tied together without the costly and heavy plastic holders filled with oasis (a green, spongy material that holds water to keep the flowers fresh). Let the florist guide you to flowers that will last a long time in hand-tied bouquets and still look pretty. Since body heat will travel up the stems of these flowers while they are in your bridesmaids' hands, some flowers will open more fully than you might want during picture taking and won't be fresh for the ceremony.

Tantalizing Trivia

In ancient times, brides wore orange-blossom wreaths to secure their bridal veils. Orange blossoms were quite expensive, so brides on a budget often resorted to using artificial orange blossoms on their veils. They would then select other flowers to carry and the flowers developed special meanings. Apple blossoms came to symbolize better things to come; clematis was considered the love vine; ivy came to represent good luck; rosebuds represented a promise; myrtle was considered the lover's flowers; laurel stood for peace. There were also flowers whose meanings made them undesirable in a wedding. For instance, yellow flowers represented jealousy, and tulips, infidelity!

Wedding Blues

Be careful about the flowers you select for your bouquets. It doesn't make sense to select the most expensive blossoms and then try to save money by hand tying them.

Sharing Flowers

Another way to save money on your ceremony decorations is to share flowers with another bride who is having her wedding at your ceremony location on the same day. Call the bride to see if you can share the expense. Perhaps you can decorate the sanctuary all in white, which will go with both weddings, and add just a splash of whatever color you prefer—the florist can remove your pink blossoms and substitute her red ones. Of course, neither of you will be able to take those flowers on to your reception site, but that will save you the transfer fee that the florist was planning to charge you anyway.

You may be able to do the same thing with your reception flowers. If your reception facility usually has two weddings in one day, and you happen to be the first one, call the bride from the second reception and ask her if she is willing to share decorations. If you are both having a buffet table and then only scattered seating for your guests, you might be able to go to the florist and design the centerpieces together, so it will work for both your weddings. You would then share the cost of these centerpieces and have only the full costs of your personal flowers.

Most major cities have wholesale floral markets where florists purchase the flowers they sell in their shops. When it comes to doing a wedding, however, these same florists do not depend on the floral market, because they can't be sure the flowers they need will be available. Wanting the very finest flowers for their brides, florists usually order their flowers in advance and have what they need flown in specifically for their wedding. This assures them the choice of the most beautiful blossoms for their brides. Of course, it does mean that the bride must notify her florist well in advance of the wedding date if she adds or subtracts a bridesmaid, or if she needs more or fewer table centerpieces than she originally expected.

Sue's Suggestions

Save money by buying flowers in bulk from a floral warehouse and arranging them yourself.

Florists usually order the flowers for your wedding 14 days before the wedding, so you should note that date on your floral contract. After that date, you usually can add to your order, but you won't be able to reduce it, because the florist will have already secured the flowers. If you do add to your order, the florist knows he or she will be able to secure the additional blossoms at the wholesale floral market in town.

Naturally, when your florist orders the flowers flown in for your wedding, he or she selects flowers that are in season. If you want a type of flower that has to be cultivated somewhere else, because it's out of season here, you'll pay dearly for it. The higher cost comes not from having flowers flown in, but where they're flown in *from!* If the florist orders early enough for the wholesaler to get the flowers from any of his or her sources, the wholesaler will hold to the original quote, whether the flowers come from Florida or California. But it only gets expensive if you ask for tulips in July and they have to be flown in from Holland!

Corsages, Throwaway Bouquets, and Boutonnieres

There seems to be a trend today to eliminate *corsages* for the mothers and grandmothers. The trend may have nothing to do with the floral budget. The fact is, most women find corsages uncomfortable and don't want to pin them on their dresses. Instead, ask mom and grandma if they would like to carry a single flower down the aisle, perhaps tied with a pretty ribbon. This flower, along with the bridesmaids' bouquets, can be used to decorate the cake table after the ceremony. Or you can carry a few single flowers along with your wedding bouquet, and after the ceremony hand one to each mother and grandmother as you and your new husband walk up the aisle. It's a lovely gesture. If you do decide to use corsages, don't get carried away. It's not necessary to honor every woman who is special to you with a corsage.

Language of Love

A **corsage** is an arrangement of flowers to be worn by a woman. A **boutonniere** is a flower or small bouquet worn at the buttonhole usually on men.

Language of Love

A **throwaway bouquet** is the bouquet the bride throws to the single ladies during the reception. Superstition says the lady who catches it will be the next to marry. This bouquet can be as simple as three or four daisies or carnations tied together with a beautiful ribbon.

Originally the groom's *boutonniere* was a blossom from the bride's bouquet. In ancient days, she sent him the blossom to let him know he was in her thoughts as she prepared for the wedding. For this reason, some florists still do not charge for the groom's boutonniere today. If your florist has it on the proposal, ask him about it; he may be willing to simply remove the charges.

Most florists do not charge for your *throwaway bouquet* as long as you don't request something very elaborate. A few flowers tied with a ribbon is not only sufficient, but safer for the ladies who are trying to catch it. If you throw your real bouquet, the weight of it could hurt someone if it hit her. Read your contract and if the florist is charging for this, you may decide to make it yourself.

Doing It Yourself: Low-Cost Decorating Ideas

Some brides choose silk flower arrangements and bouquets for their weddings. Contrary to public opinion, silk flowers are not less expensive than real ones—they just last longer. Silk flowers are less expensive only because you can save labor charges by making the arrangements and bouquets yourself. If you plan to do this, watch your local dealer carefully for when the flowers go on sale, and then purchase what you need. Or ask if the store will offer you a quantity discount. If so, figure out how many flowers you'll need for your entire wedding and buy them all at one time. You can make these decorations in advance and have friends deliver them to the reception site while you're being photographed at the ceremony site. After the wedding, you can give the centerpieces to friends as a thank you for helping.

Here are some money-saving decorating ideas you might consider:

➤ Fill a ball-shaped glass bowl with water and float one large blossom in it, put it on a mirror square, and set votive candles around it for a sophisticated centerpiece that's quite inexpensive.

➤ Use framed pictures of your groom's and your parents and grandparents and surround them by scattered petals on the seat-assignment/ place card table. This decoration costs almost nothing and adds a lovely sentiment to your wedding.

➤ Place your throwaway bouquet on the seat-assignment/place card table. It will match the wedding flowers and will be right there when you go to look for it to throw.

➤ Use fresh fruits and vegetables in your centerpieces. Deep purple eggplants and red cabbages mixed with lemons, limes, and oranges give the whole room a unique appearance, and the natural aroma of the fruits will add to the ambiance of the area. Or try mixing fruits with flowers for a unique look. If you cut a lemon or lime in half as part of the arrangement, you will really perfume the room.

➤ If you're planning a spring wedding think about using potted plants for centerpieces, perhaps placed on mirrors and surrounded by votive candles. After the wedding, use these plants as gifts or plant them in your yard.

➤ Use blossoming bulbs as centerpieces. Tall daffodils in a rock-filled shallow bowl, for example, are inexpensive, look contemporary, and smell delightful as well.

➤ Tie balloons with ribbons and attach them to plastic bags filled with corn kernels or dry beans (to keep the balloons from floating away). Then put them into mini shopping bags filled with long-stemmed daisies, for instance, that you can purchase yourself. This will give you an interesting and very professional look—for much less than you think!

➤ Wrap rented ficus trees with twinkling white or gold lights to give your reception room a romantic, sparkly feeling.

Sue's Suggestions

If you can get access to your reception location the day before the wedding, do your own decorating. You can also make all your centerpieces yourself. There are wonderful ideas as well as supplies available at craft stores. Many craft stores offer classes to teach the techniques you'll use for making your own decorations.

Sue's Suggestions

Your throwaway bouquet can also be used first as a cake topper. Set a small Dixie cup down inside the top of the cake and place your throwaway bouquet on top. Cut a small hole in the top of the cake to accommodate the Dixie cup. This works best with a solid-type icing such as buttercreme.

➤ Tie assorted sizes of white gift boxes with bows in your wedding colors and cluster them together as a centerpiece. For a festive look, lay curly ribbon right off the spool around the boxes.

➤ Use live fish in small fishbowls to add movement and color to your centerpiece. Children love to take these home.

➤ If you'd love to have elaborate, tall floral arrangements on your guest tables but the cost is prohibitive, decorate every other table or every third table in an elaborate style; then scale back on the others. Your florist can coordinate the entire look. Some tall and some short centerpieces add a beautiful dimension and variety to an overall uniform room.

Sue's Suggestions

Rather than purchasing the same type of container to hold all your centerpiece flowers, be creative and use an assortment of containers you have around your house. Most people are surprised by how many shapes and colors they find. This will be less expensive and give an interesting, unique look to the tables.

Look to the yellow pages for a school that teaches floral arranging. Perhaps you can find a teacher or talented student who will work with you on your wedding. You may be able to purchase the flowers at your local floral market and then have them arranged by the teacher or student at a significantly lower rate.

Understanding the Contract

Read your florist's contract carefully and be sure you understand exactly what you're getting. Florists sell an image, and you want to be sure they see what you see. Florists are no more gifted mind readers than any of your other vendors, so you may want to show them pictures of your likes and dislikes to be sure they understand what you're looking for. If you have no idea what you want, ask them to show you pictures of their work and tell them what you like or don't like about each photograph. This will help them understand your taste so they can design flowers that will create the look you want.

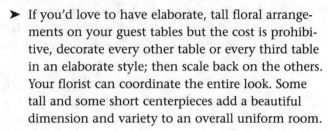

Wedding Blues

It's important to understand that approximately one third of the price of your flowers is for the actual flowers, one third is for the rental of the containers, and one third is for the labor. So if you have a $900 contract, only $300 will actually be spent on blossoms. Be prepared—$300 worth of flowers doesn't look like $900, even though it is!

Because this education process can take several hours of a florist's time, some shops charge an initial consultation fee. Also, some brides spend one to two hours with several different floral shops to get ideas, so many florists have implemented an hourly fee. Ask your florist if he or she charges to discuss plans. Most florists will apply their consultation fees to the floral costs once an order is placed.

Take a look at this sample contract from a florist and note what is included. Can you imagine the flowers?

Flowers For You, Inc.
123 Main Street
Anytown, Georgia
Phone: 123-555-5555   Fax: 123-555-6666

Wedding Flower Proposal for Suzabelle Bride

Ceremony: June 17, 1999
Ceremony time: 5:00 P.M.
Pictures to begin at: 3:00 P.M.
Location: Ridgeway Hotel Ballroom A
Reception: Ridgeway Hotel Ballroom B-C
Color Palette: to be determined

Suggested types of flowers (based on availability):

Freesia   Stock
Lilacs   Larkspur
Roses   Queen Anne's Lace
Iris   Lisianthus

Tulips in centerpieces, not in bouquets.

Overall desired look: Bride likes natural garden setting look.

The Bridal Bouquet: $150.00
Round, hand-gathered bouquet. Satin-wrapped stems and backed with bow. Roses, stephanotis, freesia, shades of white.

4 Bridesmaids Bouquets @ $60/each: $240.00
Round, hand-gathered bouquets with short exposed stems tied with elegant ribbons.

Maid of Honor: $70.00
Similar to the Bridesmaid Bouquet but a little larger and possibly more predominate in one particular color.

Toss Bouquet: $25.00

Groom's Boutonniere (Stephanotis): $10.00

20 Single-Rose Boutonnieres @ $5.00/each: $100.00
At least two weeks before the wedding, florist will need a list of gentlemen to receive boutonnieres.

4 Corsages @ $20.00/each: $80.00
Delicate mixture of petite roses and freesia in shades of pink and white. Two weeks before the wedding, florist will need the names of ladies to receive corsages. These can be designed as wrist corsages, pin-on corsages, or hand-held corsages if you prefer.

continues

---

continued

Bows and Ribbons for Aisle 6 @ $15/each: $90.00

Chuppah Jewish wedding canopy: *$400.00*
Simplistic freestanding structure with Crepe Myrtle. Tree trunks as poles which will be anchored in garden pots and decorated with natural materials, foliage, and flowers. Family talis [prayer shawl] will be used for the top.

Financial Breakdown:

Bride & Groom's Flower Expenses:

The Wedding Party	$ 675.00
Ceremony Flowers	$ 475.00
Delivery, Installation & Removal (20%)	$ 230.00
Subtotal	$1,380.00
Sales tax (6%)	$ 82.80
Total	$1,462.80

25% deposit due: January 12, 1999

25% due on May 17, 1999

Balance due on June 17, 1999 (Please ask best man or bridal consultant to have check available when ceremony flowers have been installed.)

Delivery scheduled for June 17, 1999 at noon.

Terms:

Your date on our calendar will be held for two weeks; after two weeks a 25% deposit with a letter of agreement must be received to guarantee our services. Revisions to the contract may be made at any time after contract is received.

25% of the remaining balance is due one month before the event. (In the event this contract is to be divided into "Bridal" portion and "Groom's" portion, this payment should include 100% of the Groom's portion.)

Refund Policy: Cancellation of an event prior to four weeks before the event will result in a refund of funds paid, minus a $150.00 penalty, additional expenses incurred, restocking fees, air freight and special order penalties. All cancellations must be submitted in writing.

In the event of theft, loss of or damaged props, it is the client's (the party paying the Bride's expenses) responsibility to fully compensate replacement value of all stolen, lost, or damaged items that are rented or on loan by Flowers For You, Inc.

It is the responsibility of the client to make sure that Flowers For You, Inc. has a copy of all policies that will affect the floral installation at any facility used, including the church. Please send these printed instructions with your deposit.

All flowers listed are subject to change due to occasional circumstances beyond our control, such as weather, airline mistakes, improper shipping, and Mother Nature. In the event that a flower is substituted, an upgrade usually takes place at no additional charge. Dealing with perishable products requires flexibility; using quality products to achieve your floral "look" is our goal.

Payments can be made by cash or credit card. If personal checks are to be used, they must be presented 72 hours before the event and must clear the bank before installation of floral arrangements can begin.

_____

Client

_____

Date

_____

Flowers For You, Inc. representative

_____

Date

Another contract might look like this:

Floral-Adora
678 Center Street
Anywhere, Georgia
Phone: 912-555-6789   Fax: 912-555-1234

Floral plan for the wedding of: Janet Berryman and Thomas Strikles

Wedding date	July 15, 1999
Ceremony location	Hilton Garden Hotel
Time	5:00 P.M.
Reception location	Hilton Garden Hotel (follows the ceremony in the same location)

Bridal Bouquet (pink and white cascade bouquet)		$125.00
6 Bridesmaids Bouquets	@ $45.00/each	$270.00
Throwaway Bouquet		-0-
Groom's Boutonniere		$ 15.00
8 Boutonnieres	@ $7.50/each	$ 60.00
3 Corsages	@ $22.50/each	$ 67.50
12 Aisle bows	@ $10.00/each	$120.00
9 Centerpieces	@ $75.00/each	$675.00
Room Decor—8 ficus trees	@ $25.00/each	$200.00

continues

continued

Subtotal	$1,532.50
Delivery & installation	306.50
Tax (6%)	91.95
Total	$1,930.95

Payment terms: $482.74 deposit due when contract is signed
$725.00 due on June 5, 1999
$723.21 due on July 13, 1999

Contract must be paid in full 48 hours before delivery of the flowers. Any changes in quantity or design need to be made in writing before July 1, 1999.

_____   _____
Client   Floral-Adora representative

_____   _____
Date   Date

Both of these contracts will provide flowers for your wedding. Both of these contracts list the items that you'll receive and basically tell you how those items will be used. You have to decide if you feel comfortable with the other information—or lack of information—that they contain. Can you visualize the arrangements, can you see the bouquets? Are they what you want them to be? If not, how do you know what will be delivered to your wedding?

The second contract lists only the numbers of items that you'll receive. There's no reference to a specific flower and only very limited reference to color. What if the florist you met with is called out of town on an emergency, or is ill the day of your wedding? Can his or her staff create the wedding you planned based on this contract? Will you receive what you are paying for and what you expect? This is part of the contract's responsibility as well, and once you sign it, you have agreed to what it says—make sure everything is spelled out.

The point is, contract #1 is more complete, and contract #2 leaves room for lots of interpretation. The more detailed your contract, the more protected you will be if anything changes. For instance, if the designer you spoke to is no longer working for the florist, the new designer will know *exactly* what you are expecting if you have a contract like #1. With a contract like #2, the new designer may have no idea.

Wedding Blues

Read your contract carefully and make sure that everything that you're expecting is listed there. If it's not in writing in the contract, you can't expect it to be there at the wedding!

The Least You Need to Know

➤ When it comes to bridal bouquets, smaller can be better.

➤ Your florist can give you valuable advice on what flowers to use for your wedding.

➤ Sharing flowers with another bride is one way to save money.

➤ Corsages, throwaway bouquets, and boutonnieres can be attractive and inexpensive.

➤ Some of the most attractive decorations are those you make yourself.

➤ Review the florist's contract carefully to make sure everything is spelled out.

Photography and the Music of the Night

Once you've secured your wedding date, place, and reception site, the next vendors you'll secure are the photographer and the musicians. Photographers and musicians can generally work one event per date, so you'll need to be sure that the specific ones you want to work with will be available to you.

You'll spend six to nine months planning your wedding celebration. After the ceremony and reception, the excitement will be over and all you'll have left are your memories—and your pictures! So you want to make sure they're great. When you think about photography and videography in terms of the lasting effects of your memories, they take on a different significance in the planning process and perhaps in your priorities.

In this chapter, I'll review some of the things you'll run into as you begin interviewing photographers, videographers, and musicians for your wedding. These are unique specialties and their services may not be offered exactly as you expect, so it's important to understand what you're seeing and hearing.

Professional Photographer or Talented Amateur?

Every professional photographer is not a wedding photographer. Being comfortable with a camera doesn't automatically mean you know how to photograph a wedding and tell the story of the event. *Wedding photography* requires that the photographer be able to tell a story with pictures.

Language of Love

Wedding photography is a specialized form of photography that requires that the photographer be able to tell the story of an event with pictures. It also includes being able to capture in images the important people in a couple's life without really knowing who those people are in advance.

One photographer I've worked with tells me he photographs every person who hugs the bride or groom on the theory that anyone who feels close enough to the couple to hug them is probably important to them. This way, when they review the proofs, the couple can decide who they want to include in their album. This photographer isn't concerned about how many pictures he takes; he takes as many images as possible so the couple will have the greatest number of choices in assembling their wedding album.

Choosing a Photographer

A good place to find professional wedding photographers is at a bridal show. There are usually many professional wedding photographers present, and they will have their albums available for you to review. This makes it possible for you to see several approaches to a complete wedding. It's a unique opportunity, because normally when you go to a photographer's studio, you can see only that one photographer's work, with nothing to compare it to.

Another option is to ask several of your married friends to lend you their wedding albums and compare the work of each of their photographers. Then make an appointment with the two photographers whose work you liked the best to discuss your particular wedding plans.

How do you assess one photographer's work over another's? Here are a few tips:

➤ Look at the group shots. What did the photographer select as a background for this group? Is there a painted mural in the background? Does the grandmother have a bird sitting on her head or a tree growing out of her shoulder? Is there a shadow across the bride's face?

➤ Do the bride and groom look like they're standing comfortably in the pose, or does the bride look like she's about to fall over? Can you see the detail on the bodice of her gown?

➤ Is the photograph properly lit? Now, I know you don't consider yourself enough of an "expert" to judge proper lighting, but you can tell if the skin tones look natural as opposed to too light or dark.

➤ How creative are the photographs? Are they all posed, and do all the poses look about the same, or are they creative, candid, and artistic? If some of the photos are posed, are there also some candid shots? Is this photographer telling the story of the event?

All of these things indicate the talent of the professional photographer and his understanding of the use of light and shadows to give the picture dimension and to make the couple most attractive.

The Cost Involved

While hiring a professional photographer is always a good idea, there's no question that it can be costly. In the planning of your wedding, there will always be some items that you give top priority and others that you consider less important and on which you hope to save some money. If photography is one of the items on which you want to cut costs, consider hiring a talented amateur photographer instead. You might find such a talented amateur by contacting local colleges and universities to see if they have a photography teacher or a talented student who might be willing to accept this responsibility.

If there are no photography classes on the college level in your community, check out high school classes, extension classes, your local YMCA, or even a camera store that offers classes. You may be able to locate someone who teaches these classes and will be willing to photograph your wedding. Be sure to look at the photographer's portfolio since you will not be able to check references with either satisfied or dissatisfied former bridal clients (see Chapter 2, "Is Doing It Yourself an Option?").

Be careful here—the Monday morning after your wedding, the photographs and your memories will be all that's left, so if you've saved money but don't like the photographs, your savings may not seem very significant after all.

Candid Camera

A popular style of photography today is the *photojournalist* approach. While some photographers advertise this approach as their specialty, nearly all professional photographers take a quantity of candid shots along with the more formal posed photographs. You'll want to be careful here, since the photojournalist approach means that the people in the picture are unaware of the photographer. You can get a lot of the backs of people's heads, and those shots do not tell a story of your wedding in the same way.

Wedding Blues

If you decide you want to save money on photographs, and you're going to be happy with an amateur's job, you can't complain because your photographs aren't professional!

101

Language of Love

Photojournalist photography refers to photographs most commonly seen in newspapers and magazines, often of sports figures. Generally they are action shots and the subject is not even aware of the photographer.

If you're interested in this candid approach, consider contacting your local newspaper to determine if there's a photographer at the paper who would be willing to photograph your wedding. Be prepared to negotiate price with this photographer and to explain what coverage you're looking for.

If you're being married in a church or synagogue, you must find out if there are any rules on photography at that particular location or during the ceremony. Your wedding is first and foremost a religious ceremony, and your photographer must be respectful of those rules. Professional photographers are used to working within the rules of religious institutions while still capturing the photographs you need. If you work with an amateur, you're responsible for communicating the rules and explaining their importance.

Face to Face Meeting

One of my major concerns is couples who attempt to research photographers on the telephone. Photographers differ when it comes to fees. If you're at the other end of a telephone cord, you not only can't see their work, you can't see what they are including in their packages or what that looks like when you receive it. Most of us can recognize an 8 × 10 photo, but can we distinguish between an 11 × 14 and a 16 × 20? Do we know the difference between a glossy finish and a matte finish? And what do they call that textured portrait that looks like an oil painting? Only by having a face-to-face conversation with the photographer and reviewing his work can you see what he is talking about as you see his work.

Wedding Blues

You can't research a photographer on the telephone! Knowing what the charges are will not tell you everything you have to know. You really need to see the photographer's work to make a decision about whether or not to hire that person.

Minimums or Packages?

Remember having your picture taken in high school? The *proofs* finally came and you could choose a package deal of two 8 × 10 prints, two 5 × 7 prints, and six wallet-size prints of the same proof for $8.95. Or you could order four 5 × 7 prints instead, and the price jumped to $85.00!

Wedding packages are a lot like those high school packages. They include a specific number of prints, usually in an album, for a specified amount of money. The package price is usually due by the wedding date. If the photographer does a great job and you want to purchase many more prints, or if you want to purchase prints as gifts, the price of these individual prints jumps dramatically! This seems to be a marketing technique. There doesn't seem to be any reason these additional prints should be more expensive than the originals, but they are!

Language of Love

Proofs are the first set of photographs a professional photographer shows the subject, from which orders are placed for the finished photographs the client wants.

There's really nothing wrong with a wedding photography package, so long as you understand what you're paying for and what you'll be getting. There are some questions that you should ask, such as how many proofs will you see and who selects the images that appear in your album. Sometimes the photographer puts together the album in a size that you've requested at the time you signed your contract, and you won't see the proofs at all. Sometimes you'll receive all the proofs, and you'll select the photographs for your album yourself.

Other photographers charge on the basis of a *minimum contract*. This means that the bride and groom will agree to spend a minimum amount of money with the photographer. This amount can be interpreted two ways. The first interpretation is that the couple agrees to spend a minimum amount of money on their photography and all of that is applied to the couple's album. This album will include a variety of pictures of different sizes totaling up to the amount of money agreed upon by the couple at the time they signed the contract. Here's an example:

Example 1: The contract is for $2,290.

10 × 10 photographs	$28.00 each
8 × 10 photographs	25.00 each
8 × 8 photographs	23.00 each
5 × 7 photographs	19.00 each
4 × 5 photographs	15.00 each

Leatherette album $200; leather album $350

Language of Love

Minimum contract means that the couple agrees to spend a specific amount of money with the photographer at a minimum. All of this money is applied to photographs, but all the photographs do not have to be in the couple's album—some may be placed into an album for her parents or his parents or be given as gifts. In those cases, the person who purchases that particular album pays that portion of the contract.

This couple selected a leatherette album containing 80 8 × 10 prints and six 4 × 5 prints, for a total of $2,290 (86 images in an album). The bride's parents ordered an album of 25 4 × 5 prints plus a leatherette album for $575. The groom's parents chose a leatherette album of six 5 × 7 prints and 18 4 × 5 prints for $584. The bride's grandparents selected one 8 × 10 print for $25. Two of the groom's aunts each ordered a 5 × 7 print of the whole family with the couple for $38. The total came to $3,512, with $2,290 of it from the bride and groom!

The second interpretation takes into account that most people want an album for the bride and groom, an album for the bride's parents, an album for the groom's parents, and perhaps individual pictures purchased by other guests. Since each of these people would be paying for their own photographs, this option is actually less expensive for the bride and groom. In both cases, the photographer will give the bride and groom a price list that states a price for each size print, so the purchasers can design their albums any way they want. This allows the purchaser to have more images in their album, telling a more complete story of their wedding, for roughly the same price. Here's an example:

Example 2: The contract is for $2,290.

10 × 10 photographs	$28.00 each
8 × 10 photographs	25.00 each
8 × 8 photographs	23.00 each
5 × 7 photographs	19.00 each
4 × 5 photographs	15.00 each

Leatherette album $200; leather album $350

Sue's Suggestions

Make sure your photographer knows how to dress at your wedding: A man should wear a sports coat and slacks for an informal affair, a dark suit for a semiformal affair, and a tuxedo for a formal wedding; women should follow similar guidelines. Photographers have to move among the guests to get the best shots, so they should be dressed in the most professional manner to blend in.

This couple selected a leatherette album of 60 8 × 8 prints, plus six 5 × 7 prints and 20 4 × 5 prints, for a total of $1,994 (86 images in an album). The bride's parents chose 25 4 × 5 prints in a leatherette album for $575. The groom's parents selected a leatherette album with six 5 × 7 prints and 18 4 × 5 prints, for a total of $584. The bride's grandparents selected one 8 × 10 print of the couple for $25. Two of the groom's aunts purchased one 5 × 7 print each of the whole family with the bride and groom, for a total of $38. This photographer's bill totaled $3,316, but only $1,994 of it was paid by the bride and groom.

In both of these examples, there's no mention of the number of hours of coverage. That's because photographers who quote a flat rate view the wedding as an event that they record from beginning to end. They will generally ask the bride and groom to arrive early enough to be photographed with their attendants and family before the ceremony. The photographer will also be there when the bride and groom leave the reception, perhaps eight or nine hours later.

By the Hour, By the Event ... What Does It All Mean?

Other photographers quote their services in terms of hours. They will provide coverage of your wedding for a specific number of hours, often using a specified amount of film for a predetermined amount of money. The contract may include the price of the various size prints that you may order and the cost of the album covers that you may choose. Often it will also list approximately how many proofs you will be able to view in making your selection of photographs. Once you've determined approximately how long your ceremony and your reception will be, you can determine if the photographer's time frame will work for you and whether he will fit into your budget.

My major concern with photographers who charge by the hour is that everything seems to be extra. Here's what I mean. Let's say you hire a photographer who offers you a five-hour package. You know the ceremony will last 30 minutes, the cocktail reception 45 minutes to an hour, and the seated dinner three hours—it sounds like you have plenty of time to spare. Then the photographer tells you he's coming two hours before the wedding to photograph the bride with her bridesmaids and family and the groom with his attendants and family for 45 minutes each.

By the time the ceremony is over and the photographer has completed the couple's "together" pictures, three hours and 15 minutes have passed—more than half of his allotted time—and your reception hasn't even started! By the time you dance your first dance, the photographer will be approaching you to ask if you want to extend his contract. Unless you've made other arrangements for photographing the cutting of the cake, the throwing of your bouquet, and your getaway, you'll feel obligated to extend the photographer's contract. Unfortunately, this same photographer probably told you how many photographs he or she would take in those five hours and how much each additional roll of film would be, so when you extend the contract, you are also extending the number of rolls of film you will actually use.

Wedding Blues

If you hire a photographer who works at a company that employs several photographers, specify in your contract who will be photographing your wedding. Be clear about how and when you'll be notified if this particular photographer can't be present. Some companies will show you the work of one photographer and send another to photograph your wedding.

Lights! Camera! Action!

As tempting as it may be to ask a family member to videotape your wedding ceremony, avoid this temptation! Videotaping a wedding is a relatively new concept, and it's definitely *not* as easy as it looks. As video cameras have become less costly, everyone thinks they're videographers, so you have to be pretty careful in your research. This is your wedding; it's not Hollywood. Your videographer should discreetly record the event, not direct the activities. You and your guests should not be aware of any videotaping activity, so you should speak to several references to be sure that the videographer or the equipment didn't get in the way during the event. Some brides solve the problem of the lights getting in the way by asking the videographer to work with only available light. Unfortunately, this means that the quality of your video will be quite poor, and you will have silhouettes walking down the aisle. A professional videographer knows how to set the lights so they won't detract from the ceremony or the reception.

If your clergyman or –woman allows videography during the ceremony, find out exactly what the requirements are. Where should the videographer stand during the ceremony? How much can the videographer move around?

Wedding Blues

The videographer who attends your wedding wearing blue jeans because he or she is a behind-the-scenes vendor has missed the point! In fact, the videographer will be very visible and may even create comment among your guests about his or her lack of professional attire.

You will also want to know how the videographer will edit your video. Some professionals do it in the camera; others wait until the event is over and then edit the video from two or more cameras to tell one story. If you can afford it, a multi-camera job will give you a more enjoyable video because the various cameras will get different views of the same event so you'll have a more interesting tape.

When you're researching the videographer, be sure to ask to see one wedding tape from start to finish, instead of scenes from several different weddings. If you watch one wedding all the way through, you'll be able to see how well it's edited and should be able to tell how unobtrusive the videographer was. Viewing sample tapes with scenes from several weddings tells you only that the videographer is able to capture good shots and string them all together in one tape; it doesn't tell you how talented the videographer is at creating the story of one wedding.

Sue's Suggestions

Hire the most talented videographer you can afford. Saving money here will produce a less-than-professional tape that will make you feel you wasted whatever money you put into it.

Many videographers will provide you with a full videotape of your wedding as well as an abbreviated recap tape, which condenses your five-hour wedding ceremony and reception into a 15-minute highlights tape. This is the tape you'll probably look at most often, so be sure one is included in your video package.

If, by the time you're thinking about video, most of your budget is gone, you might want to skip videography completely instead of hiring someone based only on price. Another option might be to hire a professional videographer for the ceremony only, and let

Uncle Joe do the reception. Later, for probably a nominal fee, you can ask your professional videographer to edit the two tapes together.

If you've already hired your photographer, ask him or her to recommend a videographer to you. It's helpful when your photographer and videographer work well together. If your photographer offers video as well, it's worth considering using the same company to videotape your wedding. Naturally, you should research this vendor as carefully as you would any other.

By the way, if the photographer tells you that he or she can be both your still and video photographer, *run* out of the office! The two skills are not related and one person—even someone who's very talented—cannot perform both services at one event. A photography *company* may employ both videographers and still photographers, and it can provide you with both, but don't let one person try to convince you he or she can do it all!

Choosing Your Music

Immediately after securing your wedding date and the reception site, you should begin researching the music for the reception. Even though the ceremony happens first, it's the music for the reception that you will be hiring first because you can often save money by using one of the reception musicians for your ceremony music. (We'll get to that in a moment.)

Wedding Blues

Watch out for hidden charges such as microphone rentals or mandatory additional tape copies. Also, make sure the package includes enough hours to cover your entire wedding (at least four to six hours) so you don't get hit with overtime charges.

Understanding how the reception room will handle the music will help you determine how many musicians to hire—and therefore how much money you'll be spending. Ask yourself these questions about the reception room:

➤ Is the ceiling lower than eight feet? If so, you won't need to hire many musicians to have a loud, full sound.

➤ Is there carpeting on the floors or drapery at the windows, or is the room all hard surfaces, with wood floors and uncurtained windows? If the room has all hard surfaces, there will be nothing to absorb any of the sound and a few musicians will sound like a very large group!

➤ Is there any upholstered furniture in the room? Usually ballrooms do not have upholstered furniture to absorb the sound of the band, but if your reception is being held in a room that does have upholstered furniture (sofas, over-stuffed chairs, etc.) you will have to consider it.

➤ How many guests will you be having? The ratio of musicians to guests is important—too many musicians can be over-kill.

A good way to secure your band is to ask for recommendations from friends. Find out if the band you're interested in is available on your wedding day and when you can hear the group playing at a wedding. I'm not suggesting that you crash people's weddings, but you can ask the band when and where they are playing a wedding that might be similar to yours. If the band tells you what time to come, you and your fiancé can dress up, go to the wedding, and stand in the back of the room or just outside the door for a few minutes to hear how the band sounds.

Keep these questions in mind as you assess the band:

➤ First and foremost, do you like the way they sound?

➤ Are they properly dressed for the formality of the event?

➤ Do they look like they're having a good time performing, or do their expressions seem to indicate that they're bored with either the event or the performance?

➤ What are the guests doing? Does it look like they're having a good time? Are they dancing? If guests are responding to the music, the band is doing exactly what they're hired to do—please the guests. A talented band, and especially a talented band leader, will be able to read the crowd and decide to play specific music based on what the crowd is doing.

There are groups that play for all kinds of corporate events, and they may be terrific, but if they don't know how to look out into the audience and read the mood of your guests, they may not be capable of creating an enjoyable wedding for everyone. Remember, at a corporate event, most of the people are close to the same age, and the music may be background sound rather than music for dancing. At a wedding, you'll want a group that can look up, see that no one is dancing, and change their music until they find a sound and rhythm the guests respond to.

Face the Music: Disc Jockey or Live Band?

First you'll need to decide if you want a disc jockey or a live band. There are many advantages to hiring a disc jockey, not the least of which is the money you'll save. Disc jockeys can provide the original musicians playing all the music you want at your party, and they require a minimum amount of floor space so, if you're tight on room, this can be an advantage. The disc jockey won't need to take as many breaks as live musicians do, so you'll receive more music for your dollars. With the disc jockey, however, you lose some of the spontaneity of the moment, because the DJ is limited by length of tape or compact disc. Let's say you want background music while the host introduces your bridal party—if your group walks more slowly than expected, there may be a short period without sound while the disc jockey restarts the music.

Disc jockeys generally charge by the event and you can expect them to charge between $300 and $1,200 for a wedding. Live bands charge by the musician and by the event and you could expect them to charge $750 to $1,000 for three musicians for a three-and-a-half-hour reception and $900 to $1,200 for four musicians for a three-and-a-half-hour reception. If you decide on a live band, you'll have to determine how many musicians you'll need and how long you'll want them to play. Whatever approach you use to selecting your musician or musicians, you'll want to hear them play before your wedding date, as I mentioned earlier. You don't want any surprises, so do your research ahead of time.

Sometimes it's not possible for you to hear the band playing at an actual wedding, so the band will send you a cassette or videotape of their performance. While this can be quite helpful in determining what the group *sounds* like and what they *look* like, a tape cannot show you how the crowd responds to the music or how good the group is at "reading the crowd" and adjusting their music. Ideally you will be able to both hear the tape *and* see the group in person. If this is not possible, the tape may be the best alternative you have.

Wedding Blues

While audio tapes can be a big help in deciding if you want to see a specific band in person or not, they should not be relied on solely to make your decision. Tapes can be doctored to provide a flawless sound, so if the tape sounds too good to be true, it probably is!

How Many Pieces and How Many Hours?

There is a direct relationship between the number of musicians you hire, the length of time they'll play, and what it will cost you to hire them. Naturally, the more musicians you hire, the most expensive it will be. Determine how many musicians you'll need when you talk with the band leader about what kind of music you want. Then let him help you find a way to balance this within your budget.

Next you'll decide how long the musical portion of your reception should be. If you're planning a standup cocktail buffet reception, you'll need approximately two and one-half to three hours of music. If you're planning a sit-down dinner, you might start the reception with 45 minutes of cocktails before opening the doors to the dinner-dance portion of the reception. The band should be playing when the doors open to invite the guests to move into the room, and you can expect to need three to three and one-half hours of music for this type of reception. Hiring your musicians for longer than you need will cost you more money, but it will not make a better party.

Sue's Suggestions

If it's possible for you to negotiate price directly with the band leader, do so. When the band is represented by a nonperforming agent you can expect to pay for his or her services, directly or indirectly.

Brides and grooms often tell me they want their reception to go on all night. Having spent several months planning something, it's not unreasonable to want it to last as long as possible. Weddings, however, have a rhythm to them—high and low spots. You will want your reception to end on one of the high spots, at a point when all your guests are having a great time. You'll want your guests believing they're enjoying the best reception of all time, not the longest reception of all time. Most bands offer either a three-hour contract (which you can extend in fifteen- or thirty-minute segments for an additional fee) or a four-hour contract. You will want to read carefully to determine if you have a financial advantage by extending the contract at the time you sign it rather than at the end of the evening.

While you're discussing the length of time that the band will be playing, also ask about overtime charges. If, at the pre-arranged ending time on your contract, everyone is dancing and having a terrific time and you don't want the evening to end, what do you do and what does it cost? If your contract specifies three hours at $1,200 and you want to extend it for 30 minutes, is that an additional $200 or is it more? Sometimes, a band will quote in the contract $1,200 for three hours, $1,400 for three and one-half hours, and $1,600 for four hours. If you wait until the evening of the wedding to extend the contract, the price for three and one-half hours might rise to $1,500. In that case, you would certainly come out better choosing the extra half hour at the time you signed the contract. This is a gamble—you might not need the extra time, but if you buy the extra time now, you may be able to construct your caterer and florist contracts to avoid the extra charges on their parts as well.

If you tell your florist your event will continue until midnight instead of eleven o'clock, he will plan to return at that time and your overtime charges will not begin until after that point.

Sue's Suggestions

For a big-band sound without the expense of hiring more musicians, hire a smaller band (four musicians should be plenty) with a keyboardist who can use a synthesizer. A synthesizer will give your wedding music the varied sound of a much larger ensemble.

That's the Breaks

When you hire a live band, be sure to ask the band leader to explain their system of breaks. So band members get a chance to relax, most groups schedule breaks for 15 minutes out of every 60 they are contracted to play. It's unrealistic to believe that a band can play three or four hours without such a break. Most groups will arrange to play taped music while they take their breaks, so the music will continue. If you work with your band leader closely on the flow of your evening, you'll be able to schedule breaks at times when your guests will hardly notice the band's absence.

In many cases you can request, and pay for, continuous live music. The important word here is *live*, because taped music is still music. If this is what you want, be sure to discuss this with the band leader. If you want band members on the stage for the entire reception, you can usually accomplish this by adding a few musicians so the group can rotate, allowing one musician to break while the rest of the group continues to play. You may have hired six musicians but have only four performing at any one time because someone will always be on break. There is an additional charge for this arrangement, and you'll have to decide if this additional fee is appropriate for your budget.

Music for the Ceremony

If you've decided to hire a band for your wedding reception, you may want to ask if one or two members of the band might be available to play for your ceremony as well. Many bands have members who are willing to do this, and they add a small amount of money to your existing contract for the ceremony part of your music. You should find this less expensive than hiring someone else to play just for the ceremony. It's especially cost-effective if your ceremony is held in the same location as your reception. Your musicians can come for the ceremony and then stay for the reception. Of course, the musicians that play the ceremony will arrive earlier than the rest of the band. The rest of the band will arrive and begin setting up during the ceremony so they'll be ready to strike up the band as soon as the doors open for your reception.

You can often find very talented amateurs to play for your wedding ceremony. Here are some tips on how to find someone:

➤ Check at the church or synagogue to see who has played in this facility in the past. If the church has an organ, the church secretary can probably recommend someone to play it at your ceremony.

➤ Contact the music department of your local college or high school for names of talented young musicians there.

➤ Call your local symphony orchestra and ask about referrals to either regular symphony performers or members of the youth symphony.

➤ Contact local or regional theaters in your area for the names of musicians. While they may not perform at wedding ceremonies themselves, they may have friends who do.

Sue's Suggestions

If your ceremony and reception are held at the same location, you won't need music playing during cocktail time. People will be visiting with each other and won't even miss it. But if the ceremony and reception are at separate locations, you don't want your guests walking into a silent room. You can play recorded music or hire one or two of your reception musicians to play during cocktail time.

If you're considering hiring an amateur, go hear him or her play at an upcoming wedding. If the amateur doesn't have an event scheduled, ask to meet him or her at the wedding site to play for you in the room. This will be very helpful, since the acoustics

Sue's Suggestions

Having a friend play for your ceremony, and perhaps having another friend sing, will not only save you money, but will be very meaningful to you.

of the room will have a bearing on the performance, and you don't want to discover on your wedding day that you really needed a microphone for the musician to be heard. Expect to pay a nominal charge for the musician to meet you at the wedding site for this audition; but you'll find it's money well spent!

You may have friends who play musical instruments, and they may be willing to provide music for your ceremony. Nearly any musical instrument will be appropriate if the musician plays it well. You'll want to be careful of friends who want to play for your wedding as their gift, but then expect you to hire two additional musicians to accompany them—is this a gift to you or to them?

The Least You Need to Know

➤ Select your photographer, videographer, and musicians immediately after securing your wedding date.

➤ Photographers who work on a flat-rate minimum are often less expensive in the long run than photographers who charge by the hour.

➤ Hiring a disc jockey to play recorded music at the reception is generally less expensive than hiring a live band.

➤ There is a direct relationship between the number of musicians you hire, the number of hours they will play, and the number of dollars you will pay for them.

➤ Hiring an amateur to play music at your ceremony will save you money. Asking a friend to play or sing will also provide you with lasting memories of your friendship.

Chapter 9

Sharing the Excitement

In This Chapter

➤ Making a good first impression with an elegant invitation

➤ Cost-saving options

➤ Where to buy your invitations

➤ That old black tie

➤ Addressed, stuffed, stamped: mailing your invitations

➤ Putting together a weekend planner for your guests

Invitations set the tone for your wedding celebration. The style of paper and print that you select communicates to your invited guests the formality of the event. It is also the first thing that most people see regarding your wedding. A beautiful and well-presented invitation gives your guests all the information they need to begin making their plans to attend the wedding. Important as it is, the invitation is still only paper, so this is a very good place to save money on your wedding.

In this chapter I'll discuss the differences between engraved and thermography invitations and all the ways you can have beautiful invitations on your budget. I'll also explain the elements of your invitation and the message it conveys.

Invitation to a Wedding

Your wedding invitation not only tells your guests the who, what, when, and where of your event, but also sets the tone for the formality of your wedding. It makes that all-important first impression. Even if you select the simple ecru folded paper, you are showing your personality by your selection of typeface. Are you straight and narrow like the Styvasant type or free and fluid like the Citadel letters?

Anatomy of a Wedding Invitation

First, let's talk about the parts of a wedding invitation. Traditionally, it's made up of three parts:

➤ The wedding invitation itself

➤ The reception card

➤ The response set

The wedding invitation is usually a folded piece of paper sold with two envelopes (contemporary ones generally have only one envelope). It is folded with the print facing to the outside. Many printing companies also supply sheets of tissue, which are used to keep the wet ink from smearing. The tissues may be discarded if you like. Traditionally, the wedding invitation invites your guests to the ceremony only, but if the reception is held at the same location, that information may be included, too.

A reception card is enclosed with your invitation if your reception is held at a different location or if it does not immediately follow your ceremony. The card gives the name, address, and time of the reception.

The response set is made up of a small card and a self-addressed, stamped envelope addressed to the host and hostess of the wedding. The card provides space for guests to accept or decline the invitation to your reception. The card is stuffed into the small envelope and enclosed along with your wedding invitation.

Although not part of the invitation, you should order your thank-you notes at the same time you order your invitations. These are usually the same color paper printed with the same typeface.

Engraving Versus Thermography

With a little understanding, a bride and groom can really save money on their invitations. There are two processes commonly used to create wedding invitations today—engraving and thermography. They vary widely in cost, but the finished product looks almost the same.

Engraved invitations are the most expensive invitations your can buy and start around $100 per 100 invitations. They are printed with the use of an engraving plate usually made of a combination of copper and nickel. You'll often hear the process called "copperplate engraving." In this process, the wording of the invitation is first cut or engraved into the metal plate. The wording is applied backwards, so if you look at the plate, it reads right to left, instead of left to right. The plate is then cleaned and spread with ink, which fills in the engraved letters on the plate.

The paper is dampened and laid on the plate; then pressure is applied. The damp paper is pushed into the crevices where it picks up the ink, creating the raised print on the invitation. The pressure applied to the paper will leave a slight indentation on the back side of the invitation, which is the easiest way to identify an engraved invitation. Engraved invitations are always printed on high-rag-content or cotton paper, which is strong enough to withstand the pressure that needs to be applied during the printing process. If the rag content of the paper is too low, the pressure will cause the paper to tear during this part of the process. This process is almost always used on very formal invitations, which are usually printed in black or very dark gray ink on white or ecru folded paper.

Language of Love

The process of **engraving** uses a copper printing plate to impress the image on high-rag-content or 100-percent cotton paper. It produces raised lettering on the paper that you can feel if you run your fingers over the type. Engraving is the most expensive printing process used for the printing of wedding invitations.

Twenty plus years ago a heat and powder process became available to create raised-print wedding invitations. In this process, called *thermography*, the ink is applied to the paper in the shape of the letters and words at the first stop on a long conveyor belt. Next a powder is dumped on the invitation and the invitation is heated, so that every place the powder hits the wet ink, it bubbles, creating the raised print. Then the conveyor belt moves the invitations under a strong vacuum, which sucks away the extra powder. The invitations are counted and packed into boxes and sent on to the bride. Thermography can be done on all different grades of paper.

Generally, thermography invitations cost approximately half as much as engraved invitations and start at around $41 per 100. Not only is the process less expensive, since it doesn't require the creation of a costly plate, but the paper can be less expensive, too. Thermography invitations can be formal, printed with black ink on white or ecru folded paper; semiformal printed with any colored ink on white or ecru folded paper or firm cards; or informal printed with either black or colored ink on colored paper or cards. There are some other differences between these two processes. In thermography, if a lettering style that is selected has thick letters, there could be a shine to the ink on the invitations; this won't happen in an engraved invitation. Also, thermography invitations can arrive in your home carrying a gritty residue left over from the powder that was not completely vacuumed away. This is a very minor inconvenience, and the powder can be removed with either a hand held hair dryer or a dry dish towel as you stuff the invitations.

Language of Love

The process of **thermography** uses heat and powder instead of ink to create the type on the paper. It produces raised lettering like engraving, but is a much less expensive process.

Do You Need a Reception Card?

If your wedding ceremony and your reception will be held in the same location, or if the reception site does not require an address, you can certainly put the reception information on the invitation. If you need to give an address or any other direction, the reception information must be on the matching, separate reception card so that the type on your invitation is not significantly reduced in order to accommodate all this information. There is an additional charge for this card, but it is usually not very expensive, especially if you are working with a discount dealer.

Love the look of beautiful decorative handwriting (calligraphy), but can't work it into your budget? Check with your local stationery dealers. Many have the Inscribe Calligraphy Computer, which produces hand-written, computer-generated calligraphy at a fraction of the cost of human-hand calligraphy. But please, no laser printing and no labels on your wedding invitations! Wedding invitations should be addressed by hand—that's why the Inscribe Calligraphy Computer is such a great help. If even that is too expensive, invite your bridesmaids over for an afternoon and they can help you address your invitations.

Sue's Suggestions

To cut invitation costs, avoid colored ink and embossed papers. Simple white or ecru invitations printed in black ink are your best buys. Go easy on the inserts: A reception card and response card are probably all you need. If you need to enclose a map, create one yourself and make copies to insert into the invitations.

Tantalizing Trivia

When Emily Post frowned on the use of response cards in the 1922 version of her book *Etiquette*, most people paid for wedding receptions by the pound, not the person. You might have ordered 20 pounds of roast beef and 10 pounds of turkey, and when it was gone, the reception was over. So responses were not needed. This is not the case today, and response cards are an important part of the wedding invitation.

...ot to use a response card is always the question. Brides believe that they ...ey by not including a response card and stamped return envelope with ...ons, and they will ... or will they? If you're mailing out 100 invitations, the response sets will run approximately $58.00 and the stamps approximately $33.00, for a total of $91.00. If you're paying for your reception by the person (which is how most caterers charge today) at a rate of $25 per person, and you're off by six people (only three couples), you'll spend $150 too much for food—and that doesn't include tax and tip. So, as a bride, now you know why it's so important to return those response cards. Next time you're a guest at someone else's wedding, you'll remember how much work you did preparing your own invitations, and you'll appreciate how easy it is to simply sign the response card, check it off, and pop it back into the mail.

Selecting a Type Style

Although there is no additional charge for the specific type style that is used on your invitation, selecting the right one for you may take some time. Most people don't spend enough time looking at the shape of the individual letters to know what they like. Today most stationery books show you a complete alphabet in upper- and lowercase letters for every lettering style they offer. The bride and groom should look at these alphabets and pay particular attention to the capital letters of their own first, middle, and last names.

If the invitation will have the traditional wording, where her parents issue the invitation, the bride should also consider the capital letters there. When you decide that you like the capital letters in a particular style, flip to a sample page using that style and make sure that the entire invitation is easy to read and visually pleasing. The difficult letter in most lettering styles is the "S." It can look like an "L" in many of the different styles. This is really not a problem in most cases, but if either of your names starts with an "S," you'll want to make sure you like the way it looks and that guests will be able to understand what your names are. Not everyone receiving these invitations will know both of you.

Sue's Suggestions

Don't assume you know who's coming and who's not. If you've included response cards with your invitation and someone has not responded, call that person and inquire about his or her plans. Your guest may not have even received the invitation and you would have no way of knowing.

Sue's Suggestions

To save money on postage, look for semiformal and informal invitations that offer a postcard as a response card. Postcards cost less to mail than envelopes, and because they weigh less, your total invitation will cost less to mail as well.

In some thermography invitation albums a distinction is made between *regular lettering* and *photo lettering*. The company uses this designation to charge a slightly higher fee for invitations printed in the photo lettering. The difference in price is quite nominal and you should be able to select whichever you prefer.

117

Language of Love

Regular lettering tends to be simple print styles, often block-shaped letters. **Photo lettering** tends to be fancier script lettering.

Purchasing Invitations

Okay, now where do you buy these invitations to get the best deal? Well, of course, you can shop at retail stores in shopping malls and strip centers. They will be able to show you the large stationery books with samples provided by the various companies, and will show you the differences between engraved and thermography invitations. Or you can shop with stationery dealers who work out of their homes, usually offering generous discounts, and showing you the same stationery sample books. In both these scenarios, you can expect someone with knowledge of proper etiquette to actually prepare your order, and you should be offered the opportunity to review the spelling before the order is submitted. In these instances, if your invitations arrive with either spelling, grammatical, or etiquette errors, you will have some recourse and certainly the help of the salesperson.

Several stationery companies, which you can find in the national bridal magazines, sell directly to you, the client, via mail-order catalogs. These invitations may appear to be less expensive, but the paper quality is often much poorer as well. The biggest problem here is that there is no one to review your order, and whatever you submit is *exactly* what you will receive!

Wedding Blues

The companies that print invitations will not review your order for spelling, grammar, or etiquette errors. The invitations will always be printed *exactly* as submitted. Be sure that you ask someone who was not a part of the selection process to read your invitation order before mailing it to the company. Only when the correct information is submitted can you be sure it will arrive correctly.

Some brides also have the option of ordering invitations through their companies if they work for ones that have accounts with a printing company. The idea of securing your invitations at cost can be very intoxicating. One bride who chose this route ended up having to place the entire order a total of *three* times. On the first order she forgot to include the time of her ceremony and on the second one she misspelled the church address. She probably saved 40 percent on each order, but that still means she paid 180 percent for her invitations (60 percent times 3). Had she gone to someone selling invitations from her home and offering a 20-percent discount, she would have had someone to proofread the order before it was submitted. She also would have had someone to deal with the print company on her behalf when the problems arose.

The very least expensive invitations are those you make yourself. You can compose your invitation on your computer and print it out on pretty stationery you bought at a stationery or office supply store or a discount party store. The lettering won't be raised, but if your wedding style is informal, you'll certainly be able to get the important information (who, what, when, where) out to your guests for a minimal charge. If you choose this option, get an etiquette book from the library so you'll be sure to include all the information your guests will need.

You can even make layered invitations yourself and decorate them with pieces of lace or ribbons or any other wedding motif that appeals to you. When doing this, give some thought to the envelope. Standard-sized envelopes that you can purchase at an office supply store are the least expensive, so you'll want to design your hand-made invitation to fit them.

Sue's Suggestions

If you're having a small wedding of 50 or fewer guests, buy pretty stationery and hand-write the invitations to each of your guests. It's personal and warm, and you will save money and impress your guests.

Black Tie

If you've decided to host a formal wedding and would like your guests to come in formal attire, there are several ways to communicate this to them. First, if you've scheduled your ceremony in the evening—anything after 6 o'clock—and have selected white or ecru paper with black ink for your invitation, the sophisticated guest is expected to know that the wedding will be formal. But we live in such a casual society today that many people miss these obvious clues, and couples have gotten in the habit of indicating dress on the reception card. According to etiquette gurus, ceremonies were never formal, semiformal, or informal—they were just ceremonies. But receptions could be formal; hence, the term *Black tie* could appear in the lower-left corner of the reception card.

Couples often viewed this as a commandment and were uncomfortable putting it on their reception invitations because they felt that guests who didn't own a tuxedo would be reluctant to attend if they couldn't afford to rent one (or didn't want to). So they began using *Black tie optional* instead. When a corporation or a large nonprofit organization holds an event to which people of varying socioeconomic levels are invited (the company president and the entry-level receptionist), the phrase "Black tie optional" is appropriate since you wouldn't expect all the men to wear formal attire. This phrase is *not* correct on a social invitation, however, because everyone invited to the wedding is assumed to be at the same socioeconomic level. To avoid confusion, tuxedo companies encouraged brides to use the phrase *Black tie invited,* which sounds like the suit is welcome but the man should stay home! This phrase should be avoided.

In fact, when you put "Black tie" on your reception invitation, you're simply telling the out-of-town guest that *if* he owns a tuxedo and *if* he would like to wear it, he will not be the only person in the room wearing one. It is assumed that your local guests

Language of Love

Black tie indicates that men should wear tuxedos and women should wear long gowns or dressy attire. **Black tie optional** is a business phrase that is used when people of various socioeconomic levels are invited to a business gathering. It should never be used on a social invitation. **Black tie invited**, a variation of "Black tie optional," is an undesirable phase—it sounds like the suit, not the man, is invited!

will know the formality of the location and your personal style well enough to make the same decision. This term is strictly informational and no more a commandment than if you were to put on your invitation "Ladies will wear yellow dresses."

Mailing Your Invitations

You've ordered your invitations, and they've arrived. You've checked them carefully to make sure all the information is correct. Then you addressed, stuffed, and stamped them—now they're ready to be mailed. As I mentioned in Chapter 3, "Getting Organized," the correct time to mail out-of-town invitations is six weeks before the wedding; in-town invitations, four weeks before the wedding. But, you say, I'm so anxious! I can't wait! Besides, you really want your responses soon, because you'd love to be able to invite everyone at the office if some of your out-of-town guests can't come. What would it hurt to mail your invitations eight or nine weeks before the wedding?

I know it's tempting, but don't do it! The whole idea of sending out invitations is to elicit a response—which guests are coming? When most people receive an invitation in April for an event that's taking place in June, their typical response is: "How do I know what I'll be doing two months from now. I'll put this with my bills, and next month I'll make a decision about this wedding." That's not what the bride wants. By mailing the invitation too early, she removed all pressure from the guest and eliminated any possibility of an immediate response.

If she had mailed the out-of-town invitation just two weeks later (six weeks before the event), the guest would have opened the invitation and felt the need to make a decision about attending. Guests who were sure they could not attend the wedding would immediately sign the response card, indicating their negative response, and mail the card back to the bride and groom. This would allow the bride to address invitations to other local guests she had hoped to include if she had the space. These local invitations would be mailed four weeks before the wedding since these guests would not need to deal with airline or hotel reservations. This pattern of mailing invitations in two waves is effective for brides who have to have an A and a B list. It's important to understand that the B list has to be local guests, since their invitations are mailed closest to the wedding.

Tantalizing Trivia

The United States Postal Service requires a clear, readable return address on all pieces of first-class mail that are mailed in this country. In most communities, the blind embossed return address that is an option on many engraved invitations does not qualify as "clear and readable" and could cause an invitation not to be returned to you if it can't be delivered to your invited guest. You should select a printed return address option for your invitations to avoid this problem.

What's on the Weekend Program?

About five days after invitations are mailed to your out-of-town guests, you'll want to mail a weekend program to each of them. This is a great way of ensuring that your guests will enjoy your wedding weekend, because you're telling them about every aspect of it in advance. Another benefit of the weekend program is that it can serve as an invitation to all the additional events of the weekend, so you won't have to send out other invitations. It can also provide information about transportation from the airport to the hotel, and can tell guests what to expect the weather to be like for your wedding weekend, so they'll know what to pack.

Weekend programs can be very simple, produced on your home computer and then duplicated at any quick print company. They can range from the very simple, perhaps in a letter format, to the more elaborate, with pictures, drawings, or slick papers. Whatever style you choose, weekend programs actually can be quite inexpensive. This is a terrific way for the couple to show their creativity and their personalities, and putting the program together can be a great tension breaker when the wedding details start to get to you.

Sue's Suggestions

Using a weekend program can save you the expense of printing and mailing invitations to your guests for other events of the weekend.

For their weekend program, Susie and Marc chose two sheets of 8 ¹/₂" × 11" stationery with a faint picture of a bridal bouquet and veil that they got at the office supply store (100 sheets for $9.95), along with matching envelopes ($12.75). The only other expense was the $.33 postage each of the weekend programs required. Susie did all the typesetting on her computer and printed out all 65 weekend programs herself.

Here's how their weekend program looked:

Susie and Marc's Wedding Weekend

We hope you will be coming to Atlanta to share in our wonderful celebration. Here are some details!

Hospitality Suite

A special Hospitality Suite will be open throughout the wedding weekend, beginning on Friday afternoon. Please be our guest there any time. There will be snacks, home-baked goodies, coffee, and soft drinks, as well as plenty of good conversation. We know it will be a great place to meet up with old and new friends. The Hospitality Suite is compliments of the following people:

Torie and John Carter
Lynn and Ted Morris
Sally and Fred Wallace

Friday Evening, November 19, 1999

7:00 P.M.   Prenuptial Dinner—Marriott Hotel

Hosted by Marc's parents, Judy and Frank Marsh

Saturday Morning, November 20, 1999

8:30 A.M.   Continental Breakfast—Hospitality Suite

Come by the Hospitality Suite at your leisure all day or have fun all day as you explore this great city!

6:45 P.M.   Buses pick up guests for ceremony

7:30 P.M.   Wedding Ceremony

We have arranged for a bus to take you from the hotel to the wedding ceremony at the church.

Buses will leave promptly at 6:45 P.M. from the lobby of the hotel. If you plan to drive, please refer to the directions that follow.

Sunday Morning, November 21, 1999

11:00 A.M. Brunch—Marriott Hotel—Tremont Room

Hosted by:	Barb & Clint Fox	Marie & Ralph Pullman
	Candy & Bill Karney	Renee & Mark Rowen
	Judy & Danny Marsh	Beth & Gary Sully

Jamie and Rick chose another form of a weekend program for their guests. They folded an 8 ¹/₂" × 11" sheet of paper in half and created a four-page booklet that they had printed in black ink on white paper, which complemented the colors of their wedding. At the office supply store, they found white 6" × 9" envelopes that opened on the narrow end ($22.50 for 250 envelopes). They really needed only 100 envelopes, but they were able to share the box with another couple being married a few weeks later. Printing the program cost $.16 per double-sided page, or $16.00.

Rick created the copy on his PC at work. Jamie and Rick's weekend program looked like this:

Sue's Suggestions

Purchase oversized envelopes at an office supply store and mail weekend programs and response postcards for one $.53 stamp, instead of individual $.33 stamps.

The Wedding of

Jamie Lynn Rodgers

and

Richard Alan Green

May 28–30, 1999

We hope you will be able to join us in Ann Arbor to help us celebrate our Wedding Weekend.

Delta Airlines has agreed to grant discount fares for travel to our wedding. The discounted fares include 10 percent off all "B" fares, 5 percent off all First Class tickets, and 5 percent off all excursion fares! Discounted travel is valid between May 26 and June 1. Please call Brenda Jones at Jones Travel in Ann Arbor (619-555-1234) to arrange for travel with these discounted fares.

Rooms have been set aside for you at the Westin in Ann Arbor, which is the location of most of the weekend's activities. A Hospitality Suite, hosted by Jamie's cousins, Betty and Bill Simpson, will be available throughout the weekend as a place to gather and visit between activities. The Westin has supplied reservation cards so that you can contact them directly to make your reservations.

continues

continued

A reservation card is enclosed in this packet. Please mail your card directly to the Westin, and your room will be waiting when you arrive.

We have also arranged discounted reservations at the Days Hotel, just down the street from the Westin. They have also provided reservation cards, and one is included here for your convenience.

Both hotels are in close proximity to shopping malls and Ann Arbor's mass transit system. The Westin offers a complimentary van service for transportation within a one-mile radius of the hotel for your additional convenience.

Also in this package, please find a postcard response card. This card will help us know when you are arriving, which parties you will be attending, and what your transportation needs are.

For those of you who are flying to Ann Arbor, there are several ways to get from the airport to each of the hotels, which are next to each other.

The Westin offers a courtesy van which leaves the airport every hour on the hour between 12:00 P.M. and 10:00 P.M. daily. The cost of the van is $15 per person. Follow signs to ground transportation to meet the van.

If you prefer, the Ann Arbor Rapid Transit system will take you from the airport to about a block from the Westin (where you can call the hotel at 619-555-2222 to send a courtesy van for you).

Taxi service is available from the airport ground transportation area. The fare should be about $35 to the hotel. Naturally, you may rent a car. After picking up your car, follow these directions:

Leaving the airport, follow I-95 North to exit 28 Brandon Road. Get in the left lane. Turn left onto Lenox Road. Go approximately 2.5 miles, and the Westin Hotel will be in front of you at the intersection of Lenox and Fink Roads. The Days Hotel is to your left.

Schedule of Events

Friday May 28, 1998

10:30 P.M. Informal Dessert & Coffee in the Hospitality Suite— Westin Hotel

Saturday, May 29, 1998

9:00–11:00 A.M. Continental Breakfast in the Hospitality Suite— Westin Hotel

The afternoon is yours to enjoy Ann Arbor while we prepare for the wedding. You may want to browse through the shops at either Lenox Square or Phipps Plaza Shopping Centers. Both are located about a half block from the hotel. You can enjoy a ride on Ann Arbor's rapid transit to downtown Ann Arbor to visit the art museum or the University. The Hospitality Suite at the Westin will be open all afternoon.

7:30 P.M.	Begin seating for the ceremony
8:00 P.M.	Wedding ceremony begins
8:30 P.M.	Cocktail reception
9:30 P.M.	Dinner and dancing 'til dawn!

Sunday, May 30, 1998

11:30 A.M.   Brunch at Rio Bravo, hosted by Bonnie & Bob Miller and Jean & Jerry Jessup

Rio Bravo is approximately three miles from the Westin. A complimentary van service will provide transportation between the hours of 11:00 A.M. and 2:00 P.M.. There will be transportation from the Days Hotel as well.

We look forward to seeing you! Please return the enclosed postcard and the response to the wedding so we will know when to expect you.

One groom took over the responsibility of the weekend program on his own. Matt pulled together his talent with the computer and his love of theater to create a Playbill for the wedding program for his wedding to Amy. This program turned out to be slightly more expensive because the cover was printed in two colors and there were two inside pages folded and each printed front and back creating an eight-page booklet. Matt produced 100 booklets, even though only 78 were mailed out. The booklets cost $32.00 to print the inside pages and $35.00 to print the cover. Matt selected a 6" × 9" white envelope that opened at the end, and 100 envelopes cost $12.65. Mailing the 78 packets cost $42.90.

When guests have been entertained by a variety of hosts and hostesses, it is appropriate for them to acknowledge and thank their hosts for their generosity. The polite bride makes it possible for her guests to fulfill their obligation by providing the names and addresses of all the weekend hosts. That's why you'll find this information in the weekend program. Those brides who didn't include it in the weekend program often had a page of names and addresses available in the Hospitality Suite so each guests could pick it up and write their notes when they returned to their homes.

In addition to the weekend programs, these weekend packets included a response postcard that was addressed to the bride and groom. When other people are involved in the weekend by hosting some of the events, they may choose to create their own invitation and include it in this packet or just allow the weekend packet to be the invitation. Doing this saves the cost of mailing for each of the other hostesses. This response postcard will provide a great deal of information for the bride and groom and allow them to make plans for the comfort of their guests. The postcard looks something like this:

Dear Bonnie Bride and Gary Groom:

❏ I/We will be arriving in Chicago on _____, the _____ of _____ at _____ o'clock on _____ airline's flight _____.

❏ I/We will be driving to Chicago and plan to arrive on _____, the _____ of _____ at about _____ o'clock.

❏ I/We will be renting a car.

❏ I/We will be taking public transportation to the hotel. Please include us in your weekend transportation plans.

❏ I/We will be staying at the _____ Hotel.

❏ I/We will attend the Prenuptial Dinner on Friday evening.

❏ I/We will attend the Luncheon of Saturday afternoon.

❏ I/We will attend the Sunday Brunch.

Name_____

Please respond by June 5, 1999.

The bride and groom can have these cards printed on two sides of a card stock, three to a page, so they can be cut. The cost will be roughly $.25 per page but at three to a page, only 34 pages need to be printed to give you the 100 postcards needed.

If the invitations to your out-of-town guests are mailed six weeks before the wedding, and invitations to your in-town guests are mailed four weeks before the wedding, when are the weekend packets mailed to your out-of-town guests? There are two possible times to send them out:

➤ *Mail all the packets to out-of-town guests five days after mailing the out-of-town invitations.* This assures that the guests will know about the wedding before they learn about the other weekend activities. It also allows the guests to know what is happening, so when they make their travel plans they can be sure to arrive early enough and depart late enough to attend all the events they would like to attend.

➤ *Mail a packet to each out-of-town guest as soon as the guest responds to the wedding.* While this may save a little postage for the couple, it will put pressure on them to constantly be addressing the packets and getting them mailed and it will make it somewhat more difficult for their guests to make the necessary travel arrangements in advance. Besides, if some of your guests respond later than you hoped, there may not be time for them to receive this packet, and that might make it difficult for them and for you.

Don't forget to mail weekend programs to any of your local guests who will also be attending the weekend festivities.

The hotel you've selected for your guests will print reservation cards free for you to send along with your weekend program. Be sure to get enough printed, because you'll have to pay for reorders, and they can get expensive. The reservation cards are filled out and returned to the hotel by the guest and look something like this:

Andersonville Hotel

361 Something Street, Any Town, Any State

local phone number, fax number

welcomes the

JONES-BROWN WEDDING

MAY 28–30, 1999

Guest name_____

Guest address_____

City_____ State _____ Zip Code _____

Phone_____

Credit card number_____

Expiration date_____

Signature_____

continues

continued

I prefer a

_____ king room; _____ double room; _____twin room;

_____ nonsmoking room; _____ handicap room;

_____ to be away from the elevator;

other (explain) _____

	Friday	Saturday	Sunday

\# single rooms _____

\# double rooms _____

All rooms $99 plus tax.

Reservations due by May 1, 1999 to secure this rate.

Some couples select two hotels that are close together to secure rooms for their guests. The philosophy here is that some guests may be able to afford a luxurious hotel, certainly at a discounted rate, while others will prefer the moderately priced facility just down the street, also at a discount. Sometimes it's necessary to work with more than one hotel because neither hotel is able to block enough rooms to accommodate all your possible guests. In this case, you'll need to ask both hotels to print reservation cards for you to include in the weekend programs so your guests can make their own decisions on which hotel they prefer. If the block of rooms is limited at either one of the hotels, be sure to tell that to your guests in your weekend program, so everyone will know they must respond quickly to secure their rooms. If you are working with two or more hotels, you will have to designate one hotel as "hotel central" for the purpose of organizing transportation and securing a Hospitality Suite and Bridal Suite.

Be sure to explain in your weekend program that the room rate is valid only until a certain date. After that, the rooms may still be available, but at full price. Also, tell your guests to phone the hotel at its local number to receive the discounted rate you've negotiated. (The toll-free phone numbers of hotel chains usually don't have on record any special rates negotiated by their individual hotels.)

You will be able to call the hotel reservations desk and keep up with your guests' reservations. That way you can be sure that everyone who is coming to the wedding has made a reservation at the hotel, or has told you they've made arrangements to stay somewhere else. Even though you're not responsible for your guests and their reservations, it's very considerate of you to check this area so that you can head off any errors that may occur so your guests will all feel welcome when they arrive.

Even though you've negotiated discounted rates at a hotel, some of your guests may decide to stay elsewhere—they may have relatives or friends living in your community they would rather stay with, or they may have a fondness for another hotel.

That's not a problem for you, but it would be helpful if you knew about it, especially when you are making your transportation arrangements.

The Least You Need to Know

➤ Invitations may be printed by the engraving process or by the thermography method.

➤ There are three parts to the traditional wedding invitation.

➤ The term "Black tie" is informational and perfectly correct on a social invitation.

➤ Weekend programs save you money versus printing invitations to various events, and are a good way to let your out-of-town guests know what is planned for the whole weekend.

➤ Hotels are happy to print reservation cards so your guests can book rooms directly with the hotel.

Chapter 10

More Things to Consider When Budgeting

In This Chapter

➤ Optional parties: the bridesmaids' luncheon and the groom's sports tournament

➤ Bridal shower or luncheon etiquette

➤ Getting folks together at the rehearsal or prenuptial dinner

➤ The pre- or post-wedding brunch

➤ Buying the engagement and wedding rings

➤ Do you need "Weddinginsurance"?

➤ Easy, inexpensive favors

Your wedding ceremony isn't the only event that will take place on your wedding weekend. There will be other activities planned to entertain your guests and honor your bridal party members. Therefore, all special events and activities need to be considered as you begin planning your budget. Family members and friends may offer to host parties during the weekend, but until they do, you'll need to add these events to your original budget. In this chapter, I'll talk about budgeting for bridesmaids' luncheons, showers, brunches, and more.

Bridesmaids' Luncheon

Bridesmaids' luncheons are optional parties that have different meanings to different brides. To some brides, the bridesmaids' luncheon is a party hosted by the bridesmaids in honor of the bride, to which her mother, grandmother, and aunts are invited. To other brides, it's an intimate party hosted by the bride (and maybe her mother) in honor of the bridesmaids, to which the bridesmaids and groom's mother are the only people invited. However, if the groom has a sister who happens not to be a bridesmaid, she is often included in the party. Sometimes a family friend hosts this party the day before the wedding. In this scenario the bride, her immediate female relatives, and the bridesmaids are invited. Whether this event appears on the budget or not depends on how the bride defines this event and who is hosting it.

Bridesmaids' luncheons do not have to be costly—they can be simple "hen parties" in the bride's home, with everyone in jeans, much like a high school slumber party. The goal here is for the bride to reserve some special time during the hectic wedding weekend for her very best friends. It's a good way for them all to relax and enjoy each other's company.

Sue's Suggestions

If you decide to host a luncheon in honor of your bridesmaids, keep it simple. Hold it in your home and keep the costs down by doing most of the work yourself. Remember, these are your best friends; they want to spend time celebrating with *you.*

One of my very clever brides decided to host her bridesmaids' luncheon at the beauty salon on the day of the wedding. All the bridesmaids were there, some got their hair done, some did not, but they all came to share this time with her. The maid of honor picked up each bridesmaid and her wedding clothes, while the bride and her mother stopped at a sandwich shop for sandwiches, chips, and cold drinks, so they all could enjoy a "picnic" at the hairdresser's. The bride gave the bridesmaids their gifts. Then, when everyone's hair and make-up were finished, they all left for the ceremony site together to dress for pictures. The added bonus was that everyone was on time for the wedding, because they were all together for the afternoon.

The Sports Tournament

What will the groom and the groomsmen be doing while his bride and her bridesmaids are enjoying their luncheon? Recently several of the grooms I've worked with have planned sports tournaments for the first part of the wedding day. This tournament could be in any sport or game that this groom and his friends enjoy: baseball, golf, tennis, even backgammon.

One groom rented the gymnasium at a high school for the Saturday morning of his wedding day and invited his groomsmen and ushers for a basketball game. This proved to be a great way to make the day pass quickly and keep the groom relaxed until it was time to get dressed for the big event. The main goal is to get everyone together for some activity that is relaxing and will help keep the groom calm. If the groomsmen have come to the wedding from all over the country, they will enjoy this extra opportunity to spend casual time together.

This activity usually won't have any financial impact on the budget if the groom selects a sport at a location where he's already a member. If the wedding is being held at a country club, the use of the tennis courts, golf course, and locker room can be negotiated into the wedding contract. This would have the additional benefit of bringing everyone together early to dress in one location for the wedding. If backgammon is his game, the groom could schedule the tournament in one of the meeting rooms of the hotel where the out-of-town guests are staying. If any of these reservations do require deposits, this expense should be listed as a part of the budget.

Bridal Showers and Luncheons

Being a bride has some responsibilities you may not have thought of, among them the responsibility of picking the dates and creating the guest lists for the parties given in your honor. Friends and relatives will want to entertain for you. It becomes your job to schedule these parties, because if you don't, you'll have a very difficult time attending all of them!

A bridal shower is usually a ladies-only event but throwing a couple's shower is also an option. At a couple's shower the guests are both men and women who bring gifts the couple can use together, such as picnic baskets and bar accessories. In either case, shower gifts are smaller than wedding gifts.

In addition, there are some rules about bridal showers and luncheons that you'll want to observe:

➤ *A guest is invited to only one party where a gift is required.* With the exception of your mother, sisters, future mother-in-law, future sisters-in-law, grandmothers, and bridesmaids who are invited to every event given in your honor, other guests should be invited to only *one* party. This means that if you have three showers (perhaps one given by your friends, one given by your mother's friends, and one given by your future mother-in-law's friends), you'll have to make sure that each person on the wedding list is invited to only one of them.

Sue's Suggestions

If you are having more than one shower, suggest to your family and bridesmaids that they present only token gifts, and at the very most, go together to purchase one gift for one of those showers. Weddings are very costly for your family and bridesmaids, and having to give multiple shower gifts can really become a burden.

Sue's Suggestions

How about suggesting a progressive bridal shower gift, where each gift combines to make one set? For example, at the first party, give kitchen towels; at the second, give hot pads; at the third, give a matching toaster cover.

➤ *The only people who can be invited to a shower are those who are on the wedding guest list.* If one of your coworkers wants to have a shower for you, you'll need to be quite careful if everyone in your office is not invited to the wedding.

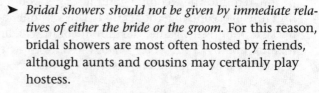

➤ *Bridal showers should not be given by immediate relatives of either the bride or the groom.* For this reason, bridal showers are most often hosted by friends, although aunts and cousins may certainly play hostess.

➤ *Sign up at a bridal registry.* While it's not considered good taste to talk about gifts, everyone knows that people invited to a wedding will buy one. Registering allows couples to communicate their taste and choices to their guests and makes shopping easier. Bridal registries have become somewhat aggressive in recent years. They want to print up cards to be included in shower and even wedding invitations, indicating that the bride and groom are registered in their store. Sorry, but this is still a no-no! Your family (mom, sisters, aunts, cousins) and your bridesmaids can spread the news for you. Of course, the hostess of your shower will tell people where you are registered, and for some reason, spreading the word this way is considered appropriate, while printing it or including the same information in an invitation is considered rude.

Sue's Suggestions

Showers should not be given the weekend of the wedding, even if you really want to include people who are not in town. Your out-of-town guests have just paid for an airline ticket, they're about to receive a hotel bill, and have a wedding gift for you in their suit-case—asking them to provide you with *another* gift isn't very kind. Ask the hostess to plan a luncheon instead!

Gifts are not the focus of a bridal luncheon. Instead, a luncheon is simply an opportunity for friends and relatives of the bride to gather and share some of the excitement of the wedding. Brides can have many luncheons, and guests may certainly be invited to more than one. Sometimes the hostess of the luncheon presents her wedding gift to the bride and groom at the luncheon, but no one else is expected to bring a gift.

Tantalizing Trivia

No one is quite sure when giving showers became a common occurrence, but one charming tale has it that the custom began when a poor Dutch miller fell in love with a girl whose father forbade the match and refused to provide a dowry. The miller's friends came to the rescue and "showered" the bride-to-be with the items she needed.

Rehearsal/Prenuptial Dinner

This party is held the night before the wedding, usually after the rehearsal, and is called a *rehearsal dinner* when the guest list includes only the bride and groom, their parents and grandparents, the bridal party, and the officiant and his or her spouse. This same event is called a *prenuptial dinner* when all of the out-of-town guests are included in the event.

Whether the event is called a rehearsal dinner or a prenuptial dinner, some of its characteristics remain the same. It should be as different from the wedding as possible. If the wedding is going to be a formal, sit-down dinner, the party the night before should be casual, perhaps a buffet dinner, a barbecue, or even a pizza party. One of the important goals of this event, especially if all the out-of-town guests are included, is to help the groom's family and friends meet the bride's family and friends. The more comfortable guests feel, the more fun the wedding will be. To accomplish this you could use name tags for each guest, or you could use assigned seating and mix the guests at each table.

Language of Love

The **rehearsal** or **prenuptial dinner** is a party held the night before the wedding. It gives people from both the bride's and groom's sides a chance to meet before the wedding. Some rehearsal or prenuptial dinners include a "roasting" of the couple.

Depending on the size of the wedding party, the rehearsal dinner could be a very small, intimate event held in either the bride and groom's home, or the home of a family member. It could also be hosted in the private room of a restaurant or other event facility.

When planning a prenuptial dinner, pay attention to the location of the event. If most of the guests have come from out of town, the host will need to provide transportation to the event for those who didn't rent vehicles. If the hosts are the bride and groom, this transportation becomes a budget item as well. There are several economical ways to do this:

➤ *Organize local members of the bridal party to pick up the out-of-town guests at the hotel and bring them to the prenuptial dinner.* This method of transportation has an added benefit—it assures that people from far away will begin to know members of the wedding, which will certainly make them more comfortable at the wedding.

➤ *Recruit out-of-town guests who have vehicles to provide rides to those who don't have transportation.* They can also travel together to other events during the weekend. This will take a little time on the bride and groom's part, but will not add any dollars to their budget.

➤ *Rent vans and/or buses.* If you choose this route, be sure to include these charges in your budget.

Of course, if none of these options are possible, then you can leave transportation to the events up to the individual guests.

Brunch

A brunch is sometimes part of the wedding weekend for the out-of-town guests. If you'll be having a Friday night prenuptial dinner before your Saturday wedding, you could schedule this brunch for Saturday morning, so while the bride, both mothers, and the bridesmaids are getting their hair and nails done, the out-of-town guests can be entertained. Of course, the ladies can pop in to the brunch and say hello to everyone before they head off to the salon. The groom, the fathers, and the groomsmen can attend the brunch and have another opportunity to visit with these guests.

If you prefer, the brunch can be held on Sunday morning, after the wedding. This gives everyone a chance to have something to eat before they take off for the airport. It also provides time for good-byes and recapping the joy of the wedding celebration. When the brunch is scheduled after the wedding, sometimes the bride and groom have already left on their honeymoon and do not attend. If they're not leaving for awhile, attending the brunch gives them a chance to visit with friends and family and to thank their out-of-town guests for coming.

Sue's Suggestions

You don't have to get carried away with your brunch. Coffee, sweet rolls, juice, and fresh fruit will make your guests *and* your pocketbook quite happy!

There are many ways to include a brunch without it becoming a costly venture. Some couples find that extended family and close friends want to be a part of the celebration and offer to entertain for the couple. This party is a good way to include them, especially if the bride and groom will be leaving for their honeymoon the next morning and won't be in town to attend the brunch.

If most of the out-of-town guests are staying in the same hotel, the brunch can be held either in the hotel's hospitality suite or in a meeting room. The hostess can bring in bagels and cream-cheese spreads, muffins, fruit, a variety of juices and home-made sweets, paper plates, and colorful paper tablecloths and napkins to create a festive feeling. The floral centerpieces from the wedding can be saved and used at the brunch. This do-it-yourself brunch is not expensive, but it can be fun and a great ending to a wonderful weekend.

The Rings

Originally marriages were finalized when the couple exchanged something of value and made a pledge to spend their lives together. Eventually this "something of value" became a ring, a circle of a precious metal with no beginning and no end. The symbolism of the ring is frequently discussed during the marriage ceremony, and over the years has become an important part of the ceremony, as well as married life.

Tantalizing Trivia

The exchange of rings dates back to at least the Egyptians. In ancient times, the husband-to-be gave his future wife an item of value, such as a gold coin, as a sign of their agreement to be married. Her acceptance signified their betrothal. Over the centuries, the coin evolved into a ring, an unbroken circle that symbolizes the eternal nature of love, the wholeness achieved through marriage, and hope for an unbroken union. In the Middle Ages, the ring began to evolve from a symbol of betrothal to a symbol of marriage. Over time, according to custom, the ring was worn on different fingers before it finally found its place on the third finger of the left hand. This finger was chosen because it was believed that the vein from this finger led directly to the heart.

The Engagement Ring

Today, many couples are marrying later in life than they did a generation ago. Often they're planning and paying for the wedding themselves with little or no assistance from their families. The engagement ring has always been optional, but today it's even more common for the couple to forego this expense than it was a generation ago. If the groom really wants to present his bride with an engagement ring, there are a few things he should know. The engagement ring becomes part of the wedding budget especially if the groom continues to pay for it after he has presented it to the bride.

When the groom sets out to select the diamond for the engagement ring, he will need to do almost as much research on the jeweler as on the stone that he finally purchases. He should select a store that has been in business for a long time and has a good reputation, and he should check that reputation with the Better Business Bureau. Before making his purchase, the groom should understand the store's return policy and feel comfortable asking questions. No one expects him to know all the answers about buying an engagement ring.

Some grooms really want to involve their brides in choosing the engagement diamond. This can be done easily by window shopping or looking at magazine ads to determine the shape of the stone the bride most admires. Then the groom can go into the jeweler of his choice and select three or four stones that are within his budget and bring the bride in to help him make the final choice and participate in selecting the setting. By selecting the price range that he is most comfortable with, the groom can be sure that the final ring will be within his budget and something that his bride will love wearing the rest of her life. This method does take away the surprise element that some grooms prefer. The groom could also make his own selection of the diamond and ask the jeweler to set it temporarily in a setting so he can surprise the bride with a ring; then they can return to the jeweler to have the diamond reset in the setting of her choice.

Once he's made his selection, the groom would be wise to have the diamond appraised by an independent gemologist (someone who appraises gemstones for a living). Naturally, he shouldn't ask the jeweler he has just purchased the ring from for a referral to the appraiser. While appraisals may vary as much as 25 percent from one to another, the groom will want to be very sure that he's purchased a diamond which is priced appropriately to its value. When the groom is secure that he has paid an appropriate price for the quality diamond he's selected, he will be very proud to present it to his bride. (If he should discover that he's paid too much for this stone, he should return it immediately.) The bride will wear this ring every day for the rest of her life, so he will want to know that it's the best stone that he could afford.

While most engagement rings have a diamond as their center stone, other gemstones are also popular. According to Cheryl Weiss, a sales professional at Maier & Berkeley in Atlanta, "While 80 percent of

Wedding Blues

Diamonds are considered a blind item. This means that most people cannot determine their value just by looking at them. Grooms should always have the diamond appraised by an independent gemologist before presenting it to the bride.

grooms present a diamond engagement ring to their brides, the remaining 20 percent of brides prefer using a ruby or sapphire as the center stone. Emeralds and South Sea pearls are also popular as center stones, but since they're very soft, they're not usually a good choice for rings that will be worn every day. Selecting a stone other than a diamond is usually not a budget decision, but rather a decision based on the bride's personal taste." Cheryl goes on to explain that rubies, sapphires, and emeralds are often as expensive as diamonds of the same carat and quality because they're much less plentiful. South Sea pearls of a fine quality can be so rare as to make them considerably more expensive than diamonds.

Most jewelers recommend that the groom spend about two months' salary for a diamond engagement ring. A lovely option is to use an heirloom stone—perhaps one that belonged to either the bride's or groom's mother or grandmother. I know of a woman who inherited a diamond from her grandmother and asked her fiancé to have this stone set into the engagement ring. What a lovely way to keep a special keepsake in the family and help the groom save money as well! In this case, the groom selected the setting he wanted his bride to wear, but he did not have to pay for the actual stone, saving a considerable amount of money.

Wedding Blues

If the groom presents the engagement ring to the bride as a complete surprise, the ring may not fit properly. The bride should immediately return to the jeweler and have the ring sized!

Whatever the groom has chosen for an engagement ring, it's important to insure it properly. If you have homeowner's or renter's insurance, be sure to read your policy to determine whether the limited jewelry coverage it currently contains will be sufficient to cover your engagement ring. If is doesn't, or if you have no insurance, now is certainly the time to purchase a policy with adequate coverage.

The Wedding Bands

While engagement rings are not a requirement of an engagement, wedding bands are an integral part of the wedding ceremony and the marriage that follows it. Even if there is to be an engagement ring, which may or may not be included in the budget, the wedding bands most certainly should be included since they're an important part of the wedding ceremony and of marriage.

Most brides and grooms participate together in the selection of the wedding band. While a great many couples select matching bands, this is certainly not a requirement of a double-ring ceremony, and each individual's personal taste should be considered. This is the one piece of jewelry that you'll wear every day for the rest of your life, and you should like it and be proud to wear it.

Wedding bands generally come in precious metals and in many styles from smooth and plain to Florentine, which has a textured look, to intricately carved. Since it's customary for the bride to wear the engagement ring and wedding band together, you may want to select the same metal for both bands. A bride may prefer to wear her wedding band on the third finger of her left hand and her engagement ring on the third finger of her right hand. If this is the case, it's probably not necessary for the bands to be a matching metal.

The most popular of metals for wedding bands is gold. The amount of gold in an item is measured in *karats* (not carats, like the measurements of diamonds). Pure gold has 24 karats, but is too soft to be used in making jewelry. When gold is mixed with other metals, the proportion and type of metal it is mixed with determines the value of the gold. For example, when a piece of jewelry is designated 14-karat gold, it is 14 portions of gold and 10 portions other metal. If the quantity of gold in an item is measured as less than 10 karats, it cannot be labeled gold in the United States. Most pieces of gold jewelry are stamped with the amount of gold in the item.

Language of Love

Karat is the unit for measuring the purity of gold. Pure gold measures 24 karats.

As you begin looking at wedding bands, you'll encounter gold jewelry that carries one of the following labels:

➤ *Solid gold* means that the item is 100-percent gold and is not generally hollow. A 14-karat, 2-millimeter wedding band runs about $30.00.

➤ *Gold-filled* means the item has a solid outer layer of a gold-colored metal injected with gold weighing approximately 12 karats.

➤ *Gold-plated* means the item contains a layer of metal covered by a layer of gold weighing approximately 10 karats.

Silver, another popular metal in jewelry, is also too soft to be used in its purest form and is therefore mixed with other metals. Sterling silver is a combination of 92.5 percent silver and 7.5 percent copper. Like gold, silver must be marked with its purity, which for sterling is 92.5 percent. Silver is 75 percent less expensive than 14-karat gold.

Platinum is a white metal that has become popular in jewelry because of its strength and resistance to heat and chemical change. It's frequently used in prongs that hold a stone into a piece of jewelry, but has become a popular metal for both engagement and wedding bands. Platinum is 50 percent more expensive than 14-karat gold.

Recently engagement rings that also serve as wedding bands have become very popular and brides are choosing not to wear an additional wedding band. While this might present a savings to the groom, since he is purchasing only one ring, he may select a more elaborate band for this purpose. Today, most (but not all) couples are opting for a double-ring ceremony, in which the bride and groom exchange bands. If this is your choice, be sure to plan for the purchase of the groom's wedding band.

Weddinginsurance

Most young people at this stage in their lives have not given a great deal of thought to insurance, except perhaps to the health insurance offered by their employers and the automobile coverage they buy for their cars. But as you start to build a new life— and especially as you begin to acquire things in the form of engagement rings and shower and wedding gifts—it's appropriate to begin thinking about insurance coverage. While coverage for your gifts and such doesn't belong on your wedding budget, there is a type of insurance you might want to consider buying. It specifically covers your wedding plans and the deposits you've made to the vendors who will be working on your wedding. This insurance is called Weddinginsurance and if you decide to carry it, it certainly belongs in your wedding budget.

Consider the story of Diane and David. They were planning to be married on June 12, 1997. On May 28 of that year, they were driving to meet their friends for dinner when a truck ran a red light and slammed into their car. Diane broke both legs and her left arm. David suffered a head injury and was briefly in a coma. Even though both eventually recovered fully, two weeks after the accident, neither of them was able to walk down the aisle, and their long-planned wedding had to be postponed. All of their vendors had required nonrefundable retainers and it looked like they'd lose all their money. All the expenses related to the postponement of their ceremony and reception and its rescheduling were completely covered by their Weddinginsurance policy.

Language of Love

Weddinginsurance is a registered trademark of a specific type of insurance underwritten by Fireman's Fund Insurance Company and provided by R.V. Nuccio & Associates Insurance Brokers, Inc. in Fawnskin, California. It's a unique insurance product specifically designed to insure against your having to pay for the same wedding twice.

The coverage can be tailored to meet the particular specifications of your wedding and the one-time premium starts at $195.00. The coverage can begin up to two years prior to the wedding. For more information about Weddinginsurance, see Appendix C, "Wedding Insurance."

Favors

Think through the favor question carefully. Even though each favor costs only a small amount, the total you'll spend could grow into an amount to be reckoned with. If the inexpensive favor is something that most of your guests will throw away anyway, aren't you just wasting your money? No one is really expecting a favor, and few will miss it if it's not there. So, if there's something on your budget that has to be eliminated, this is a good place to start.

Sue's Suggestions

Making your own wedding favors is a great way to show your creativity, and, if you allow yourself plenty of time, it can be lots of fun!

If you are determined to give your guests a small souvenir of your wedding, make something yourself. The little tulle bundles with almonds or other candies in them, tied with a ribbon and the couple's names attached, are probably the most reasonable and appreciated. This may be a way to add your creativity to the wedding. If you decide to make them yourself, however, don't wait until the night before the wedding to begin. Assemble your favors well in advance. Making them will be fun only if you can prepare them at your leisure.

Here are more easy and inexpensive ideas for favors that other couples have tried:

➤ One bride chose a pen with a light in it for writing notes at night. The names of the bride and groom and the wedding date were printed on the barrel.

➤ Another bride commissioned a local chocolate company to package a pair of beautiful truffles in a small gold box, tied with a bow, for each of the guests.

➤ Several brides chose small "silver" frames to hold the guests' table assignments. The frames became the guests' favors.

➤ Several companies produce candy bar wrappers that honor the bride and groom with their names and wedding dates or even pictures on them. Most come with an ingredients list that includes "understanding, respect, romance, and whoopie" as the ingredients of a great marriage.

The Least You Need to Know

➤ Consider hosting any of the additional parties at your own home and preparing the food yourself or picking it up at a grocery store or carry-away gourmet shop.

➤ Wedding guests should not be invited to more than one shower for a bride.

➤ Whether you're hosting a rehearsal dinner or a prenuptial dinner depends on who is invited to attend.

➤ While there are many gemstones that could be used in engagement rings, 80 percent of brides receive a diamond engagement ring.

➤ Weddinginsurance is an insurance product that will protect you from paying for the same wedding twice.

➤ Favors are a totally optional item at your wedding.

Chapter 11

Your Honored Guests

> **In This Chapter**
>
> ➤ Drawing up the guest list and addressing the invitations
>
> ➤ Assessing your responses
>
> ➤ Arranging accommodations for your guests
>
> ➤ The lowdown on discounted room rates and complimentary rooms
>
> ➤ Airline discounts
>
> ➤ Arranging transportation for your guests

This chapter is dedicated to your guests—those wonderful people who will share with you the joy of your wedding. Most couples want to share this happy occasion with the world, but that guest list would be just too long! We'll talk about how to decide who to invite, how to make them feel welcome—especially your out-of-town guests who may be traveling great distances to celebrate with you—and how to do all this while still staying within your budget.

Deciding On the Guest List

There are brides who believe the most difficult part of planning a wedding is creating the guest list—and they're probably correct! The size of your guest list will have a dramatic impact on your budget. Every estimate that you receive for the wedding is computed on a per-person basis, so you'll need some idea of your total count. That way you can make sure the guests you plan to invite can be accommodated in the facility you select.

This is somewhat tricky. You want to reserve a facility that's large enough to handle all the guests you *really* expect to attend, yet has enough "wiggle room" to accommodate additional guests if you actually have more than you expected. But you don't want such a big facility that your guests will be lost in the room if some of your expected guests are unable to attend.

In the best scenario, you should figure the cost of the total wedding before you make your final guest list. That way, because making a guest list can be a very emotional process, if you truly can't afford more than a certain number, you'll be better prepared to limit the number of people you can invite.

It's Okay to Limit Your Guest List

I am reminded of the very excited mother of the bride who, in their very first conversation, told the mother of the groom to make her guest list. The parents of the groom began thinking about all the people who had played a role in bringing their son to this point in his life and created a guest list of more than 300 people. It included his first grade teacher, who had instilled his love of learning and lived down the street, and his scout master, who had nourished his curiosity in nature and had helped him find his life's work. Even though these people had played a major role in the groom's early life, he had really not had contact with them in several years.

In the meantime, the bride's parents, who were paying for the wedding, had been making inquiries into costs and had determined that they were prepared to host a wedding of about 150 total guests. They broke this down into 50 guests for the groom's family, 50 guests for the bride and groom, and 50 guests for themselves. Imagine their surprise when the groom's family list arrived. You can also imagine the difficulty the groom's family experienced as they attempted to cut their list to one sixth of its original length, especially since they had given so much thought to the role each of these guests had played in their son's life.

The rules of etiquette give options for dealing with this scenario. If the size of the wedding is based on what you can afford and the groom's family absolutely cannot cut their list, they could pay for each of their guests who attend the wedding, above the number allotted to them. If you decide on this option, you'll need to tell them in advance exactly what it's costing you, per person, to have each guest at your wedding. This way they can decide if they can afford these additional guests or if they really must cut their list. If this is acceptable to you, and if the facility selected can accommodate these additional guests, all should be fine. If, however, the goal of the wedding is to create an intimate affair and the guest count was limited with this in mind, it's perfectly appropriate for you to decline their offer.

After All, It's Your Money

As I've mentioned earlier, I believe in the Golden Rule: The guy with the gold rules! So if you're paying for your own wedding, the decision on the number of guests should be yours. When you research the various expenses and divide the estimated cost into per-person units, you'll have a pretty good handle on the total number of guests you can accommodate. Now comes the really tricky issue of who those guests will be. There's usually not a problem when you discuss your family members and your close friends. The difficulty comes when you begin thinking about two groups of people—your single friends, who will want to bring a guest, and the people you see every day at work!

Sue's Suggestions

If you're working with a bridal consultant (see Chapter 4, "Getting Ready for the Big Day: Wedding Essentials"), she can give you a total per-person estimate for weddings in your area. With this information, you can start with a target number of guests, which is a big help!

Tantalizing Trivia

In many small communities in the United States, the custom of "open church" is still quite popular. This means that everyone in the community is welcome to attend the ceremony, while only the bride and groom's invited guests attend the reception. Even where this is not the general custom, usually the bride's family puts a notice or invitation in a community newspaper or church bulletin so people know the ceremony time and date. Some members of the community or church may choose to attend the ceremony, and some may even bring gifts, but gifts really aren't expected or required.

Inviting Your Friends

It's not necessary to invite every one of your single friends to bring a guest, especially if you would rather not have strangers at your wedding. Instead, invite your friends to bring guests only if you know the guests well enough to want them at your wedding. Otherwise, it's perfectly acceptable to invite your friend to come alone. I actually know several people who met their mates while attending someone else's wedding without a date.

Shall I Bring a Guest? Will You Be My Escort?

For example, when you invite a gentleman to bring a date to your wedding, the invitation would read "Mr. Adam Baker" on the outer envelope and "Mr. Baker and Guest" on the inner envelope. When you invite a young lady to bring a date, her invitation would read "Ms. Anne Brown" on the outer envelope and "Ms. Brown and Escort" on the inner envelope.

Even though it's perfectly acceptable to invite your single friends to bring either a guest or an escort, it's certainly more welcoming to put that person's name on the invitation if you know it. This is most often done on the inner envelope. For instance, the outer envelope might read "Mr. Adam Brown," his street, and his city; while the inner envelope would read "Mr. Brown" on the first line, and "Ms. Carrie Dorian" on the second line. When an invitation is addressed in this way, it indicates that Mr. Brown is invited to the wedding and you hope he'll choose to bring Ms. Dorian. If this couple decides to stop seeing one another before your wedding, Mr. Brown is still invited, but he should plan on attending alone. If the invitation had invited Mr. Brown and a "guest," he would have the option of bringing Ms. Dorian or any other woman of his choice. If you would prefer to know most of the guests at your wedding, you might want to re-think the use of the terms "guest" and "escort."

Bring Your Partner

Another way to handle this situation is to invite your friend who is engaged or living with someone to bring his or her "partner" on the assumption that this person truly is a part of your friend's life. It's perfectly fine to tell your friends, who don't have partners, that you've had to cut your list to accommodate people who are most special to you and regret that you won't be able to extend an invitation to their guests. Most of your friends will understand and will happily attend alone to celebrate with you. There may be others who will choose not to attend alone, and you may find that they have less time to spend with you in the future. Everything in life, and certainly in the planning of a wedding, is a trade-off and everyone who goes through this has to make choices and be able to live with these choices after the wedding.

I'm Bringing the Entire Family!

You'll also want to eliminate the phrase "Number of people _____" from your invitation response card. This question implies that you don't know how many people will be coming to your wedding and gives the guest the opportunity to include guests you may not have invited. In fact, if you've addressed the invitation to Mr. Ian Joseph and the response is returned in the affirmative, you know that *one* person will be attending. If the response card asks the number of people attending, Mr. Joseph may think you want him to bring a date, and may respond that two people will attend even though that was not your intention. On the other hand, if you've invited a couple, and one of them can't attend, you can trust that they'll write a note on the card indicating that one person will attend and one will not.

146

What do you do if you invite a single person to your wedding and that person responds to your invitation saying that *two* people will be attending? It's perfectly acceptable for you to call that guest and explain that you can't extend an invitation to the guest's friend because you've had to cut your list in order to accommodate all your friends and relatives. You'll probably want to add that you hope your invited guest will join you anyway.

Many couples tell me they are uncomfortable making this phone call, and I do understand their discomfort. The issue, though, is that it's *your* wed- ding and you shouldn't be concerned about expressing your wishes in a polite way.

Wedding Blues

Don't lose control of your guest list! By addressing your invitation correctly and eliminating the phrase "Number of people ___" you'll communicate your wishes to your invited guests and keep your number of guests in check.

What About Coworkers?

The more difficult problem often comes from the people you work with every day. They'll want to hear about all your plans and you'll then feel that they *have* to be included, but you don't even know their husbands or wives. You're probably right if you believe by inviting one, you *must* invite them all, and that can add up! One way to solve this problem is to think about work in terms of your *career* instead of your job. If someone in your office will have a direct impact on your career goals, it may be "politically correct" to invite that person and his or her spouse.

There's another solution that will be appropriate in some work situations: You may be able to invite your coworkers to attend the wedding ceremony, only. You need to be careful with this, however, because you certainly won't win any popularity contests at work by making the staff feel like "chopped liver." Honesty is always the best policy. If you can explain that you must limit your guest list for the reception for financial reasons but would like to include your coworkers for the ceremony only, you may be able to pull it off. Naturally, if the reception is not in the same location as the ceremony, this is easier to do, since everyone leaves the ceremony together and your coworkers have no way of knowing how many are going to the reception that they're not attending.

People Far Away

Almost every bride and groom have friends or distant family members who will not be able to attend the wedding. Your future mother-in-law may tell you that she knows certain people will not be able to attend, but you simply *must* invite them because they would be so hurt! The only problem is, no one, not even your future mother-in-law, can possibly know for sure that any guest will not attend until the invitation is sent and the response returned. It's important to remember that there's no mechanism in polite society for you to un-invite a guest who responds "yes" when you thought he or she wouldn't. So be careful here—if you're limited to a specific number of guests by the size of the reception site, you'll have to remove guests from your local list in order to accommodate those out-of-town guests who decide to come. You can be very sure that your Aunt Sarah is not willing to have any other guest sitting on her lap for the ceremony because you've invited more people than the church can accommodate.

Responses!

Since all the expenses of your wedding are calculated on the number of guests who actually attend, you'll want to get your guest count as quickly as possible. As I mentioned in Chapter 9, "Sharing the Excitement," etiquette experts recommend that invitations to out-of-town guests be mailed so they arrive six weeks before the wedding, and invitations to in-town guests be mailed to arrive four weeks before the wedding.

The correct response date on your response card is the third Monday before the wedding. There are some very practical reasons for this rule:

➤ Your out-of-town guests will need additional time to make arrangements to get to your wedding. They may need to make airline reservations and will certainly need hotel reservations. Sometimes the airlines offer additional discounts when reservations are made more than three weeks in advance of the travel date, so giving your guests six-weeks notice will allow them to take advantage of these discounts.

➤ Most brides discover that a high percentage of their out-of-town guests are unable to attend, allowing them to include more of their local friends and family on the guest list.

Wedding Blues

Your wedding invitation will include a self-addressed, stamped response envelope. If you have guests living outside the United States, skip the stamps on these response envelopes. Every country requires its own postage be used. If the foreign guest attempts to return your response with United States postage, the card will never be delivered.

You'll want to be sure that all out-of-town invitations are mailed on the same day and all in-town invitations are mailed on the same day. This will prevent any of your guests from having their feelings hurt if they discover their cousin in another city, or a next door neighbor, was invited to your wedding two weeks before their own invitations arrived. No one wants to feel like a second choice! If you do discover that you can invite additional guests after your in-town invitations have been mailed, the best plan is to hand deliver the invitation to the intended guest and explain how delighted you are that you're able to include them now. This is a delicate situation, but if you're honest with your friend you should be able to make him or her feel special rather than feel like an afterthought.

Welcome, Honored Guests

It's *your* wedding—but if that's all that is important to you, you could have been married at the courthouse or in the minister's study. By inviting all these guests you are acknowledging that they're important to you, and their comfort and enjoyment plays a part in your planning.

When I ask people what made a particular wedding wonderful, they never tell me it was the flowers, the food, or the band. Most people tell me they felt honored to have been invited to witness the marriage of two people so obviously in love. This feeling of "honored guest" can be created by the bride and groom, and if this is the feeling you wish to convey, it becomes your responsibility. People tend to feel honored when their needs are met before they ever have to ask.

In Chapter 9 I mentioned how creating a weekend program to send to all your out-of-town guests can

Sue's Suggestions

If you have a large number of wedding invitations going to the same foreign country, you'll save money by boxing them and sending them all to one friend in that country. Your friend can then put local postage on them and mail them from there. In addition, the invitations will probably arrive more quickly when mailed within the country.

go a long way toward conveying a feeling of consideration for your guests. Your program tells guests about hotel accommodations, the events of the weekend, and even the kind of clothing they'll need. It asks if the guest will be renting a car or if the guest will need transportation, and this gives the guest an opportunity to make the appropriate plans and you the opportunity to make the necessary arrangements.

Tantalizing Trivia

The fact that no one can ever predict who will attend a wedding was brought home to one family. Just six weeks before Marilyn mailed the invitations to her daughter's wedding, her husband Roger's great aunt passed away. Marilyn and Roger went to the funeral and connected with cousins they had not seen in several years. Ten days later another elderly relative in the same family died. When the invitations were mailed, several out-of-town cousins who had not planned to attend the wedding, and who were not expected, decided to attend, feeling that the family needed to be together for a celebration. Marilyn and Roger were first surprised and then delighted. Fortunately, they were able to afford the extra guests and the reception room could accommodate the numbers.

As the host and hostess, you're not *responsible* for your guest's room rates or for any of their expenses related to the weekend. As their friends, however, you'll want to keep the expenses as low as possible so they'll be able to share the weekend with you. There are several things that you can do to reduce some of their expenses and especially to make them feel comfortable and welcome when they arrive, which I'll cover in the following sections.

Discounted Room Rates

You're planning a wonderful celebration weekend, and you want your friends and family to share it with you, but traveling to an out-of-town wedding can be expensive. What with airfares, hotel rooms, and rental cars—not to mention appropriate clothing and a gift for the bride and groom—some out-of-town guests may not be able to afford to come to your wedding, even if they really want to. For this reason, many couples negotiate special room rates at local hotels in an attempt to reduce their guests' expenses for the weekend.

In most cities the major hotels consider themselves business people's hotels, and they created their room-rate schedule based on this consideration. Business people usually travel during the week and try to return to their families on the weekend, leaving hotels lightly booked for that time. The hotel has to employ their staff anyway, so they would really like to have their rooms filled even if they cannot get every guest to pay the same rate the business people paid during the working week.

Language of Love

A **block of rooms** refers to the number of hotel rooms held for members of your guest list. This hold is valid usually only until a specific date and does not mean that all your guests will receive rooms on the same floor. Each guest will be able to indicate his or her preference for a smoking or nonsmoking room, king, queen, or double room, or a room equipped to accommodate people with physical disabilities.

If you're hosting your wedding in a hotel ballroom, you'll be bringing additional revenue into that hotel, and you should be able to offer your guests discounts on their room rates as a part of your package. Even if your wedding ceremony and reception are not held in the hotel, you can still ask for a discount room-rate package at the hotels located near your ceremony and/or reception location. To do this, make a few phone calls to several hotels and educate yourself. Find out what the room rate is during the week and what the hotel's normal weekend specials are. Ask if the hotel is served by any public transportation from the airport, such as a regularly scheduled shuttle or limousine service, and what the fee is (if any) for this service. You may want to ask about other hotel perks, such as indoor swimming pools, health clubs, and complimentary transportation to and from local shopping malls. If you find that the hotel with the best location for your guests also has the highest weekend rate, you can make an appointment with its sales department to discuss securing a *block of rooms* for your guests if that would bring a better rate.

Most hotels will want you to book several rooms (usually about 20) in order to give you a significantly discounted rate. If you believe you'll have enough out-of-town guests, it's certainly worth your efforts to talk to the sales department of the hotel. You will not be expected to pay for these rooms; instead, the hotel will prepare a card for you to include in your weekend program so each guest may reserve a room on his or her own credit card. Don't worry if you can't fill all the rooms you booked—the room rate won't be affected.

Complimentary Rooms

If you've made arrangements for most of your guests to stay in a specific hotel, and you believe your guests will be booking approximately 20 sleeping rooms, you can ask the sales director for complimentary additional rooms—specifically a hospitality suite and a bridal suite. Most major hotels are happy to give you these rooms for the weekend if you're booking enough rooms to meet their minimum requirements.

Occasionally hotels will also give the parents of the bride or groom a sleeping room for the night of the wedding. This is definitely not a standard situation, but it's sometimes available especially when a large number of rooms have been booked by out-of-town guests. This can help your parents who may not want to drive home after a late wedding. When this is available to you, it can also be the room you use to dress in before the ceremony.

Unlike the discounted room rate, which does not change if you can't fill the number of rooms you booked, the complimentary sleeping rooms and hospitality suite may not be free if you fall below the estimated number of rooms. For this reason, don't over-estimate the number of rooms you expect to fill.

Do You Need a Hospitality Suite?

A *hospitality suite* can be a sleeping room or a meeting room in the hotel, but more often it's a suite comprised of a sitting room and often an attached bedroom. The advantage of having a hospitality suite is that it gives your out-of-town guests a place to congregate and visit during the weekend. You'll have friends and relatives coming from all over the country, you haven't seen many of them in awhile, and they haven't seen each other in awhile as well. They won't want to sit in the hotel lobby to catch up with one another, so the hospitality suite is the perfect place for them to meet and greet each other.

Once you've been assured the suite will be available to your guests, you can plan on stocking it

Language of Love

A **hospitality suite** is a meeting room, sleeping room, or sitting and sleeping room where your out-of-town guests can congregate to visit with you and with each other.

with soft drinks, nuts, home-baked sweets, chips and dips, coffee, and tea. The hotel will tell you that they must provide all the food that is served on the premises. But as long as you're discreet and respectful and don't have a catering truck back up to the hotel to unload trays of food, the hotel staff will probably not object to your providing some snacks for your guests yourself. If the suite you've been given also includes a complimentary sleeping room, you can offer this room to one of your out-of-town guests if he or she offers to tidy up the hospitality suite and get the coffee started in the morning. This may make it possible for a friend or relative to attend the wedding who otherwise may have difficulty affording the weekend.

If you've decided to host a rehearsal dinner (see Chapter 10, "More Things to Consider When Budgeting") for just the bridal party and officiant, and are feeling a little uncomfortable about your out-of-town guests having nothing to do that evening, you can host a dessert party in the suite after the rehearsal dinner. Or if friends have asked how they can help you with the wedding, you can ask them to bring in juice, sweet rolls, and coffee to provide a continental breakfast on the day of the wedding so your guests will not have to purchase breakfast. All of your guests may not attend, but it's certainly a nice gesture for those who do.

Sue's Suggestions

Don't purchase coffee from the hotel for your hospitality suite, because it will be very costly. Instead, borrow large coffeepots from friends and make the coffee yourself (or ask a close friend staying at the hotel to be responsible for this). Set up three pots: one regular coffee, one decaffeinated coffee, and one hot water for tea and hot chocolate. Don't forget the teabags and the cocoa!

Language of Love

The **bridal suite** is the room where the bride and groom spend their wedding night. Usually hotels hold their most elaborate rooms as bridal suites.

The Bridal Suite

The other complimentary room you can ask for is the *bridal suite*. If you're hosting your wedding in the hotel, chances are they'll offer this suite to you. But if the catering manager doesn't offer it, don't be shy— ask for it! Most hotels will give you the suite for the night of the wedding. If you want to stay in the hotel the night before the wedding, you may have to pay for the room for that night, but you could ask for a discounted rate for that one night. If you're having an afternoon or early evening reception and you really need to spend the night at the airport to catch an early morning flight, ask the hotel if it could arrange for you to stay in the bridal suite at its airport property. Not only is the hotel likely to provide the room either complimentarily or at a greatly discounted rate, but it's also likely to provide transportation to the airport facility as well.

Airline Discounts: Are They Worth the Effort?

Major airlines will sometimes offer your guests discounts on airfare. You can research this with the help of your travel agent. Usually, these fares are 5 percent below the airline's lowest *published* price, which is never the least you can pay for a ticket. If you have a large number of guests traveling from one city, ask your travel agent to contact the airline most people would choose to ask about a discount for your guests. Then be sure to tell your guests about it. Most airlines have several layers of fares and many specials to offer, so your guests will probably be able to get lower rates through their travel agents. But just in case there are no lower rates the weekend of your wedding, this discount will certainly be appreciated.

Even though you won't mail your wedding invitations to your out-of-town guests sooner than six weeks before the wedding, you don't have to wait until six weeks before the wedding to let your guests know about it. If your wedding is in the spring, and you usually send out Christmas cards, you can include a note in your greeting card, telling people about your wedding plans and some of the special pricing that you've secured on their behalf. This way, your guests can watch the paper for discount fares that may be even better than those the airline gave you. Preparing a separate mailing, in the form of a "Save the Date" card, is probably not a good idea. It will cost you money in postage and printing that you don't really need to spend at this point. But if you can piggy-back this information in a mailing that you would be doing anyway, you certainly should consider doing it.

> **Wedding Blues**
>
> If your guest list is not finalized and you send your wedding information to everyone on your tentative list, you're obligated to invite all of these people to the wedding, even if you discover you can't afford it! You may find yourself having to pass up inviting your local friends because more of your out-of-town friends than you originally expected are planning to attend.

How Will Your Guests Get From Point A to Point B?

If you're planning a weekend wedding, with all your out-of-town guests invited to a prenuptial dinner the night before the wedding, you'll have to give some thought to how these guests will get to the prenuptial dinner and to the ceremony and reception the next day. There are several options, such as organizing car pools or furnishing your guests with maps and allowing them to make their own arrangements. (See Chapter 10 for more on organizing transportation.)

Another option is to ask your guests if they will be renting cars. (See the weekend program in Chapter 9.) If you know a couple is planning to rent a car and you're willing to organize the travel, you can easily accomplish your goal of getting all your guests where they have to be safely, on time, and without getting lost. In addition, you can save some money, and as a bonus you'll have made sure that everyone knows each other so the wedding will be a fun celebration. When you know who's renting a car and who's not, you simply assign the guests without transportation to ride with the guests who have transportation and space in their automobiles.

You may find that you have too many people without transportation to match up with guests who have cars, so you'll have to provide transportation for at least some of the guests. If you plan ahead, you can probably rent a 15-passenger van for a 24-hour period for a nominal fee from most automobile rental companies. You'll have to provide a driver for this van who is willing to consider him- or herself a designated driver and remain alcohol-free all evening. Because you provide the driver, these vans are less expensive than renting a bus or minibus with a professional driver. If you need more than one van, they're reasonable enough for you to rent more than one.

Sue's Suggestions

It's tempting to ask members of your bridal party to drive the van, but this would be a poor choice. The bridal party will be involved in picture taking both before and after the ceremony—exactly when your guests need this transportation.

If you don't need the van for as long as 24 hours or don't have anyone to drive the van, you can rent minivans, usually 28-passenger vehicles, from bus companies. These vehicles come with a driver and are rented for a certain number of hours. You'll have to ask, but in most cases you actually get to use the vehicle for approximately one hour *less* than the rental time, because the company will charge you from terminal to terminal (so a five-hour rental gives you four hours of usable time).

Another option is to rent a large bus to transport your guests. School buses or motor coaches seat approximately 43 to 48 people. Again, the bus company will charge you from terminal to terminal. You will have less actual rental time, but having a bus is a terrific way to safeguard your guests. This way you can be sure that anyone who drinks at your reception is not getting into a car in a strange city and attempting to drive back to his or her hotel.

Whichever method you decide to use to transport your guests, get in your car and drive from the hotel to every place your guests need to be, and write out the directions. (It's much easier for a driver to follow written directions than it is to follow a drawn map.) Make sure you note any landmarks along the way.

Make sure every guest who will be driving gets a copy of the directions, as well as every guest who is a passenger, so he or she can be the navigator. If you hire a bus with a driver, assume the driver has never driven this route before, so make sure that both the driver and the bus company get copies of the maps. I further recommend that you assign a "bus captain" to each bus. This bus captain gets a copy of the directions so he or she can make sure that the bus or van driver does not make a wrong turn along the way and get lost. Of course, if a wrong turn is made, your guest will be able to assist the driver to get back to the correct route.

Considering your guests' needs and comfort as you plan your wedding is the best way to make sure they feel like the honored guests they truly are. These family members and close friends may travel long distances at great personal expense to celebrate with you, so make them feel as welcome as possible. This consideration doesn't have to be costly—if you think about it, there really are *lots* of ways to accomplish this on your budget.

The Least You Need to Know

➤ Making a guest list can be an emotional process, so it's best to know what the event will cost per person before deciding how many guests to invite.

➤ When it comes to coworkers, you might have to invite people who can advance your career, but don't invite the whole office.

➤ It's not necessary to invite all your single guests to bring a date to your wedding.

➤ It's usually possible to secure a discounted room rate for your out-of-town guests if you do your research and know what to ask for.

➤ There are several inexpensive options to help you provide transportation for your guests to and from the weekend events.

Chapter 12

Getting It All Down on Paper

In This Chapter

➤ What should you include in your budget?

➤ Figuring your budget using percentages and a worksheet

➤ Identifying your wedding priorities

➤ Estimating on the high side to spend less

➤ A comparison of costs by bridal consultants across the country

---

My daughter became engaged a few hours after my husband and I landed in Costa Rico for a combined business trip/vacation. When she and her Prince Charming called the next day, we were very excited and I was particularly eager to share my news with friends and family back home. My husband told me I was welcome to call whomever I wished, but the $9-per-minute phone calls from Costa Rico to the United States would have to be part of the wedding budget! Needless to say, no one heard of her engagement until we got home a week later!

In this chapter we'll be talking about how to get the most for your dollar by identifying what should be included in your budget, setting priorities, comparing costs, setting up a budget worksheet, and more. Probably the most important thing to know about your budget is that if you write it down and keep it up-to-date, you'll have a very good chance of keeping to it! A written budget is a living thing that needs to be modified as you work through your planning.

What's Included in Your Budget?

The main events of your wedding weekend in terms of budgeting include the ceremony and reception. Also included may be the bridesmaids' luncheon, rehearsal or prenuptial dinner, and perhaps a brunch. There is, of course, a great deal more you could choose to include, but these are the highlights and a very good place to start.

If you and the groom are paying for the wedding completely on your own, you may want to include additional items in your budget, such as the honeymoon and the engagement ring. If the groom continues to pay for the engagement ring after he has presented it to the bride, the ring becomes part of the wedding budget.

As you begin to draw up your budget, you probably know two things: You want to get married and you have "x" amount of dollars to spend on doing it. It's the process of budgeting that will help you determine how you'll turn those dollars into the wedding of your dreams. As you share your wedding plans with your families, you may find that family members want to participate in the planning. Sometimes people want to add to the funds that you've allocated to the project.

Sue's Suggestions

Generally, your budget should include anything that you would not purchase unless you were getting married. Your wedding gown belongs there, but mom's dress doesn't, since she might wear the dress again to a close friend's wedding.

You may discover that a family member wants to pay for your gown, while someone else wants to pay for the music; or there may be people who want to host events during the wedding weekend.

Wedding Blues

Money can be a touchy subject. Be discreet when you approach your family about contributing to your wedding. Don't assume they don't want to help just because they haven't offered. Perhaps they don't want to insult you, but would feel hurt if you didn't ask! Good communication is the key.

It's helpful to know this before you begin, but it's not critical. If someone comes forward and offers to host the bridesmaids' luncheon, for instance, you simply remove that item from your budget and distribute the money to some other area. This is why we say that budgets are not cast in stone; they can be changed and reworked as the situation changes. It's important to be flexible enough in your planning to be able to make the changes as they become necessary.

Budgeting Tools

There are several different ways to create a wedding budget. Some people like to work on the basis of percentages. This is often shown on a circle or pie graph, where, in the following example, 38 percent of the cost of the wedding is for the reception; 2 percent for printing of invitations; 3.5 percent for flowers; 4.7

percent for music; 5.7 percent for wedding attire; 9.5 percent for photography and videography; 14.3 percent for the engagement and wedding rings; 14.3 percent for the honeymoon; and 8 percent for miscellaneous expenses. The total for everything equals 100 percent of your budget.

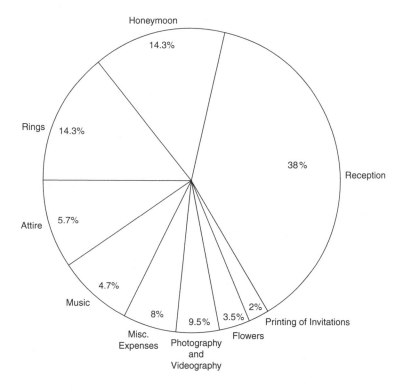

You may like to use a circle or pie graph to determine your wedding budget.

Nearly every wedding planning booklet you pick up offers a list of budget percentages for your wedding expenses, and frankly, it doesn't matter which budget percentages you decide to use as long as you use them straight through your wedding planning. It will not work out correctly if you mix two percentage charts from different budget plans, picking the percentages you want for an item depending on how much you're quoted. Whichever chart you use, the total has to be 100%. The trick is to be sure that your total spent ends up at exactly the amount that you have to spend. You're really not trying to come in under budget; instead, you're just trying not to go over budget.

Another technique is using the budget worksheet. (I include a budget worksheet for you to use a little later in this chapter.) This method lists the various items that you'll be spending money on and allows you to assign a dollar value to each one. As you begin speaking to the various vendors, you can adjust the amount you spend on any one item. This way you'll always have your bottom line clearly in view.

Your worksheet should include everything you think you might spend money on in the planning of your wedding. The Wedding Budget Worksheet shown here is very complete—you *should not* be spending money on every one of the items on this sheet! (I promise, even the most extravagant bride will not need *both* thermography and engraved invitations!)

If you prefer, you can create your own budget worksheet. As you begin, list everything you can think of that may be a part of the wedding ceremony, reception, or weekend. Talk to your recently married friends. Ask them about surprise expenses. Did they forget to plan for anything? We all learn more from the things we didn't plan for than we do from the things that went as planned. Brides often tell me they were in total control until about two weeks before the wedding. Then it felt like they were writing checks so fast they lost total track of the money. If you plan ahead and list those last-minute items on your budget,

Sue's Suggestions

If you've never worked with a budget before, a budget worksheet may be the way to go, since it includes all the details that need to be covered. Percentages can be difficult to understand, and it's sometimes really hard to put everything into an abstract figure, which is what a percentage may appear to be.

they will no longer be last minute! You may decide to eliminate some other items so you can include these last-minute ones. But be sure to list all items on your budget, even those you eliminated, because you may forget you eliminated them in favor of something else.

Tantalizing Trivia

Statistically, most couples go over their budget by approximately 10 percent. A good way to protect yourself from this overage is to include it from the very beginning! Call it "miscellaneous expenses" if you wish, but treat this just like any other part of your budget so you won't go over this amount too! You still have to be diligent to stay on your budget, otherwise you will go over budget even more. Remember, you're not trying to stay under budget—you're just trying hard not to overspend.

The most common error brides make in their worksheets is to assume that the number of guests will not affect the cost of certain items. For instance, a band is a band and flowers are flowers no matter how many of your guests attend. But in fact, every item on your budget should be thought of in terms of the price *per person*. If you invite 100 people for a cocktail buffet reception, you can figure on scattered seating for about half of them, and should order five centerpieces; but if you invite 250 guests, you'll need at least 13 centerpieces, and the larger room may need more decoration. A four-piece band may be perfect for 100 guests, but if your party is for 250 people, you'll certainly need more musicians—not just to be heard above the crowd, but to get everyone up and dancing.

In the same way, the dress you'd choose for a formal wedding of 250 people is very different from the one you'd select if you were planning an informal wedding for 60 people. All of these things must be taken into consideration when you go through your budget worksheet.

Here's how to use the following Wedding Budget Worksheet:

➤ Use the first column ("Plan") to determine your monetary priorities. Decide for yourself how important each item is to you in terms of dollars. Should you allow $5,000 for it because it's *really* important? Or $50 because it's not important at all?

➤ Fill in the next column ("Estimate") as you begin to find out the charges of the various vendors. You may find that you'll have to continue to adjust your plan as you speak to these vendors, since some vendors may be more expensive than you expected, but some may be less expensive, also.

➤ Once you've signed the contract and given the vendor a deposit, record that deposit in the last column ("Deposit"). It's probably a good idea to note the date you paid that deposit and the check number.

Wedding Blues

Planning a seated dinner wedding reception with all the trimmings? In many parts of the country you'll need to figure on paying as much as $200 per person. That means if you have 200 guests, you'll need $40,000 to pull it off! Don't panic—that includes *everything*, from your wedding gown down to the favors on the table, and if you budget for *everything*, you could find that it's affordable!

Sue's Suggestions

Be sure to do the math on your budget worksheet. If dinner will be $27.50 per person and you expect 175 people, record $4,812.50 on your worksheet, and then figure the tax and tip to make sure that your budget is accurate.

➤ The third column ("Actual") may have to be completed later. As you work with the different vendors, you may make changes in your contract that end up costing more than you expected. If you keep your budget current, you won't have any surprises in the last month before the ceremony, when everything comes due. There's a terrific feeling of comfort and celebration when you walk down that aisle, knowing you can afford your wedding!

Wedding Budget Worksheet

	Plan	Estimate	Actual	Deposit
Clothing				
Gown and veil	_____	_____	_____	_____
Alterations	_____	_____	_____	_____
Shoes, slip	_____	_____	_____	_____
Make-up, hair	_____	_____	_____	_____
Groom's tuxedo	_____	_____	_____	_____
Photography	_____	_____	_____	_____
Video	_____	_____	_____	_____
Disposable cameras (5 for $49.95)	_____	_____	_____	_____
Film developing	_____	_____	_____	_____
Blood tests	_____	_____	_____	_____
Marriage license	_____	_____	_____	_____
Flowers				
Bridal bouquet	_____	_____	_____	_____
Bridesmaids' bouquets	_____	_____	_____	_____
Boutonnieres	_____	_____	_____	_____
Corsages	_____	_____	_____	_____
Centerpieces	_____	_____	_____	_____
Decorations	_____	_____	_____	_____
Music				
Ceremony	_____	_____	_____	_____
Cocktails	_____	_____	_____	_____
Dinner/reception*	_____	_____	_____	_____
Disc jockey	_____	_____	_____	_____
Room rental	_____	_____	_____	_____
Church/synagogue	_____	_____	_____	_____
Reception site	_____	_____	_____	_____
Officiant's fee**				
Nonmember fee	_____	_____	_____	_____
Member fee	_____	_____	_____	_____
Bridal consultant	_____	_____	_____	_____
Wedding insurance	_____	_____	_____	_____
Optional items	_____	_____	_____	_____
Engagement ring	_____	_____	_____	_____
Wedding bands	_____	_____	_____	_____
Additional parties	_____	_____	_____	_____

	Plan	Estimate	Actual	Deposit
Bridesmaids' luncheon*				
Room rental	_____	_____	_____	_____
Invitations	_____	_____	_____	_____
Food and				
beverages	_____	_____	_____	_____
Decorations	_____	_____	_____	_____
Groom's tournament*				
Room rental	_____	_____	_____	_____
Equipment rental	_____	_____	_____	_____
Transportation	_____	_____	_____	_____
Food and				
beverages	_____	_____	_____	_____
Rehearsal/				
Prenuptial dinner*	_____	_____	_____	_____
Invitations	_____	_____	_____	_____
Room rental	_____	_____	_____	_____
Food and				
beverages	_____	_____	_____	_____
Decorations	_____	_____	_____	_____
Music	_____	_____	_____	_____
Equipment rental	_____	_____	_____	_____
Honeymoon*	_____	_____	_____	_____
Transportation	_____	_____	_____	_____
Lodging	_____	_____	_____	_____
Meals	_____	_____	_____	_____
Activities/				
touring	_____	_____	_____	_____
Car rental	_____	_____	_____	_____
Souvenirs	_____	_____	_____	_____
Printing/Thermography				
Invitations				
(w/envelopes)	_____	_____	_____	_____
Envelope linings	_____	_____	_____	_____
Return address	_____	_____	_____	_____
Reception cards	_____	_____	_____	_____
Response cards	_____	_____	_____	_____
Thank-you notes	_____	_____	_____	_____
Colored ink	_____	_____	_____	_____
Printing/Engraving				
Invitations				
(w/envelopes)	_____	_____	_____	_____
Envelope linings	_____	_____	_____	_____
Return address	_____	_____	_____	_____
Reception cards	_____	_____	_____	_____

continues

Wedding Budget Worksheet   (continued)

	Plan	Estimate	Actual	Deposit
Response cards	_____	_____	_____	_____
Thank-you notes	_____	_____	_____	_____
Colored ink	_____	_____	_____	_____
Postage				
Outer envelope	_____	_____	_____	_____
Response envelope	_____	_____	_____	_____
Thank-you notes	_____	_____	_____	_____
Napkins				
Beverage size	_____	_____	_____	_____
Luncheon/dinner	_____	_____	_____	_____
Cake boxes	_____	_____	_____	_____
Matches	_____	_____	_____	_____
Table cards	_____	_____	_____	_____
Place cards	_____	_____	_____	_____
Skull caps	_____	_____	_____	_____
Weekend programs	_____	_____	_____	_____
Postage	_____	_____	_____	_____
Calligraphy				
Invitations	_____	_____	_____	_____
Table cards	_____	_____	_____	_____
Place cards	_____	_____	_____	_____
Beverages				
Mixed drinks (open bar based on 2 to 2.5 drinks per person)				
Deluxe @_____	_____	_____	_____	_____
Premium @_____	_____	_____	_____	_____
House brands @_____	_____	_____	_____	_____
Additional liquor tax	_____	_____	_____	_____
Beer and wine (open bar based on 2 to 2.5 drinks per person)	_____	_____	_____	_____
Wine with dinner (based on 2 glasses per person, 6 drinks per bottle) @_____ bottle	_____	_____	_____	_____
Bartender (1 per 75 guests)	_____	_____	_____	_____

	Plan	Estimate	Actual	Deposit
Food				
Hors d'oeuvres (6–8 per person) @ _____	_____	_____	_____	_____
Cocktail buffet (15–20 per guest) @ _____	_____	_____	_____	_____
Dinner ($____ to ____ per person)	_____	_____	_____	_____
Wedding cake ($____to ____ per person)	_____	_____	_____	_____
Slicing fee/ plating fee	_____	_____	_____	_____
Tip (service & gratuity, 20% on food & beverages)	_____	_____	_____	_____
Tax on food and beverages (service is taxed)	_____	_____	_____	_____
Kosher fees (per person)	_____	_____	_____	_____
Cake baking fee	_____	_____	_____	_____
Coat check	_____	_____	_____	_____
Favors	_____	_____	_____	_____
Accessories				
Guest book and pen	_____	_____	_____	_____
Linens				
Standard linen	_____	_____	_____	_____
Special linen	_____	_____	_____	_____
Overlays	_____	_____	_____	_____
Napkins	_____	_____	_____	_____
Chair covers	_____	_____	_____	_____
Labor for installing linens	_____	_____	_____	_____
Parking				
Self-park	_____	_____	_____	_____
Valet	_____	_____	_____	_____
Transportation				
Limousine	_____	_____	_____	_____
Tip	_____	_____	_____	_____
Guest transportation				

continues

Wedding Budget Worksheet (continued)

	Plan	Estimate	Actual	Deposit
15-passenger van	_____	_____	_____	_____
Minivan w/driver (28-passenger)	_____	_____	_____	_____
Bus w/driver (43+ passengers)	_____	_____	_____	_____
Rentals				
Tables	_____	_____	_____	_____
Chairs	_____	_____	_____	_____
Dishes	_____	_____	_____	_____
Silverware	_____	_____	_____	_____
Tent	_____	_____	_____	_____
Candelabra	_____	_____	_____	_____
Archway	_____	_____	_____	_____
Gazebo	_____	_____	_____	_____
Dance floor	_____	_____	_____	_____
Audiovisual				
Lighting	_____	_____	_____	_____
Sound	_____	_____	_____	_____
Portable toilets	_____	_____	_____	_____
Miscellaneous expenses	_____	_____	_____	_____
Total	_____	_____	_____	_____
Divided by number of guests = price per person	_____	_____	_____	_____

* Continuous live music is often available at an additional price; take care to ask what that price is and how breaks are handled.

** Generally, the officiant's performance of life-cycle events is covered in the membership dues of the congregation; however, it's customary to "tip" the officiant with a contribution to his or her discretionary fund for performing at a member's wedding ceremony. If you're a member of the congregation, you can expect to pay a specific fee.

*** Total expenditure of the bracketed items below must not exceed the amount allotted for this item.

Setting Your Priorities

Once you've created your worksheet, go through it and assign a dollar figure to each of the items. The amount of money you assign to each item should reflect how important that particular item is to you. For instance, if you believe the music is the most important part of the celebration, allot more money for the musicians and perhaps less for the flowers. Another bride might think her dress is the most important element, and put the largest amount of money in that column. There may be many items on the list that are not important or relevant to you at all (such as skull caps, if you're not Jewish) and you'll not allot any money for these items.

When you've completed the worksheet, total everything up. Is this an amount that you can handle? Does it need to be reduced in any way? Look back over your projections. Have you assigned too much or too little money to a category? Make whatever adjustments are necessary and then divide this amount by the number of people you expect to attend the event.

It's important to remember when you are setting priorities, not *everything* can be equally important. There have to be some things that are less important to you than others. It's really hard to eliminate some of the lovely things that are possible to add to your wedding, but if you make everything equally important you'll not be able to stay within your budget at all.

Estimate High—Spend Less!

Since you haven't begun any of your research yet, you may actually be doing more "guess-timating" than estimating because you may not know the typical charges for items on your budget worksheet. That's okay, so long as you're working with a pencil that has a good eraser. You're just starting out at this, and no one expects you to know all the answers; besides, you're not doing this for pub-

Sue's Suggestions

One way to reduce the cost of your wedding is to reduce the number of guests that attend. You probably have not created your guest list yet, so you may want to consider this option.

Wedding Blues

If you have a $10,000 budget to plan a wedding for 100 people and you rush out and purchase a $3,000 gown, you'll really have a problem getting everything in under budget. Plan carefully so you don't come up short!

lication and no one will see it but you and your groom. When assigning a dollar amount to each item on your budget, you'll want to estimate your costs on the high side and then try to spend less than you estimated. By doing this, you'll be building in money to cover the miscellaneous expenses for the overage you may experience on some charges.

If you decide to work with an experienced bridal consultant, it's a good idea to meet with her during the initial budgeting. (See Chapter 4, "Getting Ready for the Big Day: Wedding Essentials.") Bridal consultants who have been working in an area for a while often have budget forms available to you that will show you the average prices for various services in that community. That will help you create a more realistic budget from the beginning. If you're able to secure a price-range chart for your community, use this document and select the highest range in those areas that are most important to you.

Wedding Blues

To stay on top of your financial situation and avoid going over budget, keep updating your budget worksheet each time you meet with a vendor.

Select the lowest price range in those items that are not important to you at all, and select a mid range for those things that are of medium importance to you. It will frustrate you if your research indicates that you have under budgeted every item, so get as much help as you can early on.

How Do You Know What Things Cost?

There are many factors that influence the cost of the various services you need for your wedding. Some things are simply supply and demand: The more people who want a specific item, the more vendors will offer it to you. Vendors who have earned a good reputation will be in great demand and you can expect to pay a premium to work with them. If the demand for a certain item doesn't exist in your area, that item may not be available to you. For instance, you may want to use a calligrapher to address your wedding invitations by hand, but you live in a small town where most people are not willing to pay for this service, so there may be no one advertising calligraphy there. You may have to send your invitation envelopes to someone in a larger city to have the work done at a reasonable price.

To help you determine how much money you might expect to pay for the various services needed for your wedding, I contacted members of the Association of Bridal Consultants around the United States and asked them what brides might pay for specific items in their communities. The results were interesting to me, and I hope they will be helpful to you! (For a detailed comparison chart of price ranges for communities around the United States, refer to the tear-out card at the front of this book.)

Attire

Most of the consultants responded that brides could expect to pay between $500 and $3,500 for their wedding gowns. This range would cover new gowns purchased in retail shops across the country. I was interested to learn that individual gowns might cost slightly more on the West Coast due to shipping charges, because manufacturers and distributors are located on the East Coast. The groom's tuxedo rents for between $59 and $100 across the country. In every situation, shoes were rented separately, but cummerbunds, vests, ties, studs, and cuff links were all included in the basic rental fee.

Photography

Photography prices seemed to range between $1,500 and $8,000 throughout most of the country. The consultants in larger cities reported that photographers offered packages as reasonable as $695. Most photographers quoted the minimum price they would charge for a wedding—if the bride had difficulty making decisions (and had the funds to do so) she could easily spend $10,000 on her wedding album!

Video

Video packages seemed to range from $695 for a one-camera, unedited video to $4,000 for a three-camera, edited tape. Of course, if the couple wan-ted the videographer to attend the prenuptial din-ner they could expect to pay somewhat more to add the second event. Preparing a video photo montage of the couple growing up and dating—to be shown at the prenuptial dinner and then added to the finished wedding tape—would also add to the price of this contract.

Sue's Suggestions

Hiring a photographer who works on the basis of a minimum purchase instead of a package puts you in the driver's seat. You know that you've committed to spend whatever the minimum is, but above that figure you can stop buying when you've spent enough. With some packages, you don't find out until after the wedding that everything you want may not be covered.

Flowers

Bridal consultants around the country seemed to agree that flowers can be a "blind" item. The bride's bouquet generally costs between $125 and $250. The bridesmaids' bouquets range from $20 and $95 each, with the majority of the consultants stating that $45 to $80 each was typical in their area. Corsages for mothers and grandmothers averaged between $20 and $35 each across the country, and boutonnieres averaged between $5 and $15 each.

One centerpiece for the buffet table ranged from $125 to $800, with part of the difference coming from whether the centerpiece was designed to be viewed all the way around (from 360 degrees) or only from the front (180 degrees). Centerpieces for the individual dinner tables could be found selling for $30 each all the way up to $175 each. While these prices represented ranges in the various communities, they would certainly vary depending on the specific flowers that a bride might select. There was also a wide degree of difference between the cost of floral decorations around the country, depending on the individual tastes of each bride.

Music

Musicians seemed to average between $100 and $150 per musician, per hour, when they were hired just for the wedding ceremony. When the musicians were a part of the live band playing for the reception, however, the fee changed to an average of $150 per musician for the whole ceremony. Live bands that provided music for the reception determined their pricing based on the number of musicians in the group and the number of hours they were hired to play, and they seemed to range from $850 to $10,000. Disc jockeys cost from $275 to $2,000. Some of the more expensive DJs came with light shows and costumed dancers who mixed with the guests and made sure that everyone was on the dance floor having a great time.

Invitations

The invitation sample books from which most brides make their selections are roughly the same all across the country, so there wasn't much difference in the price ranges between one community and another. The biggest difference seemed to occur when some brides selected their invitations from dealers who offered discounts, while others shopped at the mall and paid full price.

Every wedding has a budget—the biggest difference is that some brides are *in control* and other brides are *controlled by* their budgets. I hope this chapter has helped you understand the elements of budgeting and has empowered you to create your own budget to build you wedding around.

The Least You Need to Know

➤ Budgets can be interpreted either in percentages or a line-by-line worksheet.

➤ Prices for various services will vary in different parts of the country.

➤ Most couples go over their budget by 10 percent.

➤ Every item on a budget should be computed on a per-person basis. Even the cost of music and flowers will vary depending on the number of guests at the wedding.

Part 3

Sticking to Your Budget

Okay, you've written out your budget, now it's time to figure out how to protect your-self and get exactly what you want for the dollars you're willing to spend. Everyone knows you have to read a contract carefully before signing it—but do you know how what it says can affect your wedding? In this part we'll read a few contracts and point out what they say and what they mean.

You'll also want to maximize the money that you have to spend on your wedding. Sometimes this means putting things on credit cards to delay payments for a month, but paying them off as soon as the bill comes in to avoid interest charges. Sometimes it means signing contracts early to avoid price increases. Whatever it means to you, the more organized you are with your money, the more money you will have to spend.

DRESS FLOWERS LIMO RECEPTION

Money, Money, Money!

There is no "right" or "wrong" way to handle your money. Couples do it many different ways. I know several couples in which either the husband or the wife is responsible for paying all the bills from their joint checking account. All the money the couple earns is deposited into this account and everything comes out of it, including spending money.

Other couples find that the one-checking-account method just doesn't work for them. They may determine that they need one household account they each contribute to and pay all their joint bills out of. They may pay bills together from this account or alternate doing it. This way, each may have their own checking account to cover their own particular needs and into which they may deposit an "allowance" that comes from their joint account. This sometimes happens when one member of the couple doesn't record checks and the other can't deal with knowing where the money is going. Whatever system you and your partner devise for yourselves is fine ... if it works for you and if you are consistent.

Organizing Your Money

Most couples spend the early months of their marriage learning how to organize their money as a couple. Prior to marriage, both the bride and groom are usually responsible for their own bills. It's generally up to each of them to determine what they can afford based on their individual salaries and debts. If the bride decides to buy a new car, she might consult her boyfriend, her dad, or several friends, but ultimately the decision to purchase or not is hers.

Sue's Suggestions

If you're living together, use this time to experiment with different ways of handling your expenses as a couple. It's good practice for your life together, just as budgeting your wedding is good practice for budgeting your expenses after marriage.

Even when a couple decides to live together before marriage, generally they maintain separate checking accounts. If they share certain bills, such as the rent, each of them contributes his or her portion from his or her individual checking account.

Once the couple is engaged, they begin considering alternate methods of handling the expenses of their life together. Some couples decide to open a joint checking account into which they deposit both their salaries, with one person paying all the bills each month. Other couples decide to maintain their individual checking accounts, into which they deposit their salaries, and then open a third checking account into which each deposits a portion of their money to cover joint bills such as rent and utilities.

Keeping Tabs on Your Spending

If you and your groom are fortunate enough to have a savings account into which both of you have been making regular deposits, you know exactly how much you have to spend and may already have the money necessary to pay for your wedding. Having the money available makes it easier to decide how much you want this wedding to cost. For some reason, when people do not yet have the money, their tendency is to want to spend more than they can save in the allotted time. But when people have worked hard to amass these funds, they tend to want to hold on to it!

If you don't have a savings account now, you certainly can start one to accumulate the money you'll need—something like a Christmas club savings account in which you put away the same amount each week or month for "x" number of months so you'll have a total of "y" by Christmas. Be realistic, however; you won't be able to save 90 percent of your paychecks from this point on if you need that money to pay for rent, utilities, and food.

Tantalizing Trivia

There are many cultures in which money plays a part in weddings. Guests at traditional Chinese weddings give the bride and groom "lucky money" in red envelopes. The money dance is a tradition among many ethnic groups. In the Puerto Rican community, the male guests pin money on the bride's gown when they dance with her. This is also a tradition at Filipino weddings, but there the bride's guests compete with the groom's guests to see who can decorate the couple with the most money. And even in the United States, there's the "dollar dance," where male guests each pay in dollars to dance with the bride.

Places to Find Money

There are some very real things you can do to take control of your spending and save the money you'll need to pay for your wedding. Keep a record of everything you spend money on for one month. This will show you clearly where your money is going, and make it possible for you to decide which things you could eliminate to save some money. For instance, if you stop for coffee on your way to work and spend $1.50 each day, you're spending $7.50 a week. If you decide to take a cup of coffee with you from home each day, you'll save $360 in one year. If both you and your fiancé buy lunch daily and each spends an average of $4.95 a day, together you're spending a total of $49.50 per week. If you decided to brown bag it instead, your homemade lunch would cost an average of $1.50 per person or $15.00 per week. This represents a savings of $34.50 per week, and in a year you would save $1,794.00!

If you enjoy going to the movies, a simple schedule shift can really make a difference in your pocketbook. Instead of going to the evening show and spending an average of $8.00 per person, go to the matinee. (You'll spend an average of $3.50 per person.) If you typically go to one movie a weekend, you'll save $9.00 per week, which translates into $468 a year. With just these three minor lifestyle changes, you will save $2,622.00 in one year!

Sue's Suggestions

Keeping track of what you're spending money on each day is the best way to get your spending in check. You can't make major changes until you know exactly where the money's going.

Open a Special Checking Account

Once you're engaged, simplify your bookkeeping by opening a "wedding-only" checking account. If you plan to close this account immediately after the wedding, you can save additional money by ordering the minimum amount of printed checks. If there are other people who want to make contributions to the wedding, their contributions can be put directly into this checking account as well. This will keep you on top of all your payments and keep you on track. It will also help you avoid waiting for money from anyone to pay any bills. It's not important to actually use Uncle John's dollars to pay the band even if he has offered to provide the band for your reception.

Another advantage of a wedding-only checking account is that you can run your regular life out of your regular checking account and not put yourself in danger of spending your rent! If you must maintain a minimum balance in order to avoid paying service charges, that shouldn't be a problem, even though you will have to pay attention to your balance. You can almost consider that this money is earning a rate of interest equal to the service charges you're not paying on your checking account. If your savings account has been invested in a money market or other interest-bearing account, you'll want to leave most of the money there to continue to collect interest and transfer it to your checking account only as needed.

Wedding Blues

When you open a wedding-only account, make sure to look for one without monthly service charges. You want all your money to go to your wedding, not to paying service charges on your account!

Another very good plan is to get yourself a special credit card for all your wedding expenses. There are credit cards with very low interest rates. Some introductory rates are good for only a short time, but if your wedding is soon and you have the money in the bank, this should not be a problem. Credit cards can work for you. They can protect your purchases and delay your payment for the billing cycle, usually 30 days. If you always pay your credit cards in full, then the interest rate should not be a major concern. Select the card for your wedding expenses based on the perks it offers. You may be able to get mileage on your favorite airlines, discounted hotel rooms, or discounted car rentals—defraying some of your honeymoon expenses just by using your card.

Read Every Contract ... Even the Small Print

Very few people in the wedding industry will try to take advantage of you as you plan your wedding. But this doesn't mean you can avoid good business practices such as reading every *contract*. Most of the professionals you'll be working with are small businesses, and they often create their own contracts without the benefit of an attorney. For this reason, the contracts may vary slightly from client to client. The vendor will amend his or her contract each time he or she faces a new situation. The issue is not the legality of the contract or whether or not it will stand up in court. (You don't want to go to court, you want to plan a wedding!) Rather, the issue is what the contract contains. It's important to understand that once you have signed the contract you are bound by its terms and conditions, so you both should understand and agree to them before you sign the contract.

Whether the particular document is technically a contract or just a collection of terms and conditions, once it's signed, it becomes the description of the job this vendor is planning to do for your wedding. You want to be sure that the description in this document is what you want to happen. If it's not what you want, then *before you sign the document* you should either make the necessary changes or find a vendor who agrees to do what you want and need. If you sign the contract without reading it, you're responsible for its terms, whether they meet your needs or not.

Language of Love

A **contract** is the written agreement between parties that spells out all terms and conditions and serves as proof of the obligation.

Recently I read a contract from a band that said *"… if a band member is sick enough to see a doctor, the band does not have to play the event."* Like most people, I read this sentence the way I expected it to be. It wasn't until I read it out loud that I truly understood what it said. But once I did understand it, there was no way I could allow my client to sign this contract. Instead, I crossed out that sentence and substituted *"… the band member may be replaced by someone of equal or greater talent."* When the bandleader got the corrected, unsigned contract, he immediately called and was as embarrassed as he was apologetic. The wording of his contract was a total oversight, and he was mortified to think how many of his clients had contracts with the incorrect sentence. The original

Wedding Blues

Be sure to read and clearly understand all contracts before you sign them. If you don't understand exactly what something means, get clarification before signing the contract.

sentence the bandleader had planned was *"… if a band member is sick enough to see a doctor, the band **member** does not have to play the event."* It was his intention to protect himself from a client being upset because a specific musician was not playing at his or her particular event; but by omitting just one word, the bandleader had completely changed the meaning of the sentence! After the bandleader initialed the change, my bride was happy to sign the contract and pay the deposit.

While this kind of error can easily happen and the band would probably never think of not showing up at the wedding, we have no way of knowing when this oversight could turn into a loophole to get the band out of a contract they really didn't want to fulfill. So, while we fully understand that this was an unintentional oversight, if we don't call it to the attention of the vendor in question, we may later regret it.

It's reasonable for the wedding vendor to request a *retainer* when you sign the contract and are entered on their calendar. For most vendors this retainer is not refundable. Therefore, if you have any doubts, wait to sign the contract. Make sure the contract is complete when you sign it. A complete contract will tell you the total price of the service that you're hiring, how many payments there will be, and when each payment is due. If any of this information is missing from the contract, don't sign it.

Language of Love

A **retainer** is a deposit, usually nonrefundable, that secures a vendor's services for a specific date and time.

If your vendor accepts credit cards, consider charging instead of paying cash. Not only does this protect you, it allows you to defer the payment until the bill comes in and to receive whatever perks your credit card offers. Putting the payment on a credit card won't, however, change the terms of the contract that you've signed. For example, if the contract states that *"… the wedding gown is made to order and cannot be canceled or returned,"* you can expect that to be the case. Where the credit card will help you in this instance is if the bridal shop goes out of business and does not deliver your gown. In that situation, your credit card company will refund what you've paid so at least you'll be able to order one from another shop or have it made locally (if it's too late to order).

Reading your vendor contracts takes a certain amount of skill. Most brides and grooms tend to read between the lines and assume that they're seeing things the vendor may have mentioned casually, but aren't actually in the contract. Then the couple is disappointed when something they expected to have at their wedding is not there or becomes an additional charge.

A Sample Contract, Step by Step

The following is a contract offered by a hotel to a bride and groom planning an upscale, formal wedding reception.

The following contract is shown in italics; my comments and explanations are not italic.

Banquet Terms and Conditions

All reservations and agreements are made upon, and subject to, the rules and regulations of the hotel and the following conditions:

   1. Your private function has been booked on a first-option, tentative basis:

      Name of organization: *Wedding of Suzy and Jonathan*

      Contact person: *Suzy Steig*

Telephone number:	*212–555–8024*
Address:	*890 Clarence Avenue*
	Newtown, New York 01987
Date:	*Sunday, August 20, 2000*
Setup:	*3:00 P.M.–7:00 P.M.*
Reception:	*6:00 P.M.–7:00 P.M.*
	250–300 people, cabaret tables
Dinner/dance:	*7:00 P.M.–11:00 P.M.*
	250–300 people, banquet rounds
Minimum guarantee:	*Number of guests <u>275</u>*
Decision date:	*<u>March 20, 2000</u>*
Food & beverage revenue:	*<u>$15,000.00</u> plus applicable tax and service charge*

Section 1 of this contract includes the basic information: who, what, and when. It also includes the minimum amount of money this bride and groom will be spending on this event. In this particular contract, to further protect herself, the bride changed the minimum guarantee to 200 before signing this contract. As with every part of the contract, if there are any mistakes here, it's very important that you correct them as soon as you note them. This is a contract and is legally binding, so you'll not want to sign it with any errors that you can prevent.

2. *Payment method: A nonrefundable deposit of $2,000.00 is required to hold the space as definite. Please return the deposit with the signed contract no later than the decision date listed above. All deposits are nonrefundable and will be applied towards any liquidated damages due to the hotel pursuant to Section 3 of this agreement.*

3. *Function room agreements: Function rooms are assigned by the Hotel according to the guaranteed minimum number of people anticipated. Room rental fees are applicable if the group drops below the estimated attendance at time of booking. The Hotel reserves the right to change groups to a room suitable at the Hotel's discretion for the attendance, with notification, if attendance drops or increases.*

Banquet prices will be confirmed three months prior to your function. Definite menu selections must be made at least 30 days prior to the function date. There's an additional service fee of $60.00 charged for private functions with 20 guests or less.

Wedding Blues

Read the cancellation policy carefully. While no one ever *plans* not to go through with the wedding, it does sometimes happen, and it will add more insult to injury if you are required to pay for an event even if you don't host it!

Note that section 3 does not name the room that the reception will be held in and it clearly gives the hotel the ability to change the room in which the function is held. Brides expect that their event will be in the ballroom, and usually it is. But if the number of guests who actually attend are fewer than the bride expected, the hotel can change the location. The hotel is actually protecting the bride and groom as well as themselves with this clause. You would not want your 100 guests to be seated in a room that normally handles 500 people. Your guests would feel lost and the room would have a cold, cavernous feeling. This wouldn't speak well for the hotel or for the ambiance of your event.

4. *Cancellation: Should it be necessary for you to cancel this function after this letter has been signed, the Hotel must be notified in writing and will be entitled to liquidated damages (agreed not to constitute a penalty) based on the following scale:*

<u>More than 90 days to six months prior to the scheduled date</u>: An amount equal to one-half of the estimated food, beverage, and meeting room, or $7,500.00 revenue based on the minimum estimate in section 2 herein above.

<u>90 days to arrival date</u>: An amount equal to 75 percent of the estimated food, beverage, and meeting room, or $11,250.00 revenue based on the minimum estimate in section 2 herein above.

Should you cancel this function, the Hotel shall use its best efforts to resell the function and meeting room space. In the event that the hotel resells some or all of the space, liquidated damages due the Hotel will be reduced proportionately.

Payment for liquidated damages due as a result of cancellation of this agreement shall be made at the time of cancellation. In the event that the Hotel recovers some of its revenue by reselling the space, reimbursement shall be made to you after the date of the scheduled event.

Once you sign this agreement, you're committed to this hotel for this event, and you must pay for the reservation of this room if your event does not take place. This contract states that the hotel will reduce the damages in the event your wedding does not take place but it's able to rebook the space; but note, it does not state how much the penalty will be reduced.

5. *In arranging for private functions, the final attendance must be received by the Catering Office no later than 11:00 A.M. three working days prior to the commencement of the function. This number will be considered a guarantee, not subject to reduction, and charges will be made accordingly. If we do not receive a final guaranteed attendance figure for your food and beverage function by the 72-hour deadline, your organization will be charged for the expected number of persons as noted on your banquet prospectus.*

The Hotel cannot be responsible for service to more than 3 percent over the guarantee for groups of up to 500 persons. For groups over 500 persons, a maximum of 25 persons will apply.

This is a very important portion of your contract. The bride and groom should carefully note the date and time that the final guarantee is due to the Catering Office, since this will have a definite impact on your final bill. But it's not necessary for the bride and groom to give the Catering Office the total number of guests that are expected at this moment. Most weddings have last-minute cancellations as late as 24 hours before the event. Since we know from this paragraph that the hotel will prepare for 3 percent above the guarantee, it's wise for the bride and groom to reduce their total guest count at this moment by 2.75 percent. We don't want to take a chance of the hotel not having enough food, and we don't want to pay for guests who may end up not attending.

Once the guarantee has been given to the hotel, it can be increased easily—it's decreasing the number that wastes money! If you have positive responses from 263 guests, you could tell the Catering Office you're expecting 255 people. (That's 8 fewer people—2.75 percent of 263 is actually 7.23 people, but I've never seen .23 of a person!) As the time moves on, you'll probably add to your guarantee, so eventually the Hotel will have the correct number. You're not trying to avoid paying for anyone, all you're trying to do is avoid paying for guests who cancel at the last minute.

There really isn't an industry standard here. That's why it's important to read the contract and find out how much above your guarantee the caterer will prepare for. This is also not related to attendance—it's related to waste. The caterer is telling you that if 3 percent of the food isn't pretty, he will have enough to serve only the "prettiest" (not over-cooked, under-cooked, too shrunken, etc.). It does tell you, though, that he will have additional food if needed.

Sue's Suggestions

The contract tells you how much above your final guarantee they will prepare food for, usually 3, 5, or 10 percent. While you should never reduce your final guarantee by this exact amount, you can guarantee a small percentage less than this amount on your initial count.

> *A 20% service charge and a 7.00% sales tax will be applied on all food and beverage functions. Additionally, all liquor will be subject to the 3.00% Georgia State liquor tax. No food and beverage of any kind will be permitted to be brought into the hotel by the customer or any of the customer's guests or invites.*

If your food charge is $25 per person with a 20 percent service charge ($5) and 7 percent tax ($2.10) you are actually paying $32.10 per person. If you are having 200 guests, your bill will be $6,420 inclusive, not $5,000. If your guests each have two glasses of wine at $4.25 per glass and three mixed drinks at $4.50 per drink, the beverages will cost you $8.50 (+7 percent = $.60) and $13.50 (+7 percent = $.95 + 3 percent = $.41) for a total of $23.96. Tax and tip make a difference, so be sure to do the math and determine what your actual charges will be.

This clause can impact the bride and groom if they plan to stock the hospitality suite themselves. (See Chapter 11, "Your Honored Guests.") Most hotels won't mind your supplying snacks and home-baked sweets for your guests or bringing in coffee pots or cold drinks, but please be respectful enough not to back a catering truck up to the entrance of the hotel and unload catering trays. If you want this type of food, please arrange to purchase it from the hotel.

6. *Performance of this agreement is contingent upon the ability of the Hotel to complete same and is subject to labor, disputes, strikes or picketing, accidents, government (federal, state or local) requisitions, restrictions upon travel, transportation, food, beverage or supplies, and other causes, whereto enumerated herein or not, which are beyond the control of the Hotel. In no event shall the Hotel be held liable for the loss of profit or other similar or dissimilar collateral or consequential damages, whether based on breach of contract, warranty or otherwise. In no event shall the Hotel's liability be in excess of the total amount of the food and beverage contracted.*

This clause protects the hotel against anything that would make it impossible for it to host your event and limits its liability to that amount of food and beverages for which you've contracted. Hotels might not be able to host your event if their employees go on strike or if there's an ice storm or tornado, for example.

Billing procedures: The master account will be paid according to the following schedule:

$2,000.00 nonrefundable deposit due with return of the signed contract.

Balance of payment is due in full three (3) business days prior to the event, payable by Cashier's Check, Certified Check, or Cash.

This clause outlines how you'll pay your bill. You may want to have this final balance charged to your credit card, especially one that offers frequent-flyer awards or other bonuses.

Wedding Blues

If the hotel will allow you to put the cost of the entire reception on your credit card, be sure to contact the credit card company to let it know your intention. The company can extend your limit to cover this. You certainly wouldn't want this charge to be refused because it's beyond your limit!

In the event that the customer selects items which the Hotel must special order for the customer's event, the customer expressly grants the right to the Hotel to increase the prices herein quoted or to make reasonable substitutions for the event. The Hotel, whenever possible, shall provide the customer with prior written notice of such increases and the right to decide between the increased price or to accept reasonable substitutions.

Janie wants to use chivari (usually gold bamboo-looking) chairs for her wedding dinner instead of the hotel's ballroom chairs. The catering manager hasn't rented them in a while, but she remembers them at $8 per chair, so this is what she quotes Janie. When she discovers that they now cost $9.50 per chair, she contacts Janie and tells her. Janie may decide to pay the additional $1.50 per chair or to use the hotel chair covers at $7.50 per chair instead. This particular point protects the hotel if their staff doesn't do their homework before making a quote, as well as if prices change after the quote has been given.

Additional Function Room Requirements: The Hotel requires that a copy of your proposed setup specifications be submitted to us. This is to ensure all information required is complete and accurate.

If you are planning to hold your ceremony at the hotel as well as your reception, you will be expected to specify your needs for that room. These might be:

➤ An 8-by-12-foot stage should be centered on south wall.

➤ A 7-foot-wide aisle should lead to the stage from the entrance.

➤ Two hundred chairs should be set up theater style in the room, 100 on each side.

➤ Sides of the aisle should begin 6 feet from the stage.

➤ Each row should contain an even number of chairs.

➤ Chairs should be set far enough from the east and west walls to allow a side aisle.

7. The facility rental charge does NOT include:

➤ *Security Guard Services*

➤ *Drayage and placement of display equipment*

➤ *Decorations and related expenses*

➤ *Labor (i.e., carpentry, electricians)*

➤ *Lighting and electrical power to the booths*

➤ *Water supply*

➤ *Additional staging and/or dance floor*

➤ *Receiving, delivery, and storage of materials*

➤ *Hanging of banners and signs*

➤ *Excessive cleanup requirements by hotel staff*

Due to limited storage space, we request your notification in advance if you intend to have materials shipped to the Hotel prior to your arrival. It is imperative that you observe the following instructions to ensure proper handling of your meeting materials. Each item should be clearly marked with the following:

➤ *Organization name and name of the event*

➤ *Date of the event*

➤ *The name of your hotel catering contact*

➤ *The name of your organization's on-site contact*

Boxes, packages, and display materials will be accepted up to three days prior to your scheduled event. Please advise your catering manager of any special arrangements or requirements concerning your materials. The Hotel is not responsible for perishable items. A labor charge will be assessed if the Hotel's assistance is required in unloading vehicles and/or moving items to storage areas. The Hotel should be advised of any items over 100 pounds that will be displayed in any function room. There will be a charge of $5.00 per box in excess of twelve boxes.

All the items mentioned in section 7 relate to conferences and/or meetings that might be booked into the hotel. They do not relate to your wedding reception.

Sue's Suggestions

If there are clauses in your contract that don't apply to your wedding at all, ask the catering manager to cross them out of the contract. There's no reason to leave in anything that could be interpreted another way at a later date.

Most hotels have one contract that is used for weddings, meetings, and conventions, so they include everything they need to protect themselves against. As the host of a private social event, like a wedding, you have to be diligent enough to remove those things that do not apply to your event.

8. *Customer agrees to be responsible for any damage done to the function room or any other part of the hotel by the customer, any guests, invites, employees, independent contractors, or other agents under customer's control.*

The Hotel will not assume or accept any responsibility for damage to or loss of any merchandise or articles left in the hotel prior to, during, or following the customer's function.

In the event that the customer's function requires a permit or license from any governing body, local, state, or federal, the customer is solely responsible for obtaining such license or permit at customer's expense.

All of these clauses relate primarily to convention functions, but if the person installing your decorations was to damage the room, this is the clause that would protect the hotel and make you responsible for the damages.

9. *The Hotel reserves the right to assign another room for the customer's function in the event the room originally designated for such function shall be unavailable or deemed inappropriate by the Hotel.*

This clause allows the hotel to move your event to another room if the one you have booked is no longer appropriate because your event is either larger or smaller than originally intended. This rarely happens, but if your event does change significantly in size, you would want the hotel to put you in the most appropriate space.

Unfortunately, the statement does also allow the hotel to move you for other reasons that may include another, larger, event needing the space. You should discuss this with the manager and find out what recourse you will have should this happen. Make sure to write these options into the contract to protect yourself down the road.

> *This agreement shall be considered acceptable once both parties have agreed solely with the terms of the original written agreement of the contract, be it unchanged.*

_____   _____

Host of event   *Date signed*

_____   _____

Catering manager   *Date signed*

Once you sign and return this contract, it goes into force as is. If you have any other changes to make, this is the time to make them and to make sure the catering manager signs off or initials your changes.

How to Protect Yourself and Your Budget

As I've mentioned, the best way to protect yourself is to read every contract carefully and make sure you understand exactly what it means with regard to your wedding. You have two options:

> ➤ *Read the contracts yourself and make sure you understand everything.* Most wedding professionals don't write their contracts in legalese and are not trying to confuse you, so if you read the contract, you should understand it. Where the problem comes in will be in understanding what it means with regard to your wedding and how it will play out. To get some clarification on this, talk to your recently married friends and ask them candidly what they would do differently.

> ➤ *Hire a professional bridal consultant to review your contracts.* A bridal consultant can point out places where you may need to review your requests with the particular vendor. You'll probably have to spend some time with the bridal consultant helping her understand the kind of wedding you're trying to achieve and this option will cost a little money, but it should save you surprises and much more money the weekend of your wedding.

It's true for a wedding, and for everything else you pay for in your life—you get what you pay for. If you simply ask a vendor for his or her charges and hire the least expensive in each category, you'll have the least expensive wedding you can arrange; but you may not get everything you could have gotten if you understood the differences in the vendors' services.

Quoting a low basic price and then adding an additional fee for each request is not the best way to run a wedding business. But some vendors do just that because they think it helps you pay for only those things you really want. This would work well if you knew at the beginning what you needed and what you wanted, but many couples don't know until they get deeply into the planning.

For instance, you may hire a photographer and choose his five-hour package without realizing that he will start taking pictures of the bride two hours before the ceremony and the groom one hour before the ceremony. By the time the ceremony is over, he will have already been with you for half his time. If you want him to stay until the reception is over, you will be into overtime charges. Or you may want to purchase a photograph from him for your engagement announcement for the local paper only to discover that he will charge you a separate "sitting charge" for that picture.

Get a list of references from each vendor and call every person listed. A vendor will probably give you the names of former clients who were pleased with the vendor's performance and service. Asking specific questions of these people will get them talking beyond their likes or dislikes of this vendor.

You may not have even thought about extra charges until you speak to his references, but when you ask questions, you will begin to hear about other people's experiences that should begin to prompt your own questions for this vendor.

Sue's Suggestions

Instead of simply asking the references if they liked the vendor, ask more probing questions, such as: "What would you do differently if you were planning your wedding today and hiring this vendor?"

You can also contact the Better Business Bureau (BBB) on every vendor, but you need to understand what the BBB can and can't do. The Better Business Bureau is really a membership organization. If customers have problems with a member, they can lodge a complaint against the company or individual with the Better Business Bureau, but the BBB has no enforcement capabilities. All they can do is tell you that a complaint had been filed against a merchant. Whatever the problem, it has to be solved between the customer and the merchant, and it's up to you to determine how important that problem is to you and to your wedding.

I make the same recommendation to all of my clients: Take a tablet and a piece of carbon paper to every meeting and take careful notes of everything that is discussed and each decision that is made. At the end of the meeting, ask the vendor to initial your notes, date them, give him or her the original, and you keep the carbon. I believe this saves confusion and problems in every situation. This habit will help you if you're sitting around wondering if you told the caterer you want white napkins and pink tablecloths; and it will protect you if the particular professional you've been dealing with gets transferred to another facility or leaves the company completely. When there's a personnel change at your reception site, you sometimes have to start over to reconstruct everything you've planned with the previous person. If you have these notes, just make a copy of them for the new person.

And Then There's Premarital Debt!

Radio psychologist Dr. Laura Schlesinger once told a young woman, who said she was 19 and engaged to be married, that she had no business considering marriage until she was at least 28 years old! "Until you have lived on your own, paid your own rent, and bought yourself a car, you have no business considering marriage," Dr. Laura said. I'm not sure that she's totally correct, but she does make a point. Before you consider hitching your wagon to another person's star, it's best to know who you are and what you want in your life. And it's important to know that about your partner-to-be, too.

If either the bride or the groom is in serious debt, this is the time to share that information with your partner. Together you can determine how you'll approach the situation and design your plan to eliminate this debt. Technically, debts remain in the name of the person who incurred them, but creditors have the right to go after joint assets of the marriage in case of default of the debtor.

Start by assessing yourself. Where are you on the road to your career goals? Have you completed or at least started the education necessary to get a job in your chosen field? Do you live on your own or are you still a rent-free boarder in your parents' home? Are you supporting yourself? Does it seem that you have too much month left at the end of your money? Are your credit cards maxed out?

Significant debt is defined as more than 25 percent of your income being owed to anyone other than a mortgage company, from credit cards to school loans. This is the total of your debt, it doesn't have to be owed all to one person or company in order to qualify. If you find yourself or your partner in this situation, it's wise to design a payment schedule immediately and begin to end this situation of debt. If you're unable to come up with a workable plan to eliminate this situation and pay off the debts in a timely manner on your own, consider speaking to a financial planner or credit counselor to get help in this area. As long as the debt exists, it will seriously restrict your ability to make decisions for the rest of your life.

Wedding Blues

Starting a marriage in debt puts a real strain on your relationship from the very beginning. One way to help yourself out of this situation is to lock credit cards in a safety deposit box at the bank and force yourself to plan ahead and pay cash for your purchases.

Once you have determined how much you can spend on your wedding and where the money is coming from, you will want to be very sure that you know where it is going and how it's getting there. No one wants to feel that they spent money they hadn't planned on spending just because they didn't understand what they were signing. The point cannot be made often enough to read your contracts carefully and be sure that everything in them applies to your event. If some of it doesn't apply to you, have it removed from the contract before you sign it!

The Least You Need to Know

➤ There are several different ways you can set up your household "books."

➤ Keeping a record of how you spend your money is a good way to determine where you can find extra money to save—for your wedding or even that special vacation.

➤ Read every contract and all the small print. No one wants to be surprised when the final bill comes.

➤ It's not a good idea to start your wedding while either of you are in significant debt. Solve this problem before you begin spending money on your wedding.

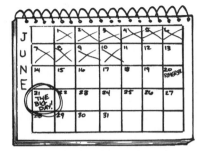

Chapter 14

Just the Facts, Ma'am

In This Chapter

➤ Wedding date and time considerations

➤ Where to hold the ceremony

➤ Determining your wedding style

➤ Start with your dreams

➤ What kind of reception would you like?

You and your Prince Charming are getting married. He's given you a ring and you've announced your plans to family and friends. You've determined how much you intend to spend on the celebration and where you're getting the money. Now it's time to decide exactly when you'll get married and what kind of wedding you'll host.

Most couples want a wedding celebration that is uniquely theirs. They want to plan an event that will both reflect their own lifestyle and make their family and friends feel comfortable and welcome. While it's not necessary to host the kind of wedding your friends have had, it's a good idea to consider what has been done in your community. Has it worked? Were the guests comfortable and happy or did they seem anxious to have it end? Why was that? What can you do to be sure that your guests enjoy your wedding?

Meet Me at the Church on Time

Time is money—you can plan to save. There's a line in the movie *When Harry Met Sally:* "When you decide you want to spend the rest of your life with someone, you want the rest of your life to start right now." This sentiment is quite true—you may not have thought much about marriage before, but suddenly, now that you're engaged, you want to get married! Taking your time to research your options as you plan the public celebration of your marriage can and will allow you to make careful choices that will save you money.

Setting the Right Date

Negotiating for the best prices on a wedding is like negotiating for other commodities; the rule of supply and demand applies here as well. Weddings happen all year 'round, but every region of the country has its popular season and off-season. If you plan your wedding during the off-season in your community, you'll have a much easier time negotiating for extras with many of your vendors.

Sue's Suggestions

De-stress your wedding planning by considering what's happening in your life. If you're still in school, you might want to plan your wedding for after graduation. Perhaps you're working on a big project at work that won't be finished for several months—do you really want to be planning your wedding and meeting this deadline at the same time?

In some southern cities, for instance, July is considered off-season, with fewer weddings per weekend in July than in either June or August. For this reason, you may be able to negotiate package prices for your reception with some of the event facilities. In many communities, January is considered off-season for weekend social events after the hustle and bustle of the Christmas season. Bands, DJs, caterers, and florists find time in their schedules and are often happy to accommodate your needs and work within your budget. However, if you live in a resort community, such as Florida or Hawaii where northerners go to escape the weather back home, you may find there is no significant savings during the winter and that the summer is actually the off-season. By understanding regional differences and being flexible in selecting your wedding date, you can save money in your wedding plans.

Even though June is no longer the busiest wedding month of the year, there are still enough girls with their hearts set on being June brides to make Saturdays in June difficult to book and even more difficult to negotiate. If you're determined to be married in June, consider another day of the week. Sunday is popular, especially with Jewish brides. If most or all of your guests live in the city where the wedding will take place, selecting a weekday for your ceremony and reception may be the easiest way to control your budget. A Friday evening wedding will allow you to negotiate the best prices with your vendors and will give you the weekend to start your honeymoon. Many wedding facilities are available and will welcome you. In addition, you'll find a complete selection of wedding vendors anxious to accommodate you and your budget needs.

Consider booking your wedding far in advance. Many vendors will allow you to sign a contract with today's rates while your wedding is a year away. (See Chapter 13, "Money, Money, Money!" for more on contracts.) In this way you'll get the benefit of a reduced rate. Not all vendors will be able to quote a price a year or more in advance and hold to it, but usually photographers, bands, disc jockeys, ceremony sites, and bridal consultants can accommodate you in this way. Vendors whose prices are affected by changes in the marketplace, such as florists and caterers, may not be able to confirm prices well in advance, but may be willing to put a cap on their price increases so you'll at least know that your charges will not exceed a specific amount.

Wedding Blues

Be sure your contract states what the fee will be and on what date charges are to be finalized so you'll not be surprised along the way.

If controlling costs and staying within your budget are priorities, you'll want to avoid the most popular weekends: Memorial Day and Labor Day. Brides often choose these weekends because they believe the extra day to be easiest for their out-of-town guests. If you're hosting a Sunday wedding, it's nice for your local guests to be able to enjoy the entire evening celebration without concern for getting to work the next day.

However, the general popularity of these holidays and the additional Monday holiday weekends (Columbus Day, Armistice Day, Martin Luther King Day, and Presidents' Day) makes them difficult to secure and affects the amount of negotiating on pricing you'll be able to do successfully. In addition, your guests will be in town longer, which may mean you'll want to host additional events to be with them, adding to your overall expenses. Thanksgiving, Christmas, Fourth of July, and New Year's Eve present another set of problems when it comes to budgeting. Not only do they book up quickly, but some vendors will add a surcharge to cover the overtime they'll need to pay their staff to work the holiday. You may benefit from using the holiday decorations the facility has in place, but your savings need to be measured against any overtime labor charges you might have to pay.

Sue's Suggestions

If you plan a Saturday wedding, most of your out-of-town guests will take off work Friday to travel to your wedding and return home on Sunday, missing one day of work. Planning a Sunday wedding could be easier on your pocketbook and not affect your guests at all. For a Sunday wedding, your out-of-town guests will travel on Saturday and return home Monday, missing one day of work—same difference!

Setting the Time

The time of day that you select for your wedding ceremony—and especially for the reception—also affects your budget. Staying away from the obvious meal times of noon or six o'clock will not only save you the expense of serving a meal, but will also save on alcohol and bartenders. Consider these options:

➤ If you get married in the middle of the morning you can serve a light brunch, and there's no need to serve hard liquor or you could offer limited mixed drinks and champagne.

➤ A tea dance reception is lovely following an early afternoon ceremony, especially in the spring and summer months. The guests will enjoy the finger sandwiches and desserts and you can easily serve champagne and fruit punch.

➤ If you would like a more formal reception, hold your ceremony in the late afternoon, serve hors d'oeuvres and mixed drinks, and your guests will be ready to go out for dinner on their own. You'll find the lighter menu slightly less expensive.

Wedding Blues

If you select a holiday weekend for your wedding, your out-of-town guests may have some difficulty getting to the wedding, and will not be able to use any of their frequent flyer points since holiday weekends are quite often blackout days.

Food and liquor are not the only place you'll save by having your wedding in the morning or early afternoon instead of the evening. Disc jockeys and bands sometimes discount their charges 20 percent or more at these off-times.

Choosing the Ceremony Site

Most couples are married in their home church or synagogue, but if you're not a member of a church or synagogue, or if that facility is not large enough to accommodate the number of guests you want to invite, you'll find yourself in search of a ceremony site.

There are any number of possibilities of locations to hold your ceremony. There may be a site that has special significance for you and the groom. For instance, if you met while attending college, the campus chapel might provide a perfect setting for your ceremony. Here is a list of other options:

➤ If you spent much of your childhood in a park and it remains a happy location for you, or if you love the idea of an outdoor ceremony, consider being married in one of the park pavilions.

➤ Some brides decide to be married in their homes or in the home of a close friend or relative.

➤ Many restaurants have private rooms that are perfect settings for wedding ceremonies.

➤ Hotel ballrooms can often be divided so that the ceremony can be in one third of the room and the reception can follow in the remaining two thirds. This way the guests will not have to change locations between the ceremony and the reception.

➤ Some communities have office buildings with beautiful lobbies that can be rented for your wedding ceremony and reception.

Before you decide on a location, check it out with a critical eye. Is there enough parking? Are there enough bathrooms? Is there any music available with this facility, and if not, is there enough power for you to bring in music and amplification on your own? If you plan to dress at the wedding site, where will you do this? Are there mirrors in the bride's room, is it near the bathroom, is it large enough for your bridesmaids, mothers, and grandmothers to dress there as well? Can you see well enough in the ladies room to apply make-up?

Wedding Blues

Bridal consultant Beverly Dembo of Dembo Productions asks each of her clients to create her guest list before securing her ceremony and reception site. "Too many couples neglect this step," she says. "They think they will have about 100 people and end up inviting 300, so the room is *much* too small. Or they plan on 200, but only 125 can attend and the room feels like a barn, and is expensive to decorate!"

What's Your Wedding Style?

Every couple wants their wedding *style* to reflect their taste and lifestyle while making their guests feel comfortable and staying within their budget. Most say they want their wedding to be elegant and their guests to have fun! While this is not difficult to accomplish, it will take some understanding and a great deal of careful planning.

The word *elegant* is defined as "richness and grace, confined by the restraints of propriety and good taste." Elegant does not mean formal. Your wedding can be elegant and still be quite informal, so long as it reflects your taste and you maintain the same level of formality throughout your planning. For instance, if you decide to host an informal wedding and select street-length dresses for your bridesmaids and sport coats and khaki slacks for your groomsmen, don't go out and purchase a formal wedding gown with a cathedral-length train for yourself! Stay consistent! You can still wear a long wedding gown, but keep it simple.

Language of Love

When used in relation weddings, the word **style** generally refers to the formality of the wedding. Do you want a formal, semiformal, or informal wedding?

In order to determine your style, think about the weddings that you've attended. Ask yourself these questions:

➤ Were you comfortable?

➤ Did you enjoy being there, or were you waiting for it to get late enough for you to quietly slip away? What made you feel that way?

➤ What did you particularly like about the weddings you hated to see end?

By identifying your own feelings about the weddings you've attended, you can approach your planning from your guests' perspective. Considering their needs will guarantee the best wedding.

If you've not attended a wedding recently, or don't remember it well enough to identify what made it terrific or terrible, ask your friends and family to share their experiences with you. You're not asking for their opinions on what you should do, but rather what they've seen or experienced, and what they thought about it. This kind of research will be very helpful and you'll avoid making mistakes you won't even think about until after the wedding. You can read descriptions of weddings in magazines and books and even rent movies with wedding scenes in them to complete your research. In a very short time you'll identify things that you really like and that fit your style, and, perhaps more important, things you don't like!

Start with Your Dreams—What Do You Want?

If you've always wanted to be married in your church or synagogue, this is where you should begin. Call the secretary and determine if the date and time you've selected are available and if there is a printed list of policies for you to review. If neither you nor your family are members of the church or synagogue, make this fact known to the secretary and ask if nonmembers are governed by the same policies. Many churches and synagogues charge a rental fee to use the sanctuary. Often this fee is significantly higher for nonmembers. Some churches also want to be sure that all their own members have first opportunity to reserve the church and won't confirm the date for a nonmember wedding earlier than 90 days before the event.

Sue's Suggestions

Some couples decide to join the congregation while they're planning their wedding. They determine that the benefits of membership and the reduced fee offered to members add up to a savings. Besides, the more they work with the staff and meet with the minister or rabbi, the more comfortable they become, making this a good place to eventually worship.

During your conversation with the secretary, determine if the officiant is available to perform your ceremony and if there's a fee for his or her services. Usually, the services of the officiant for "life-cycle events" is included in the benefits of membership in the congregation. When this is the case, it's customary to make a donation to the officiant's discretionary fund. When neither the bride and groom or either of their families are members of the congregation, most officiants charge a fee for their services. You'll want to know what the fee is and how it is to be paid. (Payment, whether a fee or a contribution to the discretionary fund, is considered to be the responsibility of the groom or his family.)

Some brides choose to be married at home and have their reception there as well. While this can be a lovely alternative, you'll have to be even more diligent if you want to keep costs under control. Every bride I've ever worked with who planned a home wedding later decided that the house needed some sprucing up to be ready for the event. Depending on the particular sprucing that's chosen, this can become costly, so plan ahead if the cost is coming out of the wedding budget as well.

Tantalizing Trivia

One couple decided to hold their wedding in the garden of the house they just purchased. The home and garden were beautiful—perfect in every way—but as they looked at everything with a critical eye, they decided the tree in the yard was too big and should be cut down. The deck needed painting, but after that was done, the house looked awful, so they painted that, too! In the end, both the wedding and the house were wonderful—but the couple had spent much more money than they had planned.

Before deciding to hold your wedding in your home—or someone else's for that matter—you'll want to consider the bathroom situation. Are there enough for the number of guests you expect to attend? If not, will you need to rent portable toilets? Give some thought to the traffic pattern in the house. Does the floor plan flow easily from room to room or can guests get trapped in a room and create a traffic jam? You may also decide to add a tent so that the outdoors becomes available to you. If you're planning your reception in a residential neighborhood, and you plan to have music, be sure to check with your county and make yourself aware of ordinances concerning noise and traffic. One way to deal with county ordinances is to invite your neighbors to your reception. This will eliminate their calling the authorities to report a noisy party, but it will add to your total reception costs.

Wedding Blues

If you want to exchange your wedding vows in a hot-air balloon or some other offbeat place, do your homework beforehand. Check with your county and state to be sure there are no specific regulations about where marriages may take place. The Yellow Pages are a good place to start.

How Do You Imagine Your Reception?

Once the ceremony site is selected and the date secured, you're ready to begin thinking about your reception site. I devote all of Part 4, "Reception Details," to reception details, but here I'll guide you through an understanding of wedding styles. You'll want to start by considering the ceremony location as a possible reception site. If you're able to do this, you'll save money because you won't have to pay a second facility-site fee and because you'll save the cost of the limousine ride between locations. If the ceremony site can handle the kind of reception you're planning and the kind of food you'd like to serve, you may be in luck! Do you want to serve punch and cake in the church social hall, a cocktail buffet (some brides call this heavy hors d'oeuvres), a buffet dinner, or a seated dinner?

Sue's Suggestions

If you didn't receive a cake knife or toasting goblets as shower gifts, don't go buy them. Your reception site can tie a ribbon around two stemmed goblets and around one knife handle and you can use theirs.

Language of Love

At a **buffet dinner,** your guests select their own food from one or more tables or stations of prepared food. At a **seated dinner,** waiters present plated meals to the guests at their assigned seats.

Many brides think that buffets are less expensive than a seated dinner. This has not been my experience. The total cost is approximately the same, but the money is divided differently. At a *buffet dinner*, the chef will not know how much food each guest will choose, so the quantity of food prepared will provide the last guest who approaches the buffet table the same selections as the first guest. For this reason, most of your money will be spent on food. At the end of the evening, most likely there will be quite a quantity of food left over. You should discuss this with the caterer in advance so you can request that leftover prepared food be donated to the hungry in your community, in your name. Not only will this provide you with a tax deduction, but also the knowledge that your celebration has been a benefit to the less fortunate members of your community.

At a *seated dinner*, the caterer will use his or her knowledge of portion control to calculate how much food to prepare for each guest, and the servings will be plated and delivered to your guests by waiters. In this scenario, some of your money will go to cover the cost of the food, but another portion will go to cover the cost of staffing the meal. The caterer will prepare slightly more food than is required for the number of people who will attend. This practice allows the caterer to serve the most attractive portions to your guests and not the portions that may appear to be overcooked or underdone simply because of their location in the roasting pan.

Your contract will indicate the percentage of food above the number you guarantee that will be prepared for your event. It's important to understand that you will not be charged for this additional percentage of food unless it is actually served. You'll be charged for the number of guests you guarantee, or the number you actually serve, whichever is greater. Once you've been through this experience, you'll forevermore be very diligent about responding to future wedding invitations you receive.

How the food is served and whether or not your guests are assigned seats at specific tables or allowed to select their own tables or even chose to stand, has nothing to do with the formality of the wedding. Read on to discover exactly what makes a wedding formal, semiformal, or informal.

The Formal Reception

For those couples who want to plan a *formal* reception, here is a list of characteristics shared by all formal weddings:

Language of Love

A **formal** reception closely follows the dictates of custom and etiquette and is generally elaborate with great attention to detail.

➤ The ceremony takes place in a church or synagogue, hotel, club, large home, or garden.

➤ The reception takes place in a hotel, club, large home, or garden.

➤ The bridal party includes a maid or matron of honor, at least four bridesmaids, a best man, plus four groomsmen.

➤ The bride wears a long gown with a royal, cathedral, or chapel train. Her veil might be cathedral, waist- or fingertip length.

➤ Bridesmaids wear long, tea-length or ballerina-length dresses, and may or may not wear headpieces.

➤ All ladies wear hosiery.

➤ If the ceremony takes place at noon, the groom and groomsmen wear cutaway coats with striped trousers and ascots.

➤ If the ceremony takes place in the evening, the groom and groomsmen wear black, full-dress tuxedos with white wing collar shirts, white piqué vests, and bow ties.

➤ Mothers select floor-length, tea-length, or ankle-length gowns in colors that complement the theme of the wedding.

➤ Invitations are white or ivory with charcoal or black ink, either with or without a raised panel border.

➤ Table linens hang to the floor, usually with a second topper cloth or overlay on top. Chairs are often covered with chair covers.

➤ Food may be served buffet or sit-down style, but all guests have assigned seats.

If the bride's taste runs to a more contemporary style, she'll select a dressy invitation that will convey this formality. A formal wedding reception would have a formal look. This would be most obvious in the attire of the male guests, most all of whom would be dressed formally. The ladies would also be dressed in formal attire; however, since fashion dictates formality, and fashion changes sometimes, you might see ladies dressed in beaded cocktail gowns at both formal and semiformal weddings. The tables would be covered with cloths that reach the floor. Sometimes there would be an overlay on the table to add either color or texture to the look. There would be floral centerpieces on the tables and, in an evening reception, perhaps candles would be included in the centerpieces. The reception could be either a served sit-down dinner, a buffet sit-down dinner, or a heavy hors d'oeuvres cocktail reception; but in any case, enough food would be offered that guests would not leave hungry. Most formal receptions include an open bar, and if it's a seated dinner, there's usually wine served to the guests with dinner. At a seated dinner, chair covers may have been selected.

Tantalizing Trivia

While the term "Black tie" on a social invitation means that a tuxedo is optional, the term "White tie" on an invitation is a commandment. Guests arriving in other than white tie and tails will not be admitted to the event. Perhaps because of the "commandment" issue of the term, "White tie" is seldom (perhaps never) used on a wedding invitation. Instead, it might be seen on an invitation to a state dinner or royal event where protocol professionals are available so no guest could be embarrassed by arriving in inappropriate attire.

The Semiformal Reception

If you really don't want a formal wedding, but want it to be more formal than informal, the *semiformal* reception may be perfect for you. Here are the characteristics shared by semiformal weddings:

➤ The ceremony takes place in a church, chapel, synagogue, hotel, club, large home, or garden. The reception takes place in a similar setting.

➤ There are 75 to 200 guests.

➤ The bridal party includes a maid or matron of honor, two to six bridesmaids, a best man, and two to six groomsmen.

➤ The bride wears a long gown with a chapel-length train or no train at all. She wears a short or pouf veil.

➤ Bridesmaids wear floor-length, tea-length, or ballerina-length dresses, or short dresses if fashion suggests.

➤ All women wear hosiery.

➤ If the ceremony is held during the day, the groom and groomsmen wear gray strollers with striped trousers, pearl-colored vests, and four-in-hand ties. At an outdoor wedding, they may wear homburgs and gloves.

Language of Love

A **semiformal** reception combines some elements of the formal reception in a slightly more relaxed way.

➤ At an evening wedding, the groom and groomsmen wear black tuxedos. In the summer they may wear white dinner jackets.

➤ Mothers wear floor-length or tea-length dresses or ensembles.

➤ Invitations are either white or ivory and printed in black or colored ink with a matching envelope liner.

➤ Table linen reaches the floor without the formal overlay cloth. Chairs are usually not covered.

➤ Centerpieces are low floral arrangements or clusters of candles with flowers.

➤ If food is served buffet style, there is seating for only about half to two thirds of the guests.

➤ Music is provided by either a live band or disc jockey, and guests may or may not choose to dance.

The Informal Reception

If you don't like the look or feel of the formal or semiformal wedding, and you want to relax and have fun, then the *informal* reception might be for you! Here are the characteristics shared by informal weddings:

Language of Love

An **informal** reception is a casual, relaxed, creative event at which the couple's lifestyle and tastes are more important than the dictates of an etiquette book.

➤ The ceremony takes place in a church, church parlor, chapel, or synagogue. It may also be held in the office of the justice of the peace or in a hotel, club, home, restaurant, or garden. The reception is held in a similar setting.

➤ There are fewer than 75 guests.

➤ The bridal party includes a maid or matron of honor, one or two bridesmaids, a best man, and one or two groomsmen.

➤ The bride may wear a white or pastel afternoon dress or suit. If the ceremony is held in the evening, she may wear a long, simple gown. She may wear a hat, veil, or just flowers in her hair.

➤ The bridesmaids wear dresses in a simple style that complements the bride's attire.

➤ Mothers and all women in the bridal party wear hosiery.

➤ The groom and groomsmen may wear dark suits for an evening wedding, or pastel shirts with linen jackets and dark trousers for an afternoon wedding. They may even choose khaki slacks, pastel shirts, floral ties, and no jackets for a daytime, outdoor, summer wedding.

➤ Mothers select something in keeping with the bridesmaids' attire, and fathers dress in clothes similar to the groomsmen.

➤ Invitations may be printed or hand-written with colored ink on colored or patterned paper.

➤ Table coverings may be paper, plastic, checkered, or chintz.

➤ Food may be served on paper plates, with plastic flatware and disposable glassware, or china with flatware and glasses.

➤ Food is more casual than gourmet, and beer, wine, and soft drinks replace hard liquor at an open bar.

Sue's Suggestions

Let guests know you're planning a formal wedding by including the phrase "Black tie" on the corner of your reception card.

As you can see, there really isn't much difference between the formal, semiformal, and informal weddings. It's clear, however, that the fashion gurus don't like bare legs on women any time of the year or in any degree of informality! The major difference has to do with the number of total guests invited and, as I have said, this is the determining factor in the cost of your wedding. The most effective way to cut your costs is to cut the number of people invited to your wedding. You can still wear a beautiful, if slightly less elaborate, gown, and your bridesmaids can probably wear the same dresses you've fallen in love with. (That may be a contradiction in terms—does anyone fall in love with bridesmaids' dresses?) The groom and groomsmen may still wear tuxedos, but if you plan a semiformal wedding, and hold your guest list down, you'll save money—and not just on the gifts for your attendants!

I think it's important to state here that these criteria come from the etiquette gurus of days gone by. We currently live in a more relaxed society in which very formal weddings may have only two attendants and informal weddings may have more than 75 guests. This is your day—pick your own style!

The Bridal Party

On your wedding day you'll want to be surrounded by your best friends and so will your groom, even if that means that you'll have five attendants and he'll have eight. Having an equal number of attendants really isn't important. Trying to add attendants to make it even can really be costly. When you add to your bridal party, you're also adding to your guest list. If you'll be inviting 100 guests to your wedding and your bridal party includes 13 single people, by the time they each invite a guest, you have 26 more people on your guest list—so one fourth of the people at your wedding will be the bridal party and their guests. Remember that you'll need additional food, additional band members, and additional centerpieces to handle these extra guests, and all of this will cost you additional money. It's not necessary to invite a guest for each member of your bridal party.

One future bride and groom watched carefully as several of their close friends preceded them down the aisle. It seemed that there was so much stress involved in the planning that the whole process took on the feeling of a chore, instead of something happy and fun. When the groom finally proposed they decided that they would not subject themselves to this whole planning cycle. Instead, they invited their friends and family to an engagement party in the private room of a lovely restaurant. As the guests arrived, they were served cocktails and hors d'oeuvres in a separate area. Everyone was mingling and didn't seem to notice that neither of their hosts were anywhere to be seen.

Soon the future groom's brother invited everyone into the dining room to be seated. When the guests were all at their tables, a harp in the corner began to play and the future bride's and groom's parents entered the room, each carrying one of the chuppah (Jewish wedding canopy) poles. They walked to the center of the room's permanent dance floor and spaced themselves so the chuppah created a canopy. A rabbi entered the room, followed by the groom and his brother. The bride's sister entered followed by the bride. The bride was dressed in a lovely, informal wedding gown and carried a bible with a single white orchid attached to it. She joined the groom under the chuppah and the ceremony took place. It was nearly over before the guests realized that they were witnessing a surprise wedding—and the surprise was on them!

After the ceremony, dinner was served to all the guests. A disc jockey provided music from a corner of the room and everyone danced the night away. Especially the newlyweds! During the evening the bride's mother was overheard telling a friend that her daughter had called her yesterday and asked her to arrive at the restaurant a few moments early so a photographer could take a few family pictures. She thought nothing of the request, and didn't even know what had been planned until the groom asked her to help carry the chuppah down the aisle!

This couple's budget looked like this:

Clothing:

Bridal gown	$275.00*
Veil	38.90*
Groom's suit	-0-
Photography	1,000.00*
Video	1,000.00*

Flowers:

Bride's bouquet	20.00*
Bridesmaid's bouquet	17.50*
4 boutonnieres @ $7/ea.	28.00*
Centerpieces	200.00*
(10 tables @ $20/ea.)	
Delivery fee	75.00
Chuppah rental	180.00*

Music

Ceremony	200.00
DJ	350.00
Room rental	-0-
Linen	-0-
Rabbi fee (discretionary)	200.00
Printing	125.00*
Postage	16.50
Telephone response	-0-
Thank-you notes	30.00*
Postage	16.50
Open bar: 100 × $9	900.00*†
(2 drinks per person on average)	
Hors d'oeuvres: 300 × $3.25	975.00*†
(3 hors d'oeuvres per person on average)	
Dinner and dessert	2,800.00*†
($28.00 per person)	
Cake: 100 × $1.35 per person	135.00*†
20% gratuity on † items	962.00
7% tax on * items	608.05
Total wedding	**$10,152.45 for 100 guests ($101.52 per person)**

* Taxable item
† Item on which gratuity is paid

This couple would tell you that the amount saved on the aggravation factor of the planning was priceless. For other couples, the simplicity of the wedding would have left too much lacking.

There are many things you can do to control the costs of your wedding, beginning as soon as you become engaged. You will be most successful if you plan to save by making selections that tend to be less expensive (like selecting an off-season date) rather than trying to cut costs on the most expensive choices. If you are diligent, you will have a beautiful, stress-free wedding within your budget.

The Least You Need to Know

➤ A Saturday night summer wedding is one of the most expensive times to be married.

➤ Consider being married during an off-season or at an off-time in your community.

➤ To really save, select a day and time when your food choices can be lighter.

➤ Because formal weddings tend to be larger than semiformal or informal weddings, they tend to be more expensive.

Part 4
Reception Details

Your reception will be the most expensive part of your wedding, so you'll want to clearly understand all the components of the reception. First, you'll have to decide how much of the reception you want to plan by yourself and how much you want specific vendors to do for you. Then, if you decide that you want to select your own vendors, you'll get busy researching each component of the reception. This can be so much fun, tasting cakes, listening to bands, meeting disc jockeys and picking flowers—sometimes it feels like you're six years old, clutching a dollar and staring into the candy case trying to decide what you want!

In many ways that's what you're doing. You've already determined that you have the money, so all you have left to do is create your fantasy. So let's get started!

Chapter 15

Eat, Drink, and Be Married!

In This Chapter

➤ The one-stop shop reception versus doing it yourself

➤ How do you find a caterer?

➤ Is there a financial difference between hosting a dessert reception, seated dinner, or buffet?

➤ All about beverages—beer, wine, or an open bar?

The reception is the most expensive part of your wedding planning and will not only take the most money, but the most planning. The reception is really your opportunity to express your own personality as you create a celebration that truly reflects your lifestyle. Since you have never planned a wedding reception before, the task may seem overwhelming, but it's not. Like everything else, if you take it one step at a time, you'll find that it's both easy to accomplish and fun.

Start by thinking about how you like to do things. Are you a hands-on kind of person who likes to be involved in every detail, or would you be happier just to plan a broad outline of the event and let someone else fill in the specifics? Either way, there's a reception site that will fill your needs—some will do the work for you while others expect you to handle every detail. In this chapter I'll tell you about the one-stop-shop and the do-it-yourself receptions, and what you need to create the perfect reception for your wedding!

The One-Stop-Shop Reception

A one-stop-shop reception can be held in a hotel, club, restaurant, resort, or any facility that can provide everything you need for your wedding. It handles all the food, supplies the linens, and supplies the bartenders and all the beverages and setups. Usually it has tables and chairs that are available to you at no additional charge. You can decide what you want to serve and how you want the room to look. You may even have a selection of linen to choose from and some centerpieces available to you; but the facility does all the work.

Generally, these one-stop-shop facilities have a short list of vendors to perform whatever services they do not provide and you may be required to work with one of these vendors. The facility seldom quotes a room rental fee; instead, it usually prices the food person, which generally includes everything that is offered. When a couple decides on a *destination wedding*, they'll be best served if they select such a one-stop-shop reception site, since they won't be around to interview and select the various vendors that they'll need.

While one-stop shopping can be a plus for the working bride who has limited time to meet with individual vendors, it does have a few drawbacks:

Language of Love

When you have your wedding in a location away from your home city, it's called a **destination wedding**—a place you travel to simply to get married, sometimes accompanied by guests. Some couples select a honeymoon destination and get married there.

➤ Sometimes the staff at these facilities are so used to doing receptions a certain way that they're unwilling to accept your input, and your reception may look like it was created with a cookie cutter—just like everyone else's and without your personality. You'll need to be politely assertive to convey your wishes, and if you determine before signing the contract that this will be a problem, you may be best served by selecting another location.

➤ You may not be able to negotiate prices with a particular vendor because he or she is the only one the facility allows to provide this service. You can expect to pay something for the convenience of having everything taken care of for you, but you'll have to determine what this convenience is worth to you.

The Do-It-Yourself Reception

The do-it-yourself reception is exactly that—you do it yourself! For example, you might choose to hold your reception at a hotel, restaurant, or perhaps the clubhouse of your apartment complex. This room may come with two eight-foot tables and six chairs, but everything else you'll need, you'll have to provide on your own.

You may find that you'll pay less for the food in this situation, but you'll have to break down each charge to discover if you'll really be saving any money. There's nothing wrong with a do-it-yourself reception if you can arrange to have someone else do it with you! The problem seems to be that while you may save money, you'll definitely spend more time researching the items you need. Finding the right supplier for each of these items and making arrangements to have them delivered to the site can be a full-time job.

On the day of the wedding you'll have a lot of things to do, and sitting at the reception site waiting for the tables and chairs, then the linens, flowers, and food may be more than you can actually handle. Keep in mind that each rental company will want a signature and a check when they deliver their items, so someone must be there to receive the items. These same companies will need to pick up their belongings after the wedding, so you'll need to arrange for someone to pack everything up and wait until it's all collected—while you're on your honeymoon.

Here's one story of a do-it-yourself reception that didn't go so well. One bride was convinced that she could arrange a do-it-yourself reception and save money. She scheduled her ceremony for late in the afternoon so she could arrange to be at the reception site having her hair and make-up done while everything else was delivered. She hired the chef at a local carry-out gourmet shop as her caterer because she really loved his food. He agreed to hire sufficient staff to set the tables and serve the guests. The caterer suggested she hire four servers for a total of four hours each at the rate of $60 per hour—a total of $960! When the bride found out how expensive the staffing would be, she decided that she and her bridesmaids could set all the tables before the ceremony. She decided she would need the staff for only two hours instead of four, and she was sure that three people could serve her guests in a timely manner. She was so proud of herself because she saved $780.

Wedding Blues

Remember, you usually get what you pay for, so take the advice of the professionals you trust. If you cut the wrong corner, your wedding will not turn out as you expect, and the money you save may not be as important when you look back on it as it seems to be right now.

She scheduled a simple ceremony in a lovely park a short walk from the reception site. The plan was that all of her guests would drive to the reception site, park their cars and congregate either on the covered patio with her, or on the lower level of the site with the groom. At the appointed time, the groom would lead the processional of his family and friends, including his attendants, down the street to the park, and the bride's friends, family, and attendants would follow. Some of the older guests were driven to the park in a van that had been rented for this purpose.

Once at the park, some of the elderly guests had the option of sitting in the 20 chairs that two of the groom's friends had borrowed from the reception site. The rest of the guests stood around the area. The bridal party came through the break in the chairs and the guests parted for them. The group was quite joyous as they walked back to the reception site. The reception was to begin with about 40 minutes of cocktails on the patio before guests were seated for dinner. Unfortunately, the tables had arrived later than expected, so the bridesmaids had not been able to finish setting them before the ceremony and had to complete the task when they returned. It took much longer than expected to set places for 188 people, so cocktails lasted 40 minutes longer than planned.

During cocktails the caterer ran out of hors d'oeuvres and the guests consumed all the beer and wine, including the wine that had been purchased to be served with dinner. Once people got into the room and were seated, the dinner was delicious, although some people were just being served as others finished eating and the couple were cutting their cake.

Wedding Blues

Choosing a do-it-yourself reception does not mean that you must actually do it yourself. Enlist your friends to do some of the busy work, but make sure you give each person a list of responsibilities so he or she won't forget the tasks in the excitement of the moment.

The bride and groom were not planning a honeymoon at that time. Instead, they took just the weekend (it had been a Thursday ceremony) and planned to be back at work on Monday. Monday morning the rental company called the groom to report that they were 20 chairs short when they picked up the order at the reception site. Apparently his friends had neglected to collect the 20 chairs from the ceremony site and return them to the reception site. The groom immediately drove to the park, but the chairs were gone. The bride and groom were forced to pay for the chairs, a total of $400.

Hiring Your Own Vendors

If you've decided that you don't want a do-it-yourself reception where you do all the work, or a one-stop-shopping reception where you do none of the work, but often make none of the choices, a combination of these two styles may be the perfect answer for you.

You'll need to hire the vendors that will actually provide the goods and services that you need. You can find these vendors in a variety of ways:

➤ Interview some of the vendors your reception site recommends.

➤ Visit bridal shows and meet vendors in every specialty.

➤ Hire a bridal consultant who has recommended the vendor to you.

➤ Check the vendor's advertisement in a local bridal magazine.

➤ Call the vendor who was used by your friends.

All of these methods will introduce you to wedding professionals, but none of them will guarantee that you'll have the wedding you want. In order to be sure of that, you need to meet the vendor face to face (never sign a contract while at a bridal show) and discuss your ideas for your wedding. Judge the vendor's reaction to what you say. Is the vendor listening, or do you get the impression that the vendor's humoring you, that the vendor believes he or she really knows what's best for you?

Before you hire anyone, check references carefully. Ask former clients if they were pleased with the vendor's performance. Did they have the wedding they wanted? You won't save any money if you select a vendor based solely on price and then discover that you didn't get the service you were expecting.

Tantalizing Trivia

I know of a bandleader who would take the bride and groom aside moments before their reception and say to them, "Just relax and enjoy your reception, I'll take care of everything you need." Very comforting, isn't it? The only problem is that he would then go into the reception room and play whatever *he* felt like playing, paying absolutely no attention to the couple's requests and instructions. The music was always excellent, and the guests always had a wonderful time, but it wasn't what the couple had requested. Future brides and grooms considering hiring this band asked for references and called the former clients. The clients all said the music had been good, but not what they had requested or expected. Eventually couples stopped hiring this band and the group disbanded.

As you begin negotiating with various vendors, follow these tips:

➤ Try to hide your excitement and enthusiasm about items you've fallen in love with. A vendor will be less likely to respond to a request for a reduced fee on a particular item if he or she believes it's your absolute favorite!

➤ Determine how busy this vendor already is around the date of your wedding. If this particular vendor is very busy, he or she won't be very open to negotiating for anything lower than the regular fee. If, however, your wedding is scheduled for a time when this vendor has few events on the calendar, you may find the vendor to be quite willing to negotiate the price with you.

Sue's Suggestions

You should listen to the professional when it comes to hiring enough waiters to get the food out to your guests while it's still hot. But when it comes to selecting the music, you know what's best! Allow your band the flexibility to change the music to get the group up and dancing, but don't give them the freedom to play music you don't want to hear.

Wedding Blues

Don't shop price only. Nancy and Stan were offered a $500 savings if they paid their photographer in cash. They had no written contract, but Nancy had taken notes so they were very disappointed when they received 100 proofs instead of the 400 they were promised. Then, it took over a year to receive their finished album. With no contract, Nancy and Stan had no recourse—they just had to wait.

➤ Remember that you generally get exactly what you pay for, so be sure you know what it is you want. If you cut the proposal down too far, the vendor may accept the contract, but you won't get the job you were expecting.

➤ When you make a purchase, be certain you receive a receipt indicating how much you've paid and what remains due. If you pay by check or credit card you're further protected. *Professional* wedding vendors will not offer their products at a lower cost if you pay cash; so if someone makes this offer to you, you should refuse it, tempting as it may be. In a cash transaction you'll have no proof of payment and no way to claim you didn't receive what you paid for. Good business practices apply to planning a wedding just as they do to any business transaction.

Selecting Your Caterer

Chances are you didn't give much thought to *caterers* before becoming engaged, so now that you need one, where do you look? As with all vendors for your wedding, you'll begin by speaking to friends who have recently been married. Then look in the regional bridal magazines in your area. These magazines' primary purpose is to create a place for vendors in your area to advertise their services. Advertising is expensive for the vendor, so seeing a company in one of these magazines tells you that they've been around for awhile and are making money. That doesn't mean you'll pay more for their services. More likely it means that they've been in business long enough to make a profit and plan to be around long enough to serve you and the brides who come after you. The Internet may be a place to check for caterers in your area, too. More and more vendors are creating Web pages to advertise their businesses.

When you've checked all of these sources and keep finding the same caterers, you'll know they are the people to speak to about the food for your wedding. Meet with at least three caterers and don't get carried away by what appears to be the least expensive caterer until you fully understand what is included in this vendor's service. If you simply ask a caterer for his or her charges and hire the least expensive one, you'll have the least expensive wedding you can arrange—but you may not get everything you could have gotten if you understood the differences in the caterers' services.

Brides learn quickly how to compare "apples to apples" when comparing catering costs, but to get you started, here are some things you should ask each caterer about:

Language of Love

A **caterer** is a person or company that prepares food or refreshments for wedding receptions and other special occasions.

➤ *Menu and food items.* Get a complete "description.

➤ *Linens.* What are your choices for buffets and guest tables?

➤ *Table decor.* Get a complete description of the decor for your buffets and guest tables.

➤ *China or disposable dishes.* Are they included?

➤ *Beverage.* What will be served? Iced tea? Punch?

➤ *Cake-cutting fee.* Is there one? Are plates included?

➤ *Bar fees.* What does it include? Labor? Setup? Corkage?

➤ *Gratuities.* Are they included? How much?

➤ *Taxes.* What items or services are taxed? What is the percent?

➤ *Cleanup services.* Are they provided after the event?

➤ *Deposit.* Find out if any or all of the deposit is refundable and under what conditions.

➤ *Delivery and setup fees.* Is there a separate fee for these services? How much?

Caterers provide the food for your reception, so you need to know what their food tastes like. Every company has a different policy on this, so you'll need to ask how this can be accomplished before the contract is signed. Most caterers will provide you with a tasting of the meal that you've ordered shortly before your seated-dinner wedding—after you've signed their contract. The purpose of the tasting is to let you sample the meal to be sure the seasoning is to your liking and the presentation is aesthetically pleasing to you. While every caterer hopes that you'll like everything exactly as it is, this is when they really want you to speak up if there's anything you'd like changed. Most caterers provide a tasting only if you're having a seated, served dinner menu, not a buffet dinner. Usually there is no charge for a tasting but the caterer does not provide it until after the contract has been signed.

Can You Bring Your Own Caterer?

If the facility has its own catering staff you'll be obligated to use this staff. Some facilities do not have on-site caterers, but instead use an exclusive caterer or provide a list of approved caterers for you to choose from. In a do-it-yourself type facility, a list of approved caterers offers the best of both worlds. You get to choose the caterer who can best match your ideas of food and decor, and you can negotiate to get to the price you were hoping to spend. Most important, you have the knowledge that you're working with a caterer who meets all the state health code and licensing requirements. This can be a major issue if someone gets sick and you want to be sure you're not liable for damages.

Sue's Suggestions

Ask the caterer to prepare an extra dinner while preparing for his or her next catered affair and allow you to *purchase* it. This may not be the menu you were planning to order, but you'll be able to determine the quality of the caterer's food.

Most caterers (and reception sites that offer catering on site) work on a minimum basis. This means there's a minimum amount of money for which they'll schedule an event. This minimum covers their hidden costs: the lights, heat, custodial services, rent, telephone—any behind-the-scenes expenses that are a part of their business. Caterers know how much it costs them to stay in business, and how much they need to earn as a minimum above the cost of food, labor, tax, and tip for the events they cater. When they offer you a quote on your wedding, they're actually quoting you this minimum. They may break it down into the number of people you're planning to serve, so that you can see that the food will cost you "x" per person, but there's still a minimum on the event.

For example, if you told the caterer you'll have 250 people, the caterer might quote you a price of $5,625.00 (plus tax and tip, sometimes stated as "plus/plus"). When you divide this amount by 250 (the number of people), it comes out to $22.50 per person. Don't forget, however, if your guest list drops to 185 people, the price will still be $5,625, but then it's $30.41 per person. When speaking to your caterer, always state the lowest reasonable number of people in attendance. If you quote the highest number, you'll be paying for this amount whether that number attends or not. If you quote the lowest reasonable number, your bill will increase by only the per-person price, since the minimum necessary for the caterer to stay in business has already been covered.

Using the previous quote covering 250 people for $5,625.00, if 275 people attended, the bill would increase to $6,187.50 (by adding the additional 25 people and multiplying by the original $22.50 per person). When reception sites state a minimum, it will vary by the time of day and day of the week. For instance, the Saturday night minimum is often higher than the Sunday afternoon minimum. Understanding this can help you plan your wedding for a day and time that is most beneficial to your pocketbook.

If you've decided to include ethnic foods, ask if the caterer knows these foods, or if you can bring in a chef or some dishes from a specific restaurant. While some caterers will work with you on this, many do not want to risk it, because their license is at stake. They may offer to make the dishes for you, using a family recipe, or even ask a member of your family who is a talented cook, to come in and teach them. This can be a great alternative, and you may actually have the best of both worlds with this arrangement.

Dessert Reception, Seated Dinner, or Buffet?

What do you want to serve at your reception? If your goal is to have the loveliest possible reception and stay on your budget, you'll want to consider this question very carefully, because the food is definitely the most expensive single item on the reception budget. If you avoid the obvious meal times, you can have a beautiful reception for a rather large number of people. So if you can't reduce the number of people you *must* invite, the best plan is to design your wedding and reception so that food becomes a smaller issue. If you plan a one o'clock ceremony, for instance, you can have a lovely dessert reception for a fraction of the cost of a reception that includes a meal, whether you serve that meal by a buffet or as a seated dinner.

Many brides and grooms think that a buffet reception is less expensive than the seated dinner. But in fact, in most locations they cost about the same. The main difference seems to be in the amount of actual food that is prepared. Earlier I explained that at a buffet reception your guests will stand in line to select their food. The caterer has no way of knowing in advance how much food any one guest may put on his or her plate, so the caterer will prepare more food than he or she would normally prepare if the meal was plated and served to each guest. The caterer wants to be sure that if the first 10 guests pile their plates high with food, the last 10 guests will still get plenty to eat. So, you're paying for a large quantity of food. No one expects the caterer to be able to exactly predict how much food to prepare for a buffet. Keep in mind, you can still have a seated dinner, even if you select buffet service. In this case, each guest will be assigned to a specific table, and after selecting his or her food from the buffet, will return to the assigned table. Tables will be set with silverware and glassware, but not with china, because each guest will get china at the buffet table.

Sue's Suggestions

When holding your reception in a hotel or other wedding facility that offers catering, ask what the minimum is for the time of day you plan to hold your wedding. Some facilities will give you this information only if you ask for it directly.

Tantalizing Trivia

Wedding traditions have varied throughout the ages and from culture to culture. At seventeenth-century English weddings, an elderly neighbor would throw a plateful of shortbread at the bride when she entered her new home. The waiting guests would scramble to get a piece of this shortbread which was considered very lucky. In India, before a Hindu couple is married, they are escorted to a pond where the Goddess Ganga is invited to the festivities. A pitcher of water is taken from the pond and relatives bathe the bride and groom in this water. They are then offered the only food they will eat that day, a meal of fried fish, curd, and flattened rice.

You could also plan a cocktail buffet reception. In this option, the food you select will be served in bite-size portions—something many people call "heavy hors d'oeuvres." This reception could be slightly less expensive than a buffet or seated dinner. The savings, however, will not be in the food costs, since you'll order enough hors d'oeuvres for each guest to feel satisfied. While you might select four to six hors d'oeuvres per person before a seated dinner, at a cocktail buffet you'll select 18 to 25 hors d'oeuvres per person. The main difference here is that you'll have seating for only about half your guests, so your guests will not be able to cut their food while balancing a plate and a drink. The money you save will not be on food. Instead, you'll save money on your centerpieces and, if you've selected special linen and/or chair covers, you'll certainly save by not seating everyone.

Wedding Blues

When seating is provided for only half the guests, the other half of the guests generally do not stay very long at the reception.

As I mentioned earlier, the seated dinner is not really more expensive than either the buffet dinner or the cocktail buffet. That's because the caterer will be able to plan almost exactly the quantity of food that is served. The caterer knows how large each portion should be, and you'll tell him or her how many people you'll be having. The savings that you'll recognize from the diminished quantity of food will easily cover the cost of the staff to serve your guests.

A surefire way to save money is to select the menu yourself, without giving your guests a choice of entrees. If you offer a choice, the caterer will charge you for two different entrees and you'll incur an additional expense in communicating with the waiters.

216

You'll need a place card for each person at the table telling that person where to sit. Some of these place cards need to have a sticker on them indicating which person gets which meal.

For instance, if the choice was chicken or fish and the majority of the guests chose chicken, then all the people who requested fish dinners get a silver star on their place cards telling the waiters these are the people who get fish. It will fall to you to communicate this information to the waiter for two reasons:

1. It will slow down the service of the meal if the waiter is forced to ask each guest their choice.

2. Since guests often don't remember what they chose and answer with what they feel like eating at the moment, the caterer might run out of one dish, and people who actually requested it will have to eat the other choice.

What about the menu? If you select chicken or pasta dishes you'll definitely have a lower food bill than if you choose beef, veal, or seafood as your main entree. Be careful about the other dishes served at your wedding, too. To cut your costs, make sure that all the ingredients are in season and readily available. If the caterer has to fly in asparagus because it's out of season, you'll certainly see a difference in your bottom line.

If you plan an evening ceremony you can have a lovely dessert-only reception for considerably less than a meal, regardless of how it's served. You can have an elaborate sweet table (sometimes called a Viennese table) and serve the wedding cake. Complement the sweets with truffles, chocolate-dipped strawberries, pineapples, apricots, or marshmallows, and a fruit display. You can serve enough champagne or other sparkling wine for a toast and then a coffee bar, where guests can add liquors, shaved chocolate, or even whipped cream to their choice of regular or decaffeinated coffee. You'll want to be a little bit careful here. Some people suggest serving a wedding cake with each layer a different flavor; but, while it's attractive, it's more expensive. The reason is, guests will want to taste several of the flavors, so you'll need more cake.

Sue's Suggestions

When determining the menu for your wedding reception, select food you like, prepared the way you want it prepared. As long as the food is fresh and attractively presented, the majority of your guests will enjoy it. Trying to select a dish that *everyone* loves is not realistic, and, anyway, your reception is no one's last meal!

Whatever you plan to serve at your wedding, if you've invited children, request that a kid's menu be available. Choose kid-friendly foods, which are usually less expensive, and remind the caterer to be careful with the portions since children usually eat very little. You'll also want to remember the children when making decisions about your bar, since they'll not be drinking any alcohol, but may drink several soft drinks.

Sue's Suggestions

A children's menu is appropriate for a sit-down dinner reception, but not for a buffet. At a buffet, the child's parent will select the food for the child to eat.

Is there another way to control the cost of the food at your reception? Most definitely! The accuracy of your guest count is critical! Brides typically make two errors in this area. First, when they begin interviewing their caterer they talk about the number of guests they plan to invite, without taking into consideration the fact that not all of the invited guests will attend the wedding. This becomes an important factor as we work through the planning process.

Let's say that you'll be inviting 250 guests to your wedding. You will, of course, look for a facility that can accommodate 250 people; but you should be aware that typically a percentage of those guests will not be able to attend. (The Association of Bridal Consultants estimates that on any given weekend approximately 20 percent of the invited guests will not be able to attend.) When you speak to the caterer, however, you'll ask for a quote on the smallest realistic number you can serve. Be realistic. You know that everyone will not be able to attend your wedding, much as they might like to, so don't penalize yourself by being too enthusiastic.

Next, read your contract carefully. Most caterers will prepare for a percentage above the number of guests you actually confirm. Typically this percentage is 3 percent, 5 percent or, in some very rare cases, 10 percent above the number you confirm. The caterer will also indicate when he or she needs your final count—usually 72 hours before the event. Understand that you'll end up paying for the number you specify at that time or the number you actually serve, whichever is greater. Three weeks before the wedding, the caterer may ask you how many people you'll have. Since your responses are due by the third Monday before the wedding, you may actually have a pretty good idea of your numbers by this time. However, if you name a number, this is the number you'll be charged for, even though there are three more weeks to the wedding. Your correct response is, "I still don't know—there are so many undecided people."

On the Monday before the wedding you'll give the caterer your numbers, minus a percentage. If the contract says that your caterer will prepare for 5 percent more than you quote, I recommend reducing your count to the caterer by 2.75 percent. Not so much that caterer could possibly be unprepared, but enough to handle any last-minute cancellations. If you've confirmed 168 guests on Monday and your number drops to 162 people, which is not at all unreasonable, you'll have paid for 6 people that will not attend. If, however, you've confirmed 160 guests on Monday and only two couples cancel (so you actually have 164 guests), you can call the caterer as late as Saturday morning and add four people easily. This way you pay for all you serve, but don't end up paying for people who don't show up. There's no point in wasting your money!

If you have the time and the inclination, you can cook the food for your reception yourself. (See Chapter 2, "Is Doing It Yourself an Option?") Of course, if you want to do this, you'll have to select a reception site that allows you to bring in your own caterer. Deciding to cook for your reception does not mean you have to cook everything yourself. You can contact a caterer and order one or two dishes that need to be made at the last minute, or you could ask your grocery store produce department to prepare large vegetable trays and dips that you can pick up. Dishes, stemware, flatware, and linens can be rented, or you can choose colorful, patterned paper and plastic. It's difficult to predict what the food for the reception will actually cost, since that will depend on what you decide to serve and how many guests you plan to prepare for.

Wedding Blues

Don't assume anything! Jennifer was positive all of her friends would attend her wedding so she skipped the response cards to save some money. She told the caterer to prepare for 210 guests but only 174 people actually attended her reception. If only she had included response cards with her invitations, she might have *really* saved some money!

Beer and Wine or an Open Bar?

Most people believe that offering an *open bar* is very expensive and that offering a beer and wine reception, instead, is the way to save money. This might be true in some situations, but it's not true at every reception. There are actually lots of ways to make sure your guests enjoy the beverages of their choice and protect your pocketbook as well.

Did you know there are two ways to present an open bar? You can have a *per-person* bar or a *consumption bar*. If your reception is held at a hotel or other facility that handles the liquor, most suggest an open bar in a per-person package, and this may sound like good advice, but is it? You'll pay a set fee for every guest that attends your wedding. For instance, you may pay $25 per person for every man, woman, and child in attendance. If you have 100 guests at your wedding, your bar bill will come to $2,500, plus taxes and tip. This may not sound like a lot of money, but let's examine it another way. If the average price per drink is $5, a per-person package assumes every person will consume five drinks. If you know you have a heavily drinking group, you probably would be wise to go for this package, because it puts a cap on your bar bill

Language of Love

An **open bar,** also called a hosted bar, is paid for by the host and the guests may order their drinks free of charge. The facility charges on a **per-person** basis (meaning a set fee for every person in attendance) or on a **consumption** basis (meaning you are charged only for the drinks your guests actually consume).

even if some of your guests consume more than $25 worth. But what if you know that many of your guests simply do not drink, or may consume only one drink each? For this to be economical, you'll have to have one guest who drinks nine drinks, for every guest who drinks only one. Think about your guest list—do you have guests who can consume nine or more drinks during the length of your reception? Would they be falling-down drunk? Is that what you want?

Tantalizing Trivia

Even though etiquette experts generally agree that cash bars are not appropriate during a private social occasion, if it's common within your circle of friends, then you should not dismiss the idea. Another alternative is to offer beer and wine at an open bar and provide mixed drinks on a cash basis. Or, for example, pay for the first $500 of the bar bill, and after that, allow guests to purchase their own drinks. Whatever you choose, include a nonalcoholic beverage, such as lemonade or iced tea, with the meal so guests will have the choice of a free beverage.

If you generally know the drinking habits of many of your guests, you may decide to select a consumption bar for your reception. This means that you'll be charged only for the amount of liquor, beer, wine, and soft drinks that your guests actually consume. You're taking a risk, because it's possible for your bar bill to exceed the amount presented in the package—but more often than not, it doesn't, and this can be a savings.

The obvious question that comes with a consumption bar is, "How do they know how much my guests drank?" The answer is, the facility doesn't know in advance of the event, but it has a formula for determining how much liquor was consumed at a party. The facility will start the evening with full bottles of liquor on the bar, several cases of wine, and a quantity of beer. The bottles of beer are easy to compute. They started the evening with "x" number of bottles, and at the end of the evening they have "y" bottles left; ($x - y$ = the number of bottles served) × the charge for each bottle = the cost of the beer. (See, high school algebra does come in handy!) For wine, the staff knows how many drinks come from each bottle. You're charged for each bottle opened. Let's say the evening starts with 40 bottles of wine, and each bottle contains six drinks. If at the end of the evening the facility has 10 bottles unopened, they know that 30 bottles were used (even if one of them still has a drink in it) and you're charged for 180 drinks ($6 \times 30 = 180$).

The challenging item is the hard liquor. To compute the amount of hard liquor consumed, the staff checks each bottle that was opened. Each bottle is assumed to contain 10 sections of 2.7 drinks each. (Some facilities figure 27 drinks per bottle, but other facilities use a different number—28 or as much as 30 drinks per bottle. Ideally, the facility computes the number of *ounces* per bottle and makes each shot one ounce. Remember, if your guest asks for a double, the drink will be counted as two drinks.)

So, if the bottle still contains $^3/_{10}$ of the liquor at the end of the evening, then $^7/_{10}$ were consumed, times 2.7 drinks, and you're charged for that number of drinks. If you had three bars at your wedding, and at the end of the reception three bottles of scotch have been opened, here's how the facility figures what to charge. One of the bottles is poured into the second bottle in hopes of bringing it to full capacity. Whatever remains is then added to the third bottle. With the first bottle empty, the second bottle full, and the third bottle missing $^4/_{10}$, it is determined that your group consumed $14/10 \times 2.7$ drinks of scotch.

This process is repeated with each kind of liquor at your bar, and a total of liquor served is determined. You're then charged for that amount of liquor. For example, in Georgia, hard liquor is taxed 3 percent more than the 7 percent state tax added to wine and beer, for a total of 10 percent. Check the tax situation in your location as well—3 percent doesn't sound like much, but it can become a big figure as your liquor total increases.

Couples frequently ask how to find out if the facility told them the truth about how many drinks were consumed. How do they know the staff didn't pour a bottle of liquor down the sink, or serve the wine to another group or to their staff? The answer is always the same: If you don't believe that you're working with honorable people, don't host your reception in this facility! No matter how careful you are, there's a point where you absolutely must trust the staff, because there's no way you can check everything and still enjoy your reception. Wedding facilities are not in business to take advantage of you! They also are very concerned about their reputation and your referrals, and, if you believe you were taken advantage of, it's very unlikely you'll say positive things about the facility to your friends. So this really should not be an issue.

Sue's Suggestions

Ask your banquet sales manager how the liquor is computed in the facility you've selected for your reception, and be sure you understand the procedure. It's never safe to assume that every facility does it the same way, and signing a contract without understanding can only lead to unhappiness when the bill is presented.

Many couples believe that a beer-and-wine reception is the most economical way to go. I remember calling a hotel once to ask for help in creating the "ultimate budget worksheet" shown earlier in this book. I asked for current pricing on the deluxe, premium, and house-brands bar, and then, almost as an afterthought, I asked the banquet manager how much a couple could expect to save if they choose a beer-and-wine reception. Her answer really shocked me. She told me that when a couple requests a beer-and-wine reception, the staff practically dances in the halls, since this is usually the most expensive reception they can host. She explained that guests tend to consume much more beer and wine than they do hard liquor. One of the reasons for this is that beer really tastes best when it's ice-cold. So if a guest starts drinking a beer and puts it down to dance, the guest gets a new one when he or she comes back, because the old one isn't cold anymore. Also, according to this hotel banquet manager, people don't get the same buzz from beer as they get from hard liquor, so they aren't as concerned about drinking more. Wine is similar in that people tend to put down their wine glasses to dance and later get another one before the first one's finished.

You can, however, protect your pocketbook if you give the staff some very specific instructions. At a sit-down dinner, where wine is served with dinner, ask the waiters not to pour wine in anyone's glass without asking if the guest prefers red or white wine. If the guest declines wine, his or her glass should be removed from the table so later waiters won't accidentally fill the glass. Ask the staff not to remove any half-empty glasses from the room without asking the guests if they're finished.

If your wedding reception is held in a facility that allows you to bring your own beverages, the situation changes completely. You can go to a discount liquor store and, with its guidance, purchase all the liquor, setups, beer, wine, and soft drinks that you'll need for the event. You can hire your own bartender, who is paid for his or her services with no connection to the amount of hard liquor, beer, or wine that is consumed. If you purchase more alcohol than you actually need, you can take it home and stock your own bar.

If you are bringing your own beverages, be sure to find out if the facility provides anything for the bar. Some places will provide glassware, others will also supply setups (lemons, limes, olives, cherries, soft drinks, mixers, and ice). Still others do not provide either glassware or setups. You'll need to know what is included in order to create your own shopping list.

The reception is the celebration part of your wedding, and it should be as exciting to plan as it is to attend. Food and beverages will be your most costly items, but since you know that from the beginning, you can plan carefully to make the best and most economical selections. Most caterers are aware of a bride's desire to stay on budget and will be very willing to assist you with this effort. For many people, alcoholic beverages add to the festivity of a wedding reception. If this is true of your family and guests, you needn't be frightened of the cost. With careful planning you can afford to serve whatever you choose and stay within your budget.

The Least You Need to Know

➤ Do-it-yourself receptions may cost less than one-stop-shopping receptions, but you'll need the help of friends to pull it off.

➤ One-stop-shopping receptions can look like cookie-cutter receptions if you don't get to add your own ideas.

➤ Plan your reception at a time of day that does not require a meal to be served.

➤ Control the size of your guest list.

➤ If you can bring in your own alcohol, buy it from a wholesale or discount broker.

Chapter 16

I Could Have Danced All Night

In This Chapter

➤ Hiring your entertainment: disc jockey or live band?

➤ The importance of a wedding script

➤ Your musical soundtrack

➤ Reading an entertainment contract

Most communities have several very talented music providers who would love to work your wedding celebration. The task ahead of you is simply to find the one that's right for you. In Chapter 8, "Photography and the Music of the Night," we spoke about budgeting for the musical portion of your wedding; in this chapter we'll take a closer look at the choices you have within that budget.

This day is about the two of you, so the entertainment you engage should reflect your tastes. If you would never go to a rock concert, there's no point hiring a disc jockey that specializes in rock-and-roll. Similarly, if you love contemporary music, why would you hire a band that dresses in spats and pinstriped suits and plays big band music? You also want someone who can create a diverse enough musical event to please your parents and guests and keep everyone on the dance floor!

Selecting Your Entertainers

You've probably already decided if you want a disc jockey or a live band at your wedding based on what you believe you can afford. But how do you decide *which* disc jockey or live band is appropriate for your event? You can serve the most wonderful food and have the most beautiful decorations, but if the music is lousy, the party won't be fun and your guests won't have a good time. How do you find the right entertainers for your event?

Finding a Disc Jockey (DJ)

The most obvious answer is to hire the disc jockey you loved at your friend's wedding; you had a great time at that wedding and thought he (or she) was terrific! But what if you haven't been to a wedding recently, or if the last DJ you saw wasn't good? What then?

Start by asking your friends and co-workers if they know a great DJ you can contact. Once you have the names, be diligent and do your own research—everyone has different tastes, and just because someone else hired this entertainer and liked the job he did does not mean he's appropriate for your event. Call the disc jockey and get the names of other brides and grooms he's worked with, then call them and get their opinions. Watch him work at a wedding and note how he interacts with the crowd. Does everyone seem to be having a good time? Would *you* be having a good time at this wedding if you were an invited guest? Is the disc jockey introducing the music, or does he have a cast of dancers that get into the crowd and make sure everyone is dancing?

Sue's Suggestions

For a fun twist, hire an interactive disc jockey for your reception. This disc jockey really gets involved in the party, either himself, or by bringing a group of male and female dancers who will dance with guests at your wedding to make sure everyone has a great time.

Wedding disc jockeys usually advertise in local bridal magazines and in the yellow pages, so you will probably be able to get names and phone numbers there as well. While pricing is important, you won't want to make a decision based on price alone. The least expensive provider may be newest to the industry or may be less well equipped to handle your needs. Listen carefully to what is included in their overall package and you may discover that there is very little financial difference between one DJ and another when you consider everything that's included.

It's important to feel comfortable talking to the DJ over the phone. You'll get a feeling for the DJ's personality during this initial phone call, and that's important, since his personality will influence his DJ style. Professionalism is also important; you should be able to detect a nonprofessional attitude during this first phone call. If you detect a lack of professionalism or a personality that rubs you the wrong way, my advice is to move on. Their attitude is not likely to improve between now and your wedding.

If the disc jockey you like the best happens to be new with the company, don't necessarily write him off—trust your instincts. Check out the company's references to be sure that they are reputable, and then hire the disc jockey you like the best.

Remember, everyone was new once, and sometimes fresh enthusiasm will add a spark to your wedding that a more seasoned disc jockey may not offer you.

Discuss the disc jockey's "requests" policy. You want to hire a disc jockey whose cassette tape and compact disc libraries are broad enough to allow your guests to make requests. You also want to work with someone who has enough of an understanding of the flow of a wedding to play requests at the right time, or to avoid playing a request that wouldn't be appropriate with the mood you and he are trying to create. Forcing a disc jockey to play every request when it is made will result in an uneven and less fun party.

Wedding Blues

There are people whose sense of humor may be seen as funny in some crowds and crude in others. With a disc jockey the personality is critical since it's generally his or her voice that is heard throughout the evening. If you don't like the DJ on the phone, you won't like him better in person!

You'll want to get references on the disc jockey who will be working your wedding. His company may have been around for years, but you won't have any way of knowing if he joined it last year or last week. Being the new kid on the block is not necessarily a bad thing, as I mentioned earlier, but not knowing about it may be.

There are several questions that you should ask when comparing disc jockeys:

➤ Do you use professional equipment?

➤ Do you provide a back-up system in case of emergency?

➤ Are you insured?

➤ Do you belong to any professional organizations or trade groups?

➤ Are we guaranteed the DJ of our choice on the day of our event?

➤ How many years of experience do you have?

➤ May we call three of your references?

➤ How will you be dressed?

➤ How early will you be there to set up?

➤ Will you allow requests?

The answers will lead you to the most professional disc jockey you can find.

Choosing a Live Band

Many brides believe that live music is the chief ingredient in keeping their wedding reception moving. Some love the elegant touch the look of several tuxedo-clad musicians on a bandstand add to their event. But finding the right band to fill your entertainment needs can be challenging.

You'll want to see the band you're considering in person at a wedding so you can see for yourself how they interact with the crowd. You're looking for their level of energy and excitement. Energy is infectious, and if the band (or the disc jockey) exhibits it, your guests will feel it and will respond.

Sue's Suggestions

If you hire your band through an entertainment agency, be sure to get the band leader's direct phone number so you can discuss any special musical requests with him directly. If the band doesn't know your first dance song, they may either be able to learn it in time or play a CD of it—but they must know in advance.

It is critical that you feel comfortable with the entertainer you select, which means that you definitely need to meet him or her before signing the contract. Anyone who tries to talk you out of the using the music you prefer, who doesn't ask about the kind of wedding you're planning, and who is otherwise difficult or disinterested in your event is not acceptable. Bands may play weddings every weekend, but they have never played at *your* wedding before, and the bandleader's demeanor should underscore the fact that he or she knows the difference.

The responsibilities of the entertainer are not merely in making great music, but in giving your party personality (which is dictated by the bride and groom) and controlling the pace of your reception. During your interview, you should expect the bandleader to ask you nearly as many questions as you ask him. For instance, he should want to know where your reception is going to be held; he should want to know what kind of music you want to listen to and might ask which is your favorite radio station or musical group. Naturally, he'll want to know how many people will be coming to the reception. He may even ask how you met and questions about your courtship. As he begins to get a sense of your musical likes and dislikes, he may suggest music that he thinks will work at your reception. Let him know if you don't like his suggestions, because he will learn your tastes with each response.

It's easy for all wedding professionals to believe that the success of your event depends totally on your being wise enough to hire their services. The photographer really believes that his pictures of your wedding will be the most important part of the event. At the same time, the florist is convinced that his flowers and decorations will set the perfect stage for your beautiful wedding, that without his skill it would never be as wonderful as you had imagined. The caterer is just as sure that the food that he presents will be the crowning touch you need for everyone to have a great time. In fact, none of these people are more important than any other—it is each vendor's ability to be a team player that really creates the wedding of your dreams. (Of course, everyone knows the bridal consultant is really the captain of the team, and that without her nothing runs smoothly!)

Tantalizing Trivia

The band is always "*sooo* loud"—what can be done about that? The members of the band usually set up the stage so the speakers and amplifiers are turned toward the audience, not toward the band members. The band members actually cannot hear how loud the band sounds to the guests. You should assign one person who will let the bandleader know when the music is too loud. This is a good job for whomever is actually paying for the band; since their name will appear on the check at the end of the evening, the band will be highly motivated to respond when asked to lower the volume.

Your Reception "Script"

When you are working with a bridal consultant, you will plan out the evening with her (or him) and a written script will be created and distributed to the vendors in advance of your event. If there is no consultant involved, you will have to assume the responsibility of notifying all the vendors of the schedule yourself, but please do so in consultation with your bandleader since he will have the most experience and know what works the most smoothly. In any case, the schedule needs to be communicated to every one of your reception vendors, from the florist to the baker to the limousine driver, so everyone knows what your plans are and can help you accomplish your goals. Remember, your vendors are all members of your team.

Weddings have a rhythm to them that is different from other events. There are high points in your reception, such as when you first enter the room and share your first dance. There are also quiet times, while the guests may be eating their meal and talking to one another and don't need musical accompaniment.

A skilled bandleader, with wedding experience, is aware of the unique pace of each wedding reception. He is the most visible team member, and his attention to the timing and flow of your event has a dramatic impact on food being served hot and the cake being cut on time. The music at your wedding controls the flow of the event, so it's essential that the bandleader or disc jockey have a copy of a carefully planned timetable—the same one that has been distributed to the caterer, photographer, and videographer. This way everyone knows the approximate timing of each part of the reception. You don't want the music to stop when the dance floor is full of people having a great time, but you also don't want your food served cold and your cake cut after your guests have left.

As master of ceremonies, the bandleader knows how to move the guests from the dance floor to their tables so hot food can be served and then how to get them back up to the dance floor for more dancing. He'll know when to take a break so toasting can begin and how to energize the guests after the break so they return to the dance floor for more dancing after the father/daughter dance. If he is very skilled, the guests won't even be aware that their movements have been tightly controlled and orchestrated. They will only know that they have had a wonderful time at a perfect wedding.

Sue's Suggestions

Be sure to ask your caterer to provide meals and a break room where the band or disc jockey, photographer, and videographer can rest and eat. The staff meals do not need to be the same food you are serving your guests—a sandwich, chips, and a cold drink will do.

The "Soundtrack" of Your Wedding

Have runs you ever seen a romantic movie and left the theater humming the music from the soundtrack? You probably weren't even focusing on the music as the male lead gathered his lover in his arms and kissed her tenderly—but every time you hear that music from now on, you remember that scene. The movie director worked very hard to create that scene, and music was a big part of it.

Now you're planning your own big moment, and choosing the perfect music is a big part in creating it. There are so many moments in a wedding ceremony and reception that can be enhanced by the right music that the task may initially seem daunting. You shouldn't fear, however—there's a great deal of reference material available to help you at the library, in all the bridal magazines, and even on the Internet (see Appendix B for a listing of sources).

Selecting Your Ceremony Music

When it comes to selecting your ceremony music, the best place to start is by soliciting the opinions of the person you've hired to provide it. If you've decided to use the organist at your church, for example, he or she will be able to suggest music that has been played previously at weddings in your church. Sometimes you can even meet the organist at a church and ask him or her to play a part of the piece for you on the organ so you can get the full effect. You will certainly want to ask if there is any music that is *not* considered appropriate if you are being married in a church or synagogue. Some religious institutions require that you use *sacred music* during your ceremony, while others are perfectly fine with *secular music*. Usually this will be listed in any printed material you've been given, but be sure to ask if you don't see it there.

Whether you have decided on a brass quintet, string quartet or trio, harp and violin duet, or even a single keyboard for your ceremony, you'll want to speak with those musicians for guidance. You'll want to be sure that the music you select sounds best when played on the particular instruments you have chosen, and the musicians can certainly guide you here.

Basically, for the ceremony, you will need music for the prelude, processional, bridal entrance, and recessional.

The prelude, or pre-nuptial concert, is the background music that is played as your guests are being seated before the ceremony. Since there will be approximately thirty minutes of prelude, you can select several different pieces to be played during this time. This can be any kind of music that you enjoy. It could be *classical music* such as:

➤ Handel's *Water Music (Air)*

➤ Bach's *Air on a G String*

➤ Mozart's *Ave Verum Corpus*

➤ Bach's *Jesu, Joy of Man's Desiring*

➤ Schubert's *Serenade*

Or you might choose a more contemporary theme and select show tunes such as:

➤ "The Music of the Night" from the *Phantom of the Opera*

➤ "All I Ask of You" from the *Phantom of the Opera*

➤ Theme from *Beauty and the Beast*

➤ "One Hand, One Heart" from *West Side Story*

➤ "Through the Eyes of Love" from *Ice Castles*

Language of Love

Sacred music is dedicated or set apart for the service or worship of a deity and is worthy of religious veneration. **Secular music** relates to non-religious themes, and while it may be played during a religious service, is not religious in nature.

Language of Love

Classical music is music that relates to the late eighteenth and early nineteenth centuries, characterized by an emphasis on simplicity, objectivity, and proportion. This music was written in the European tradition and is distinguished from folk music, popular music, or jazz.

Once the guests are seated, the processional music begins. Generally this is one piece of music that has an identifiable beat so your bridal party can walk at approximately the same speed. It is particularly helpful if this piece of music can also be played over and over again without a break and then faded out when appropriate. This is important because it will be very difficult to know exactly how long it will take the party to walk down the aisle. As people get nervous, they often walk faster than anyone expected, and you will want the musicians to be able to continue the music until everyone is in their places. Of course, once they are, you will want the music to end and not have to be played until the musicians come to the end of the piece. Some popular pieces used for processionals include:

➤ Clarke's "Trumpet Voluntary" (Prince of Denmark's March)
➤ Stanley's "Trumpet Voluntary"
➤ Pachelbel's "Canon in D"
➤ Charpentier's "Prelude to Te Deum"
➤ Vivaldi's "Concerto in D Major"
➤ Mozart's "Wedding March" (from the *Marriage of Figaro*)

It's not necessary to select one piece of music for the groomsmen and another for the bridesmaids unless you have a particularly large bridal party. If you have 4–8 attendants each, they tend to walk quickly enough that changing music gives the processional a "chopped-up effect." Of course, if the aisle is very long, or if you have 10 or more attendants each, two pieces might work very well. The bridal party usually enters in single file mimicking the bride and groom who are single when they enter the ceremony and a couple when they leave, so the bridal party generally leaves the ceremony in pairs. The groom usually enters the ceremony to the same processional music as the bridal party, but different churches often have a different custom for when the groom enters.

The third piece of music played during the ceremony is the music announcing the bride. Generally this music begins with a fanfare to herald her coming down the aisle. We are accustomed to hearing Wagner's *Bridal Chorus* (from Lohengrin) or Mendelsohn's *Wedding March* (from *Midsummer Night's Dream*), both of which are sometimes called "Here Comes the Bride," but there are actually several other pieces that are frequently used. Among them:

➤ Purcell's "Trumpet Tune in C"
➤ Handel's "The Arrival of the Queen of Sheba"
➤ Walton's "Coronation March"
➤ Beethoven's "Ode to Joy" (from the Ninth Symphony)
➤ Grieg's "Triumphal March"

After the couple is pronounced husband and wife the musicians begin playing the recessional music. This very upbeat music usually has a quicker tempo than the music chosen for earlier in the ceremony and is played until the entire bridal party and all the guests have exited the room. There are many choices for this music, a few of which are

➤ Mozart's "Exsulate, Jubilate"
➤ Bach's "Brandenberg Concerto No. 4"

➤ Geminiani's "Concerto Grosso in D Minor, Op. 2"

➤ Campra's "Rigaudon"

➤ Vivaldi's "The Four Seasons" (Spring, Allegro)

Tantilizing Trivia

Christian brides may also choose to include "Joyful, Joyful, We Adore Thee"; "Love Divine, All Loves Excelling"; "All Things Bright and Beautiful"; or "Simple Gifts" in their ceremonies. Jewish brides may choose "Dodi Li"; "Jerusalem of Gold"; "Erev Ba"; "Erev Shel Shomshanim"; or "To Life, To Life, L'Chaim" as a part of their ceremony.

Some couples select another piece of music that is played at the beginning of the ceremony for the seating of the mothers and grandmothers. This can be an additional piece from the processional list above, or a particular favorite of one of the mothers. It was widely reported that Joan Rivers was escorted down the aisle at her daughter Melissa's extravagant wedding to *Hey, Big Spender*.

And for Reception Music ...

The really fun part comes in choosing the songs for your reception soundtrack. There are so many moments that can be highlighted by the right music: your entrance; your first dance; the dance you share with your dad and the dance the groom shares with his mom; the music you cut your cake to; the music you toss your bouquet to; your last dance. Again, a good place to start is with your disc jockey or bandleader, who can suggest music that he has used in the past. In most cases, if you have a favorite that he doesn't mention, you have enough time to secure the CD so it can be learned. Don't wait until the last minute to go over songs with your musicians!

Some brides and grooms ask their musicians to provide music during cocktails. If you would like to do this, you are probably looking for a selection of background music. Your guests will be visiting with one another, eating and drinking—*not* concentrating on the music—so music may not be necessary if dinner will be accompanied by a live band. When the doors do open, the band should be playing something upbeat and celebratory, that draws the guests into the ballroom. The particular piece has changed over the years but many brides choose *Celebrate!* for this opening number and it certainly does set the mood in an upbeat way. Often guests go directly onto the dance floor and dance for a few moments until the bride and groom are ready to make their entrance.

The First Dance

Once all the guests are present, the bandleader will ask the guests to find their places and help him welcome the bride and groom. The couple enters the room and weaves their way between the tables and on to the dance floor for their first dance. There are several wonderful choices of music for the first dance. Some couples decide to take dance lessons in advance of their wedding date so they choose "their song" early and learn to dance to it. Some couples decide on a specific dance, like a waltz, fox trot, or tango and then search for a song they like that has that beat. Some possible choices include:

➤ "It Had to be You," Kahn, Jones

➤ "The Way You Look Tonight," Kern, Fields

➤ "When I Fall in Love," *Sleepless in Seattle* version

➤ "True Companions," Marc Cohn

➤ "May I Have This Dance for the Rest of My Life?" Sam Cooke

➤ "Fly Me to the Moon," Frank Sinatra

Couples decide to dance together, alone, on the dance floor throughout their song, or to only dance a portion of this first dance song and then have their parents break in to dance with them. The purpose of this "change partner" first dance is to capture pictures of the bride and groom dancing with both sets of parents and sometimes their honor attendants quickly before the dance floor gets very crowded.

Since the purpose is pictures, it might be helpful to know the order that works best. First the bride and groom dance with each other. Then the bride's father cuts in and dances with her while the bride's mother dances with the groom. When the photographer has photographed those two couples, the groom's father cuts in and dances with the bride, the groom's mother dances with the groom, and then the bride's parents dance together. When the photographer has photographed these three couples, the groom's father hands the bride back to the groom and begins dancing with his wife, so the photographer can get a picture of the groom's parents dancing together. As this happens, the bandleader invites the bridal party onto the dance floor. All this happens very quickly and could take place during just one song, or the bride and groom can dance together for the whole first dance and then have their parents cut in at the beginning of a second piece of music.

Father/Bride and Mother/Groom Dance

The first dance is not to be confused with the father-daughter dance, which generally takes place later in the evening before the wedding cake is cut. There was a time when every bride danced with her father to "Daddy's Little Girl," but things have changed a lot. Today, many brides and their fathers select songs that have a special meaning for the two of them. One bride chose to dance with her dad to the music they had celebrated to when they completed the Boston Marathon together. She felt it would always be "their" song.

Sometimes the music selected is more generic so the groom can dance with his mother at the same time. There are some terrific songs that work very well for both fathers and brides and mothers and grooms. A few that come to mind include:

➤ "What a Wonderful World," Louis Armstrong

➤ "I Wish You Love," Trenet

➤ "Because You Loved Me," Celine Dion

➤ "Butterfly Kisses," Bob Carlisle

➤ "Someone to Watch Over Me," Gershwin

Pick something that will have meaning to you, your dad, your groom, and his mother. You'll look back on this for years to come.

Ask the bandleader what he normally plays while you cut your cake. You might like what he chooses, or you may want to personalize this ceremony with your own music. One of my particular favorite pieces for the cake cutting is the Beatles tune "When I'm 64," because the chorus asks "Will you still need me, will you still feed me, when I'm 64?"

Wedding Blues

It is customary for the bride to dance with her new husband before she dances with any other guests at the wedding, so it's a good idea to schedule this first dance immediately after the couple enters the reception. Remember to keep it short. Your guests are standing around watching and they will enjoy it more when they can participate, so have the band leader invite everyone onto the dance floor as quickly as possible.

Tantalizing Trivia

After the cake is cut, some bandleaders begin playing a *tarantella*, a traditional wedding dance within the Italian community. At a Jewish wedding, the *hora* generally follows the cutting of the cake—male guests lift the bride and groom on chairs and everyone dances around them. At a Polish wedding, this is a good time for the money dance, when polkas and mazurkas are often played. If you don't have an identifiable ethnic group in the room, you might want to follow the cutting of the cake with a "city dance," where, for example, guests from San Francisco dance as the bandleader plays "I Left My Heart In San Francisco" and they stay on the floor as the bandleader continues with "New York, New York" and the New Yorkers join them. If you consider your attendees carefully, you and the bandleader can come up with enough songs to get everyone back to the dance floor.

What *Does* That Contract Say?

As with every professional that you hire for your wedding, you should receive a contract from the bandleader or the disc jockey. The following is a sample contract showing what should typically be addressed.

AGREEMENT FOR PERFORMANCE ON MUSICAL ENTERTAINMENT

This agreement made on this day, <u>Wednesday, March 2, 2000</u>, by and between <u>Beth Bride and Gary Groom</u> (hereinafter referred to as CLIENT), and <u>Brian Leslie dba Magical Music</u> (hereinafter referred to as MM). The purpose of this agreement is to state the terms, conditions, and services MM will render to CLIENT.

PERFORMANCE:

Date:	Saturday, July 11, 2000
Location:	The Markham Golf and Country Club *1600 Pennsylvania Avenue* *Macon, Georgia 31201*
Event:	Wedding Reception
Shows:	Three 45-minute sets between *8:00 P.M. and 11:00 P.M.*
Set-up:	Guests will arrive at 8:00 PM
Requested Attire:	Formal
Payment:	In consideration of said performance, CLIENT agrees to pay <u>$3,200.00</u> (three thousand two hundred and no/100 dollars).

Deposit in the amount of <u>$1,600.00</u> made payable to MAGICAL MUSIC to be received by <u>April 1, 1999</u>.

Balance due on the evening of the engagement, prior to the performance. Said balance to be paid in <u>cash</u> or <u>certified check</u> payable to MAGICAL MUSIC.

Cancellation: *CLIENT may cancel any performance prevented by fire, casualty, strike or any other cause not within the control of CLIENT, by written notice no later than 60 days before the the scheduled engagement date. Failure of CLIENT to comply with this cancellation provision will result in a cancellation fee of <u>$1,000.00</u> and <u>loss of deposit</u>.*

MM may cancel any performance prevented by illness, accident, riots, strikes, epidemic or any other condition beyond the control of MM. If MM has received a deposit for said performance, MM will return said deposit within 10 days of cencellation.

Sound stage and lighting requirements:

    A. Sound System for the event to be provided by: MM

    B. Lighting for the event to be provided by: MM

> *In the event MM will be providing sound and lights, CLIENT agrees to provide <u>six (6) twenty (20) amp circuits</u> for said performance.*
>
> *CLIENT agrees to provide all staging necessary for Performance. 16' × 30' preferred, 12' × 24' Minimum. If this requirement is not feasible, all alternatives must be discussed with <u>BRIAN LESLIE</u>.*
>
> All precautions must be taken to ensure that said stage is securely assembled (i.e., no cracks or spaces between sections), to guarantee safety of all band members during performance.

Dressing Room: CLIENT agrees to make the best possible effort to provide a private dressing area equipped with mirrors and adequate seating for 9 band members and crew. CLIENT further agrees, when possible, to provide ten (10) clean hand towels for MM's use prior to performance.

Food & Beverages: If guests are provided with meals, CLIENT agrees to provide MM with 9 *said* meals.

                          CLIENT agrees to provide the following BEVERAGES:

                Three-quarter case of non-carbonated water

                Three-quarter case of beer

                Twelve assorted soft drinks (Coke, Pepsi, 7-Up)

                Two quarts cranberry juice

                One quart orange juice

                One pot hot coffee

                One pot hot water / assorted teas

Special Provisions: _____

                _____

                _____

Let's review the above contract, paying special attention to those things shown in *italics*. Macon, Georgia may have only one Markham Golf and Country Club, but there may be two places in your community with similar names, so you will want to be sure that the exact address of your reception location appears on the contract, not just the name of the facility. It's terrific to know how many musical sets will be included, but you also need to know how long the band will perform, what time they will start, and what time they will finish. This band will also take three 15-minute breaks. They don't tell you a) if they are willing to play overtime, or b) how much overtime charges will be. Both of these things should be clearly stated in your contract, just in case you want to extend the contract.

Wedding Blues

Making sure the exact address of your reception appears on your contract can be important if your reception is scheduled at a hotel chain. Your city may have several Marriotts, Hiltons, or Holiday Inns!

The balance of the payment is due in *cash* prior to the performance. It's really not a good idea for anyone to be carrying $1,600.00 cash with them to the wedding. Plan to stop by the bank and get a certified check before the wedding day.

This band's whole cancellation clause is confusing with regard to weddings, and frankly, I would not advise a client of mine to sign a contract with this clause in it. Exactly what does it mean if the reception facility burns down 60 or more days before your wedding? Would you move your reception, or cancel it, and if it happened within 20 days of your reception and you moved the reception, would you be penalized for changing the location? If a family emergency, such as a serious illness or death, caused you to re-schedule your reception, wouldn't you expect to hire the same band for that new date, and wouldn't you expect your deposit to be applied to this new date? Besides, illness and death seldom happen on schedule, 60 days or more before the event. Furthermore, if you and the groom decided 70 days before the reception not to get married and notified the band, is that considered "beyond the client's control"? Would you get your deposit back? Why should you have to pay the band an additional $1,000.00 if it is beyond your control?

In addition, the band offers you no recourse if they have to cancel—and in fact their cancellation policy is very slanted in their favor. If there is illness in the band, chances are it will be one member of the band—not all nine. Couldn't they just hire a substitute drummer if theirs takes ill? This paragraph goes on to say "if MM has received a deposit for said performance." What does that mean? That if they have not received a deposit, they have not been hired, so they don't have to be concerned about cancellation?

The bottom line is simple: If your band presents you with a contract with either of these clauses in them, pin them down and make sure you fully understand what is meant in each instance. Write that definition on the contract, and then decide IF you want to hire this band. You should not feel obligated to do so and these policies are definitely not protecting *you*.

Their requirement as to amplification may be difficult for you, as the client, to guarantee. You will have to contact the reception facility and make sure that this requirement can be met. Most reception facilities will already have enough power for most bands, but there may be some historic locations that do not, so be sure to check before signing.

The size of the bandstand requirement is another issue. Sixteen by thirty feet is really quite large and many reception facilities will not be able to accommodate this amount of space. It probably isn't a problem in a hotel ballroom, but there are many locations where this will be a problem. Be sure to speak to your banquet manager and check on this dimension before accepting this contract.

The section titled "Special Provisions" is blank on this sample, but this is where you would write any changes that you have made to the contract. Make sure that both you and the bandleader initial and date each page of the contract, especially any changes that are being made. You don't want any confusion about what was changed and when it was changed.

It is appropriate for the band members to be fed—they will be working long hours on your wedding day, since they will have to both set up and take down their equipment when the event is over. Instead of just a three-hour performance, in fact they may be investing nine or ten hours to your job. But the issue here is *what* they will be fed. This contract actually says that the band expects to be fed the same meal that you are feeding your invited guests and that is neither necessary or appropriate. Instead, a break room should be provided with a buffet setting of sandwiches, chips, cookies, and soft drinks. This band has requested specific beverages; it shouldn't be difficult to arrange for most of their beverage requests. However, I'll bet that *you* don't drink on the job! Why would you let *them*?

Some brides need to be empowered to understand that this is *their* day and it is perfectly acceptable for them to speak up and tell a bandleader that some of the terms of his contract are unacceptable to them. Don't be afraid of losing "the best band in town." Chances are this one is just one of many great bands, and you'll know that as soon as you point up these difficulties with the contract. A truly great band will have no difficulty making the changes you request and doing a wonderful job for you. If you run into a bandleader who doesn't have that attitude, keep looking—this is probably not the right group of musicians for you anyway!

As the bride and groom you need to take an active role in selecting the music for your ceremony and reception. The musical soundtrack of your day is a lot like your fingerprint, and distinguishes your wedding from all others done by this particular set of musicians. Naturally, the bandleader or disc jockey can recommend music for you, and probably even play a few bars of an unfamiliar piece so you will know what it sounds like, but the decision is always yours!

The Least You Need to Know

➤ Both disc jockeys and live bands can fulfill your musical needs.

➤ Some religious institutions require you to play religious music for your ceremony, but others do not have that requirement.

➤ Mixing your musical choices between classical and contemporary music can make the wedding truly reflect your tastes.

➤ Most cities have many wonderful bands, so you should not feel you have to agree to unreasonable demands in order to secure a specific group of musicians.

➤ Read all contracts carefully and make sure you understand them.

Chapter 17

You Ought to Be in Pictures

> **In This Chapter**
>
> ➤ What to look for when you interview a photographer
>
> ➤ What does the contract say?
>
> ➤ How important is a photographer's assistant?
>
> ➤ Spotting the scams

Wedding photographs are works of art and wedding photographers are true artists. Their "models" are the beautiful real women we know, whose emotions and love photographers catch in the blink of a shutter. Photographers make it look so easy that many of us think that we could be photographers, too. Trust me—wedding photography is definitely not as easy as it looks! Be very careful not to skimp on your photography budget. After your wedding, the pictures are all you'll have left and that makes them pretty important!

Interviewing a Wedding Photographer

It's never a good idea to begin a telephone conversation with a wedding photographer by asking what he or she charges. You may get a quote for a basic package, but you need to see the photography first. If you've decided that your wedding photographs are important enough be taken by a professional, you'll want to hire the most talented professional you can afford. The only way to do this is to *look* at the photographer's work and *then* discuss the pricing. If you don't like the photographer's work, why would you even care about the price? If you like the work, be honest about what you can afford and let the photographer tell you what he or she can do within your budget. For example, you may discover you can afford to have your ceremony photographed but need to make other, less expensive arrangements for the reception.

Tantalizing Trivia

One bride selected a friend, who was a professional photographer, to photograph her wedding. Unfortunately, he was an architectural photographer, not a wedding photographer. First, he photographed every posed shot with a Polaroid camera to be sure he liked the composition and light. Then, everyone had to stand still while the photo developed. After that, he took the "real" shot. That meant people had to hold their poses for a minimum of 90 seconds per shot. Now, 90 seconds doesn't sound like a long time, but when you're holding a pose, it can seem like forever!

Who's in This Picture?

When you're looking at beautiful photographs in which everyone looks so calm and relaxed, you probably can't even imagine the circumstances under which these photographs were taken. For instance, families today aren't as simple as they once were, and it takes a very sensitive photographer to take the time to understand "who goes with whom" so he can capture a group shot.

Most professional wedding photographers seem to have a mental list of the photographs they must capture, and they try to go through that list in roughly the same order at each wedding, so nothing will be left out. When members of the wedding party are not ready at the appointed time, the photographer must be able to change directions quickly and capture other shots on his mental list—without forgetting to take the ones he or she planned to start with first. Emotions run high as the time for the ceremony nears and guests begin to arrive, and sometimes the photographer has to complete the posed pictures after the ceremony very quickly, especially if another wedding is scheduled in the same church.

Sue's Suggestions

Well before the wedding, make a list of the group shots you know you'll want. Assign this list to one of your family members or close friends who knows the people and will gather them together for the group shot. Give the photographer a copy of your list and the name of the person who will be helping.

Is the Photographer for You?

When you're meeting with a photographer for the first time and are looking at the photographs, decide how you feel with that person. Are you comfortable with this photographer? Remember, you'll spend more time on your wedding day with the photographer than with any other person, except your groom. If the photographer's after-shave or cologne gives you a headache, or if you're uncomfortable in any way, your face and body will show it in your photographs.

Most photographers have albums that include their favorite pictures from several weddings. Since it follows that the photographer would put his or her best work in these albums, ask if you could see one *complete* wedding. This will tell you more about the photographer's work over a whole event. As you look at the photographs notice if they all seem to look alike. Are all the pictures in traditional poses or are *candid* shots included? Are all the photographs in color or did the photographer include some black and white photos as well? When you look at the candid photos, do people look natural? Were people caught in awkward angles? Are you looking at the backs of most people's heads?

Are shadows covering the bride's face? Can you see the detail on her gown, or does the gown look flat and does the bride's midriff appear slightly wide? Did you know that if the bride is turned slightly, the lights on the camera pick up the detail of the lace on her gown and she'll look slimmer? Also, if the bride and groom each put one foot back and shift their weight to it, they'll look (and feel) more comfortable and natural in the photograph.

Pay particular attention to the backgrounds in the pictures, do they distract you? Are there flowers or birds coming out of the subjects' heads? As you turn the pages of the album, do you get a sense of the emotion and excitement of the wedding? Does it look as if the photographer is creative both in the way the book is arranged and in the way the photographs were taken?

Some couples hire a professional photographer for the formal sitting and the ceremony, and then set out disposable cameras for their guests to use at the reception.

Wedding Blues

Many photographers get grouchy when Aunt Sarah comes over to tell them how to arrange a photograph or in what order to take the pictures. To keep your photographer happy and to get the best pictures, keep family members away while the photographer is concentrating on taking the posed pictures. After that, the photographer will probably gladly listen to Aunt Sarah's suggestions.

Language of Love

In photography, **candid** shots are natural, unposed photographs. Often the subject is unaware he or she is even being photographed.

This can be a great alternative, because your guests will take lots of photographs of friends enjoying the reception—there's no way a professional photo could capture *all* your friends.

Here are two important things to remember if you use disposable cameras:

1. Assign someone to collect the cameras at the end of the reception and deliver them to you.

2. Be sure to add the cost of purchasing the disposable cameras (remember, you'll probably need cameras *with* the flash, which are slightly more expensive) and developing the photographs to your budget!

Wedding Blues

I once watched a "photojournalistic photographer" walk around the room with his camera held arm's length above his head, snapping photographs constantly as he walked. When the proofs were delivered to the bride, they were all crooked, the images weren't centered, some were blurred, and in most cases the lighting was too dark. Though he called it photo-journalism, it was simply poor photography!

The photojournalistic approach is a popular style of photography used today. While some photographers advertise this approach as their specialty, nearly all professional wedding photographers take candid shots in addition to the more formal, posed pictures. Photojournalism refers to the type of photography most commonly seen in newspapers and magazines, often of sports figures—action shots in which the subject is not even aware of being photographed. If you're interested in this candid approach, consider contacting your local newspaper to determine if there's someone there who can photograph your wedding. You'll have to be prepared to negotiate price with this photographer, understand fully what you'll receive, and explain what coverage you want of your wedding. It may be possible for you to pay for the photographer's time and the film, and then have the photographs developed yourself.

You should ask the same questions of every photographer you interview, so you'll have the same basic information for each of them, which you'll then use to compare. You'll want to know how long the photographer has been in business. You'll also want to know what percentage of the business is wedding photography. If a photographer has been in business five or more years, and most of the business is weddings and/or bar mitzvahs (the celebration of a Jewish boy's religious coming of age at thirteen), then the photographer's probably pretty comfortable telling a story with photographs. Be sure to ask how soon after the wedding you'll receive the proofs and how long it will take to get the completed album after placing the order. You'll want to know who selects the final pictures to go in the album—the photographer or you. Another question brides often forget to ask is how long the photographer keeps the negatives—important information if you need additional prints later, or if your album is ever destroyed.

Understanding a Photographer's Contract

It has been my experience that photographers don't all speak the same language when talking about their services. The couple often needs an interpreter to understand what one photographer is offering as opposed to another. Since couples tend to ask only about costs, they may select the most reasonably priced photographer, only to discover later that another photographer, who sounded more expensive, actually would have cost them less in the long run. As with every other vendor, reading and understanding the contract is your best defense.

Johnson Photography

1675 Proseptia Drive
Somewhere, Kentucky 54546

Phone: 555-1234   Fax: 555-5678

The Package includes:

Full-day coverage for two photographers. Jay Reynaird will cover the event in a photojournalist style using primarily black and white film, while Victor Johnson will cover the event in the more traditional style using medium-format color film.

The Charges:

The charge for our service is $2,000, to be paid in thirds, one third to confirm the date, one third within 30 days of the wedding date, the final third due on delivery of the proofs.

This fee includes a $1,000 credit to be applied to our à la Carte Price Menu.

A la Carte Price Menu

<u>Individual Print Prices</u>:

20" × 24"	$150.00
16" × 20"	$100.00
11" × 14"	$ 60.00
8" × 10"	$ 20.00
5" × 7"	$ 12.00
4" × 5"	$ 7.00
Wallet-size @ $2.00 ea. (minimum order of two per image, page of 8)	$ 15.00

Artist canvas prints on stretcher frame are an additional 50%. Black and white prints are an additional 50%.

Album Prices:

8" × 10" Album (full-size bride and groom album): $200 for cover plus $30.00 per page ($120.00 per panoramic page); each page holds two images.

5" × 7" Album (bride and groom or parent's album): $100.00 for cover plus $15.00 per page; each page holds two images.

4" × 5" Album (parent's album or gift album): $75.00 for cover plus $10.00 per page; each page holds two images.

Photo Thank-You Cards:

$125.00 (quantity of 50); includes wallet-size photos, thank-you cards, and envelopes.

Gift Folio Prices:

Tri-fold 8" × 10" folio:	$125.00
Bi-fold 8" × 10" folio:	$ 75.00
Bi-fold 5" × 5" folio:	$ 25.00

Preview Album Prices:

Small Wedding:	$299.00
Medium Wedding:	$399.00
Large Wedding:	$499.00

Preview albums are due back to Johnson Photography within one month from delivery unless they're purchased by the bride and groom. Value of preview album is deducted from deposits if not returned within this time limit.

Deposits

All deposits must be used within six months of preview album delivery or balance is forfeited. Prices do not include Kentucky state tax where applicable. Johnson Photography accepts cash, checks, Visa, MasterCard, and American Express.

In Mr. Johnson's contract, the bride and groom have a $1,000 credit to be used on their wedding album. This will provide 24 8" × 10" photographs at $20 each for $480.00; 12 pages at $30 (each holds two photographs) for $360.00; and one $200 album for a total of $1,040.00 plus tax. If the couple wants more photographs, they would have to pay an extra charge. This photographer requests that the original contract be completely paid in full when the preview album is delivered. This means that additional photos will be paid for after the wedding.

Another wedding photographer in the same community had a very different contract, offering three different packages:

Bourough Studios
1000 Spring Road
Anywhere, New York 10028

Phone: 555-0987   Fax: 555-6543

Silver

Our Silver package includes your choice of a custom-designed, Art Leather album, nine hundred dollars ($900.00) in finished photographs, selected from sizes 4" × 5" to 10" × 10"; or a flush-mount, library-bound Leather Craftsmen album with thirty-four (34) 8" × 10" photographs.

The Silver includes six hours of photographic coverage One hour of photographic time may be applied to a prewedding love-story photo session. An 11" × 14" photograph taken on your wedding day and one 24-print, custom-designed 4" × 5" Art Leather parent album is included in the Silver package for <u>$2,350.00</u>.

Gold

The Gold package includes your choice of a custom-designed, Art Leather album and twelve hundred fifty dollars ($1250.00) in finished photographs, selected from sizes 4" × 5" to 10" × 10"; or a custom-designed, flush-mount, library-bound Leather Craftsmen album with fifty-four (54) 8" × 10" photographs.

The Gold includes up to seven hours of photographic coverage. One hour of photographic time may be applied to a prewedding love-story photo session.

Also included in this package is one 11" × 14" photograph taken on your wedding day; two custom-designed 24-print 4" × 5" Art Leather parent albums, and two gift folios each containing two 5" × 7" prints for a total of $3,200.00.

Platinum

The Platinum package includes wedding coverage by two photographers. The second photographer will capture your special day in a black-and-white photojournalistic style. The first two volumes include 120 photographs, selected from sizes 4" × 5" to 10" × 10", and two panoramic two-page photographs. The third volume includes thirty (30) black-and-white photographs selected from the photojournalistic coverage.

The Platinum packages includes up to nine hours of photographic coverage. One hour of photographic time may be applied to a prewedding love-story photo session. Two 36-print, 5" × 7" library-bound Leather Craftsmen parent albums, and 10 gift folios each containing two 4" × 5" photographs are also included with the package.

In addition, the couple may select a formal studio or environmental engagement-portrait session or a formal studio or environmental bridal-portrait session. From this session you'll receive one 20" × 24" and two 11" × 14" portraits. You'll receive 100 wallet-size photographs to include with your thank-you notes.

The Platinum package is $8,000.00.

<u>Studio Policies and Information</u>:

$750.00 retainer required to reserve the wedding date. Balance of photography package selected is due 20 days prior to the wedding.

Upon return of the originals, any additional orders require a 75% payment at the time the order is placed. The final 25% balance is due upon completion of the order. No orders will be delivered until the final balance is paid in full.

Any photograph taken in color may be printed in black and white.

If table shots are requested, one 5" × 7" photograph of each table photographed *must* be purchased.

Additional time will be billed at $100 per hour or part of hour.

Originals are the property of the studio and must be returned within three weeks. Any other arrangements must be made prior to the originals leaving the studio.

It is ILLEGAL to copy or reproduce professional photographs without written permission. Violators of this Federal law will be subject to its civil and criminal penalties.

<u>Wedding Albums and Photographs</u>:

1 12" × 24" panoramic	$140
1 16" × 20"	$ 99
20 4" × 5" photos	$385
1 11" × 14"	$ 60
20 5" × 7"	$480
1 10" × 10"	$ 27
32 4" × 5"	$580
1 8" × 10"	$ 26
32 5" × 7"	$725
1 8" × 8"	$ 23
32 8" × 10"	$915
1 5" × 7"	$ 19
20 8" × 8"/6" × 8"	$550
1 5" × 5"	$15 add.

1 4" × 5"/5" × 7" pages	$ 6
1 4" × 5"	$ 14 add.
1 8" × 8"/8" × 10" pages	$ 8
1 set of 8 wallet size	$ 25
Originals/proofs	$ 11

Library Bound Parents Albums:

20 Gift Folios 5" × 7"	$545.00
Duo 4" × 5"	$ 35.95
32 5" × 7"	$760.00
Trio—4" × 5"	$ 53.95
32 8" × 10"	$985.00
Trio—5" × 7"	$ 65.95
add 5" × 7" pages	$ 6.00
Collection of 8: 4" × 5"	$129.95
add 8" × 10" pages	$ 9.00
1 Deluxe 8" × 10", 4 4" × 5"	$103.95

Johnson Photography's package sounds great—a full day of coverage, two photographers. How could you beat it! Well, if you use Johnson's price list and select everything offered in Bourough Studio's Gold package you'll actually spend $3,926.00, or $726.00 more than Bourough's Gold package. The point is, before you decide which is least expensive, you need to know what kind of a shopper you are. Will you want copies of everything or will you be happy with 20 photographs in an album? If you think you'll eventually purchase a lot of photographs, you may want to reconsider who is the least expensive for you! One more thing—generally parents' albums are paid for by each set of parents, so you may not actually be paying the whole bill.

Wedding Blues

If your professional photographer allows your friends and family to take pictures during the wedding, ask them to wait until after the photographer has taken the posed picture before snapping their own shots. You really don't want Uncle Bob stepping in front of the photographer to take his own picture first. Let the photographer do the job he or she is being paid to do.

Sue's Suggestions

Most photographers' contracts have a clause stating that the photographer is the only one who can photograph the wedding. If you have a family member or friend who loves to bring a camera and snap away, be sure to discuss this with the photographer ahead of time. If the photographer will not agree to your friend or relative taking pictures, consider hiring a different photographer.

Sue's Suggestions

If you really want a wedding album, but you just don't have time to put one together, ask a friend to do it for you. Purchase all the film yourself and recruit friends to take pictures at your wedding. After you get the film developed, take them to your friend so she can assemble your album for you.

While you'll want to be wary of photographers who offer a low-priced package and then charge you large additional fees for everything extra, there's really nothing wrong with a wedding photography packages in general, so long as you understand what you're paying for and what you'll be getting. Be sure to ask, for instance, how many proofs you will see and who selects the images that appear in your album? Sometimes the photographer puts together the album in a size that you've requested at the time you signed your contract, and you won't see the proofs at all. Sometimes you'll receive all the proofs and you'll select the photographs for your album yourself. Personally, I prefer the latter—this is your wedding and the photographs will be of your family. The photographer may have no idea who is important to you, so there may be no pictures of your favorite aunt in your album unless you have the opportunity to select a photograph that may have her in the background.

Assistants Are Very Important

When you're interviewing photographers be sure to ask if the photographer brings an assistant and, if so, exactly what the assistant's responsibilities are. Generally, an assistant helps to carry the photographer's equipment. This could be additional cameras, tripods, backdrops, extra batteries, and film. Having help transporting all that equipment in and out of the church or synagogue and on to the reception site makes a lot of sense. In addition, because the photographer will be using a minimum of two cameras, the assistant can be reloading one camera while the photographer is using the other. This makes the amount of time the bride and groom have to stand still go so much more quickly. The assistant can be using the light meter and reporting the measurements so the photographer can spend the time behind the camera. The assistant also directs the auxiliary flash for the photographer when additional light is needed for a specific shot.

> **Tantalizing Trivia**
>
> One photographer arrived at a wedding with only one camera. He photographed the entire ceremony and three hours of the reception without noticing that his camera was malfunctioning. When the film returned from the lab he was mortified to learn that he didn't have a single picture of the wedding! That's why photographers carry two cameras—if one's not working, they may lose some pictures, but not the entire wedding. As the consumer, you should certainly ask your photographer how he or she avoids similar problems and how he or she protects you from losing your wedding memories.

Very often, the photographer's assistant is a novice photographer who may photograph some of your reception. If so, you'll have two cameras covering the action instead of one. You certainly have a right to ask to see the assistant's work before your wedding; but don't be too concerned. The assistant will probably be taking candid action shots, not formal, posed shots for which lighting and angles are critical.

Avoiding "Bait and Switch"

Some photography studios employ several photographers. Some of these photographers may have earned a very favorable reputation in your community, and you may want one of them for your wedding. When you're in the studio looking at the albums on display, be sure to ask who photographed the ones you particularly like, and write that person's name on your contract. If the contract reads that XYZ Studio is responsible for the photographs, you'll have no way of knowing *who* will actually be in sent to your wedding. While it saddens me to think this could ever be done on purpose, I'm know there are studios that are purposely vague about who will be photographing your wedding. Some studios even lead you to believe a certain photographer will photograph your wedding, when, in fact, that photographer is already booked for another event. You'll want to make sure your contract states the name of the photographer you're expecting—the one whose work you've seen, and whom you've met. This should be all the protection you need to have the photographer you desire. Photographers, like bands, can work only one wedding at a time, so you'll want to research and hire your photographer as soon as possible after you confirm your date.

The Least You Need to Know

➤ Everyone who owns a camera is not a wedding photographer.

➤ When reading the contracts of two photographers you liked, you may be surprised to learn that the one you thought was the least expensive really is not.

➤ Be sure your photographer brings an assistant to your wedding. It will make the photographer's job easier and your posing time shorter!

➤ When dealing with a large studio, find out exactly *who* will photograph your wedding and make sure that person's name is on your contract.

Chapter 18

Flowers, Linens, Decorations, and Themes

In This Chapter

➤ Finding the perfect florist for your wedding

➤ Understanding a florist's contract

➤ Is that flower in season?

➤ Aren't silk flowers a great idea?

➤ Decorating with balloons

➤ Do you want to keep your bouquet?

In some communities, no matter what decorations you decide on—fresh flowers, silk flowers, candles, or balloons—you will be working with a florist. In other communities, you will be working with an event decorator if you want decorations other than flowers. In either case, you need to hire a person or company who can create the decorations, deliver and install them, and then return to the facility and remove them at the end of your event. Whatever your decision, this chapter should help you find the perfect provider for your needs.

Selecting a Florist

Flowers have been a part of weddings almost from the beginning of time, but selecting a florist is as difficult today as it ever was. One good place to begin is your reception facility. Ask the banquet manager to recommend florists who have worked there successfully in the past. It's very helpful if the florist is familiar with the facility and knows what works well there. Sometimes the florist will be able to show you photographs of the way he or she has decorated the room for other brides, which will certainly give you ideas. Then the florist can suggest floral arrangements or decorations that he or she knows will meet your needs.

Tantalizing Trivia

Flowers, herbs, and wheat were once strewn along the bride's path to link her progress with the symbolic blessings of nature. This is still observed when a flower girl tosses rose petals in front the bride's path as she walks down the aisle. Traditionally, the bride walks on a floor strewn with flower petals to guarantee a smooth and joyous path in life. Nature is brought into the ceremony in the bouquets and boutonnieres of the wedding party and by floral decorations at the ceremony and reception sites.

Sue's Suggestions

Be prepared for your first meeting with a florist. List all the members of your bridal party—bridesmaids, groomsmen, and all the relatives who will need corsages or boutonnieres. Bring a swatch of fabric from your bridesmaids' dresses, along with a picture of your dress and one of the bridesmaids'. This will help the florist prepare an appropriate proposal for you from the very beginning.

Most communities offer many choices in florists. One choice is a retail florist shop that specializes in weddings. This means that the shop employs designers and others who can assemble centerpieces, bouquets, and corsages and deliver them to the church and reception site. To give you ideas, the florist will often show you picture albums of arrangements and bouquets the designers have created for other brides. If you're meeting with the designer affiliated with a retail shop, ask about staffing. Does the shop have enough people to deal with walk-in business on a weekend and still get your wedding flowers delivered in a timely manner? Does the shop have enough staff to decorate your reception hall if more than drop-off service is required?

Another choice is a floral designer who is not affiliated with a retail floral shop, but runs a floral design studio. This type of designer has staff who can create whatever you need—from bouquets and flower arrangements to scenery, to custom-designed backdrops for the band area, to archways for your guests to enter through. This type of designer has arrangements with floral suppliers all over the world and will design the wedding especially for you, taking into consideration your likes and dislikes and all your dreams. This designer's staff has no responsibility for walk-in business, so they concentrate totally on your event and on making it perfect. Like the retail floral shop, this designer owns his or her own delivery trucks and refrigeration units, so flowers arrive fresh and beautiful at the wedding.

Often communities also have independent florists who work out of their own homes. Perhaps they teach floral arranging at a local adult education facility and are willing to accept the responsibility for your wedding on the weekend. They'll probably own their own refrigeration units, so your flowers will arrive in the best possible condition. They may not own their own trucks, and their staff may be independent contractors, instead of permanent employees. Floral designers frequently employ a full-time staff of artists and designers and submit bids to decorate corporate events, fund-raising events, and other year-round events during the week, in addition to decorating weddings on the weekend. In some cases, independent florists limit their work to weekend social events so, while the independent florist may work full time, meeting with clients, looking at facilities, and researching flowers for an event, the staff may only work on the weekends.

Sue's Suggestions

The size of a bouquet should be in proportion to the height and dress style of the person carrying it. If your bridesmaids are of radically different sizes, choose a bouquet for the smallest and add different lengths of ribbons to balance the larger girls. No one should be overwhelmed by the bouquet.

Unfortunately, we can't make a blanket statement that independent florists are the least expensive, and retail shops and designer services the most expensive. In each situation the retail florist may be more or less expensive than the design service, and both may be more or less costly than the independent florist. Everything depends on the bride's needs and wishes.

For this reason, it makes particularly good sense to come up with a plan for your wedding and present the same plan to each florist you interview. If you tell one person that flowers are not really important to you—all you need are bouquets for the bridesmaids and you, and a few bud vases for the reception—and tell the next person that you want to feel like you're walking into an indoor garden, their quotes will be very different, and you won't have any idea which is the more reasonable! So clip out some pictures from magazines, and try to discuss the same sorts of things with each florist. Naturally, each person you interview will make suggestions, many of which you'll like and want to incorporate into your plan, but try to hold those ideas for later—after you've received the other florists' proposals and can compare them to one another. Otherwise you're confusing the issue.

In all cases, florists are artists, and this sometimes means they may not be great at paperwork, so you might have to wait a little longer to receive their written proposals. Don't get frustrated, they're trying to put a look into words in such a way that you'll be able to see their creations simply by reading the words on the page. This is not as easy as just typing out a list of flowers, sizes, and prices. Every wedding has its own proposal because it has its own look. They can't just say, "six centerpieces at $65 each." They need to describe the centerpieces and the bases so you get the picture in your mind's eye.

A Sample Designer's Contract

Here is a floral proposal that will give you a good idea of the kinds of things you can expect to see.

Floral Proposal prepared for Barbara Bride and Greg Groom

by

Eventscapes Ltd.
1234 Main Street
Atlanta, Georgia 56788

Phone 404-555-5678   Fax 404-555-9012

Event: Wedding and Reception
Date: Saturday, June 19, 1999
Photos: Start time to be determined
Time: Ceremony at 5:00 P.M.
Location: Ceremony   Cathedral of the King
           Reception   Grand Hyatt, Atlanta

The Personal Flowers

The bride's bouquet will be a perfect compliment to her sparkling personality and sophisticated gown as we gather several varieties of roses, all in a vibrant citrus-inspired hue. The roses will vary from buds to full blooms. Joining the rich coral, orange, fuchsia, and yellow will be blooms of fragrant white freesia for a refreshing floral aroma. Touches of the "good luck" wedding flower, stephanotis, will add a touch of tradition. The flowers will be the focus of the tight design because no greenery will be showing as per your request. The stems will be tightly wrapped in sheer ivory ribbon and tied with a streamerless bow.

The groom's boutonniere will be rich yellow freesia and stephanotis to complement his bride's bouquet.

The five bridesmaids will each be presented with a bouquet that will both complement their gowns and resemble the bride's bouquet. Fresh blue hydrangea will make up most of the bouquet, which will be accented with vibrant coral roses and deep purple lisianthus. These will be full bouquets, presented in traditional bouquet holders to provide a water source for the delicate hydrangea. Just like the bride's bouquet, there will be no greenery showing. The maid of honor's bouquet will be slightly different, with a cluster of coral roses at the center, accented at the edges with fresh blue hydrangea.

The groomsmen and the two fathers will wear an orange freesia blossom combined with yellow solidago, backed by a large flat-leaf eucalyptus for a unique presentation that will be striking against their tuxedo lapels.

The mothers and grandmothers have decided against corsages.

The Ceremony Decorations

The sanctuary will be decorated with the same flowers the bridal party is carrying. When guests arrive they'll immediately notice the hand-painted aisle runner decorated with flowers and ribbons. The aisle decorations will be high enough so that no guest will have his or her line of vision impeded by the full bouquets of summer greenery accented with coral and yellow roses and tiered candles that add romantic soft lighting to the already beautiful sanctuary.

On each side of the stairway to the altar will be similar bouquets of summer greenery and coral and yellow roses. These bouquets will not have candles in them, since the permanent altar greenery will be enhanced with dozens of votive candles of varying heights to add a soft glow.

The Reception Decorations

Each dinner table will be covered with heavy ivory damask to the floor. Each cloth has a one-inch welting at the edge to keep it flowing around the table. The chairs will be covered with matching ivory damask chair covers.

The tables will be centered with a silver obelisk to add dramatic height and creative interest as it rises approximately 46 inches from the tabletop. This obelisk is divided into three sections. The top will feature a fresh floral fantasy; again the flowers will be in the citrus-inspired hues but with white tuberoses added for fullness, volume, and wonderful summer fragrance. Ethereal white organza ribbon streamers will come from the flowers to lead the eye to the second level where four votive candles will add the magic and romantic flicker of lush candlelight. The third perch of the stand will feature a design of fresh ivy vines, colorful filler flowers, and sugared fruit enhancements such as lemons and limes. This bottom presentation will be full, but tight, so as not to obscure the conversation line between the guests around the table. On the table will be four more votive candles presented in hollowed-out pomegranates for an unexpected aromatic treat!

The cake table will also be covered with the ivory damask linen topped with a white sheer organza over cloth crumpled and dotted with fresh rose petals. The cake will be surrounded by the bridesmaids' bouquets. A pin light will illuminate the cake table to make it a focal point in the room. There will also be a simple hand-tied bouquet, reminiscent of the bridal bouquet, for the bride to toss later in the evening.

The barren wall behind the bandstand will be covered with a backdrop of ivory brocade topped with an ethereal layer of ivory chiffon. The backdrop will be up-lit for more elegance. The top of the backdrop will be decorated with bouquets of hydrangeas and greenery to create an effective focal point complementing the entire wedding. The backdrop will hide the service doors and exit sign on that wall.

At the end of the night, we will return to strike this beautiful setting and rewater the flowers which we will deliver to Scottish Rite Children's Hospital to be enjoyed for the coming days!

Summary

The Personal Flowers

Bride's bouquet	$150.00
Groom's boutonniere	8.00
5 Bridesmaids' bouquets @ $50 each	250.00
2 Fathers' boutonnieres @ $7 each	14.00
7 Groomsmen's boutonnieres @ 6.50 each	45.50
TOTAL of personal flowers	$467.50

The Ceremony Decorations

Aisle pedestals topped with bouquets	$400.00
Hand-painted aisle runner	150.00
Candles for altar planters	100.00
TOTAL of ceremony decorations	$650.00

The Reception Decorations

22 Table presentations @ $95 each	$2,090.00
Backdrop behind bandstand	200.00
23 Tablecloths @ $12 each	276.00
220 Chair covers @ $6 each	1,320.00
TOTAL for reception decorations	$3,886.00
TOTAL of all decorations	$5,003.50
Set up / breakdown	704.02
Sales tax	460.00
GRAND TOTAL	$6,167.52

We will require a signed contract and a 50% deposit of the total contract amount to guarantee the decorations listed here for the noted date. The balance will be due and payable no later than noon on the Friday before the event.

Pricing will be guaranteed on contracts signed by April 15, 1999. We also require that the product order count not decrease after June 4, 1999, approximately two weeks before the event.

All linens and chair covers described are rental items only. We will come back at the end of the event at the agreed-upon time to collect these linens and chair covers. In the event of damage beyond reasonable repair or if any of the linen is missing through theft or loss, the responsibility for monetary compensation or replacement will be on the client.

The descriptions of flowers above are subject to availability. If substitutions need to be made, only the best quality of flowers would be used, keeping your look intact.

Important Planning Calendar Dates

April 15, 1999	Suggested Last Date to Contract
Upon Contracting	50% Payment Due
June 4, 1999	Minimum Order Guarantee
June 18, 1999	Final Payment Due

Thank you for considering Eventscapes, Ltd.

As you can see from reading through this proposal/contract, the staff at Eventscapes, Ltd. spent considerable time thinking about what the bride told them about her likes and dislikes. The bride obviously likes color and wanted something different for her large, formal wedding. This proposal is written in such a way that most people would be able to imagine many of the elements that are described here.

What Is a Seasonal Flower?

There was a time when ordering flowers out of season meant you were adding unnecessary dollars to your floral contract. While that's still true of some flowers in some locations, it's not true everywhere. Today many flowers are in-season at some place in the world all year round, and, since most wedding florists fly flowers in anyway, this has become less

Wedding Blues

It's considered very bad form for a bride to allow any other florist to see another florist's proposal for the purpose of bidding this event. Florist #2 should *always* be able to duplicate florist #1's proposal for less money, because he or she didn't need to invest any time in creating it or researching the price of the blossoms listed.

of an issue. Florist seldom purchase flowers for a wedding at the local floral market, so selecting flowers that are in-season in your community is not much of an issue. Since many brides don't know which flowers are in-season, this chart might help you know which flowers, in which colors, are available in which season.

Beautiful Flowers All Year Round

Spring

Anemones	White, blue, red/violet, yellow
Calla lilies	White with yellow center
Carnations	Available in many colors
Daffodils	Available in many colors
Day Lilies	Cream, orange, red, yellow
Delphinium	White, rose, lavender, blue
Forget-me-nots	Blue with yellow or white center
Gardenias	White, very dark green leaves
Iris	White, blue, violet, yellow, orange
Lilacs	White or lavender
Lilies of the Valley	White
Violets	White, blue, purple

Summer

Anemones	White, blue, red/violet, yellow
Asters	White, pink, rose, purple
Bachelor Buttons	White, pink, blue
Canterbury bells	Blue, purple, pink
Chrysanthemums	White, yellow, red
Daisy	White, yellow
Day Lilies	Cream, orange, red, yellow
Delphiniums	White, rose, lavender, blue
Iris	White, blue, violet, yellow, orange
Roses	Available in many colors
Stephanotis	White
Straw Flowers	White, yellow, orange, red
Zephyr Lilies	White, yellow, shades of pink

Fall

Anemones	White, blue, red/violet, yellow
Calla Lilies	White with yellow center
Chrysanthemums	White, yellow, red
Daisies	White or yellow
Day Lilies	Cream, orange, red, yellow
Delphiniums	White, rose, lavender, blue
Zephyr Lilies	White, yellow, shades of pink

Winter

Chrysanthemums	White, yellow, red
Spray Orchids	Sprays of white, some purple

Many flowers are available year round through florists, including baby's breath, carnations, orchids, and roses. Of course, this is only a partial list of wedding flowers. There are many more varieties that work well. Let your florist guide you.

Silk Versus Fresh Flowers

Some brides think they'll spend less money on their flowers if they used silk bouquets instead of fresh-flower bouquets. In fact it's the other way around—silk flowers are usually slightly more expensive than fresh flowers. But there are some advantages to working with silk flowers that could make them a good choice.

If a bride or her mother enjoys flower arranging and would like to tackle arranging their own flowers, silk flowers really are the way to go. Well before the wedding weekend they could visit both the ceremony and reception sites and determine what arrangements and bouquets will be needed. It might even be helpful to diagram each facility and number the locations of each arrangement. Over the next several weeks and months they can make the arrangements for those specific locations, and number the arrangements to match the number on the diagram. Knowing in advance exactly where an arrangement will be used will allow them to create arrangements to fit a specific alcove or shelf. For example, the arrangement for the buffet table could be created to be viewed from all angles (people will be walking around the buffet table), while arrangements for the altar will be viewed only from the front. The diagrams and the numbered arrangements will prove to be a terrific time saver on the wedding day when everyone's so busy. As the car is unloaded, the numbers on the arrangements will

Sue's Suggestions

Go to the library and look through magazines or books to get ideas for arrangements you might want to use at your wedding. The florist will have pictures to show you as well.

indicate exactly where they're to be placed. If an arrangement from the ceremony is to be used again at the reception, another friend can move it and get it into the correct place simply by checking it's number and referencing the diagram.

Using a silk bridal bouquet makes it possible for the bride to have her portrait sitting well in advance of the wedding and still have the same bouquet on her wedding day. Typically photographers often use silk bouquets for these sittings, but then the portrait displayed at the reception looks different if the bride carried fresh flowers on her wedding day. By using your own silk bouquet for your sitting and the wedding, your portrait will look just like you did on your wedding day.

Sue's Suggestions

Unlike fresh flower arrangements, silk flower arrangements are easy to move from one location to another. Since there's no water in the containers, they can be transported in the trunk or back seat of a passenger vehicle if necessary.

Silk bridesmaids' bouquets make wonderful, lasting gifts for your bridesmaids. They can be used just as they are and inserted into a vase to complement any room decor, or rearranged to fit a special spot in the attendants' homes. Wherever they're used, the bouquets will serve as a constant reminder of your special day and special friendship.

Of course, fresh flowers have their advantages as well. They add a look of luxury to a wedding celebration and an aura of freshness. Depending on the flowers selected, they can add a wonderful fragrance to the event. In addition, fresh flowers have a natural, sometimes even imperfect, look that adds charm to a wedding. Silk flowers are sometimes so perfect they appear stiff, and this can show in photographs. Some people like that look, others do not.

Balloons as Decorations

Versatile, colorful, and festive balloons can transform your wedding reception and help you save money on decorations. Today it's possible to mix balloons and flowers, and many florists can supply balloons for your reception. If your particular florist does not offer balloons, he or she will certainly be able to recommend a balloon artist to you, someone that the florist has worked with in the past. To display for you the magical difference balloons can make, balloon artists often show before and after pictures of the rooms they've decorated.

Wedding Blues

It takes time to fill balloons with helium and work them into floral arrangements or arches for your reception. If you plan to do this yourself, be sure to enlist lots of help and allow plenty of time!

You may decide to have a high/low look on your tables—the low tables decorated with flowers and the high tables decorated with balloons tied with colorful ribbons coming out of a low floral arrangement or anchored in some other appropriate way. The guests could enter the reception by walking under a balloon arch decorated with tiny twinkle lights. The dance floor can be decorated with balloons, and there can be another balloon arch over the disc jockey. If your wedding will be held in a tent, balloons can decorate the tent poles and cover the ceiling of the tent, adding color to the inside. Instead of petals or bubbles, balloons can shower the couple as they leave their reception.

Another wonderful send-off is to have a balloon release as the couple leaves the church. If you decide to do this, helium-filled balloons should be delivered to the church and stored inside the front entrance. The bride and groom will step aside after coming up the aisle and let their bridal party hand each departing guest a balloon as they come up the aisle. The guests would then form double lines leading from the church to the limousine. When everyone's outside the church, the bride and groom will run through the lines and guests will release their balloons as the couple passes, creating a sky full of colorful balloons and no cleanup at the church!

Preserving Your Bouquet

The decision about preserving your bridal bouquet probably should be made early in your wedding planning since there are several methods of preservation available. Some flowers are better dried, while others work better in a pressed bouquet; so if you particularly want your bouquet preserved in one way or another, you should take that into consideration when choosing your bouquet.

There are several methods of preserving your wedding bouquet you can try yourself. You can air dry the flowers on a shelf for four to six weeks until they're completely dried, and then put them under a plastic or glass display dome. Some flowers, such as daisies and Queen Anne's lace, can be pressed and used to decorate your wedding album or framed with your wedding invitation. If your bouquet contains ivy, the ivy can be rooted and will continue to grow in your new home.

It's also possible to find professionals in your community who will dry your bouquet and put it into a framed shadow box, or press the flowers into a picture frame. It's important to understand that most flowers darken when they're either dried or pressed, so be prepared for them to look somewhat different from what they looked like fresh. Occasionally the artist will paint the pressed blossoms to bring them back to their original color. If you've decided to have a local professional preserve your

Sue's Suggestions

If your reception is held at a facility that employs a full-time staff (a hotel, reception site, wedding hall), you may be able to arrange to have your bouquet refrigerated and picked up the day after the wedding by either the local floral preserver or an overnight shipper. Refrigeration tends to keep flowers fresher and make them easier to work with.

bouquet, make your arrangements before the wedding and be sure to get the bouquet to the professional as soon after the wedding as possible. Most people who preserve bouquets will tell you that the sooner they can get started with your flowers, the better their results will be.

If you plan ahead, you can find a few companies in the country that preserve flowers and will send you treated boxes in which to pack your bouquet and then ship it back to them the day after the wedding. Two such companies who do wonderful work are: The Flower Press in San Antonio, Texas (1-800-771-7560) and Keepsake Floral in Orlando, Florida (1-800-616-5337). But you'll probably find several others listed in the back of the national bridal magazines. If you contact these companies before your wedding day, they'll send you brochures listing your floral preservation options and price lists.

Sue's Suggestions

If you plan to dry your flowers yourself, do not put them in the refrigerator. The cold will simply delay the drying process and may cause the flowers to mildew before they can be completely dried.

The Least You Need to Know

➤ Professional florists may work out of retail shops, design studios, or from their own homes.

➤ Today most wedding florists have the flowers for weddings flown in, so selecting flowers that are in-season is less of an issue.

➤ Silk flowers are not always less expensive than fresh flowers.

➤ Balloons will add height to your centerpieces and are a great way to decorate large reception halls.

➤ Make arrangements to preserve your bridal bouquet well before the wedding so the flowers will be freshest when the preservation begins and you'll get the best result.

"Moving" Memories of the Wedding Day

When video cameras were first introduced to the general public for home use less than 20 years ago, they were large, heavy, and cumbersome—too impractical for the average person to lug around a wedding reception. Besides, how could anyone be sure a power source would be available? What's more, the batteries for these cameras were big, heavy, and didn't last particularly long.

A lot has changed since those days! Video cameras are much smaller now, their batteries last much longer, and we're all quite comfortable popping a tape into our VCRs. In fact, most of us who still own movies filmed by those old cameras would love to convert them to videotape, so we could watch them without setting up that bothersome movie projector and screen. The improved, easy use of today's video recorders has created a whole new wedding professional and a new reason for brides to be informed.

Selecting a Professional Videographer

Start with your friends who've been recently married, and ask to see their video-tapes—all the way through! This can be a chore in itself, since wedding videos are only slightly more interesting than vacation films, and usually much longer! Pay close attention to the way the video is edited. Did the videographer remove things that don't need to be there? Does the camera stay focused on one place during the ceremony, or does it zoom in on the bride's face when she's speaking and the groom's when he takes his vows? How is the lighting? Can you see the bridesmaids coming down the aisle? If you're reasonably pleased with the videos, ask your friends if they would do anything different if they hired the same videographer today. This will get them thinking about whatever problems they may have had; if they share them with you, you'll be able to avoid those same problems.

Next, speak to your photographer. Photographers and videographers work together all the time, and some get along better than others. It's true throughout the wedding industry that each vendor believes that whatever he or she is providing is the most important service. We all wear blinders and each of us is convinced that, without our work, your wedding will be a complete failure! In fact, as you've probably discovered by this time, a wedding is a team effort. (That's why bridal consultants like to think of themselves as team builders, pulling everyone's needs together so the bride and groom's wishes are fulfilled.) Some videographers are more sensitive to the needs of the photographer and will stay out of the way. In the same way, some photographers will work around the videographer. So ask your photographer whom he or she partic-ularly likes to work with, and then review that videographer's tapes. If you're considering hiring a specific videographer, it's a good idea to call your photographer and discuss your choice. If the photographer tells you they don't work well together, you may want to reconsider your selection, or bring them both together to see if you can help them work out their differences.

Most brides want wonderful still pictures and believe that they are more likely to look at their wedding albums or show them to friends than to look at their videos. In an ideal situation, the photographer and videographer will work as a team; the videographer will be respectful of the photographer's work and not flood the scene with light, and the photographer will give the videographer a chance to capture the action as needed.

Another place to look for a videographer is at local bridal shows or fairs in your community. In most places these shows are scheduled in January, February, and March; but recently shows are being held in late

Sue's Suggestions

Some photographers employ video-graphers in their studios, and both professionals work together quite well. You may want to interview these videographers in addition to the others that you discover. You need not feel obligated to hire a videographer from the photogra-pher's company, however. You have the right to hire the most talented professional you can afford in every position.

summer for those brides and grooms who are planning winter weddings. Usually videographers bring monitors to the show to advertise their work. The problem is, you can't really tell much from their display tapes, because they splice together a collection of their favorite scenes from several different weddings, so you never get to see one whole wedding from beginning to end. That's the only way that you can get a real measure of the videographer's talent.

Tantalizing Trivia

I remember one videographer who came to me, asking me to send him business. I asked to see one whole wedding that he had shot and edited. I was shocked to see that he had cut off all the heads of the bridal party as they came down the aisle. I asked him about that, and he explained that the minister allowed only an unmanned camera on the altar during the ceremony. The videographer had to guess how tall the bridal party was, because he couldn't adjust the camera once the ceremony began. Why did he bring me this tape? It was the *only* wedding he had ever videotaped! Needless to say, I do not send my brides to him.

Ceremony and reception-site coordinators can be another valuable source of referrals to videographers. Often they get to know the videographers when they discuss site rules with them, and they'll know who are the easiest ones to work with. There's also something to be said for hiring a videographer who is familiar with the facility that you're using. He or she knows where the loading dock and the electrical outlets are located. This makes your day run more smoothly, because they won't be constantly looking for things.

You'll find videographers advertising in your local bridal magazines and you may even find some local videographers advertising in the national magazines. (See Appendix B, "Looking for More Information?" for a list of the national bridal magazines.) If you call any of these professionals, be sure you ask for references and be

Wedding Blues

Extra charges on videos often include editing, titles, voice-over (narration), and interviews. Be sure to ask if there are any additional fees when you read the initial contract so you're not caught by surprise.

diligent enough to speak to those references, as well as preview the tapes the videographers send you. It will always benefit you to know what former clients think of this professional *after* working with him or her.

Now that you know where to get names of videographers, what do you ask them once you get an appointment? Here are some questions you'll want to ask each videographer:

➤ What kind of equipment and recording tapes does the videographer use? Are they high quality?

➤ How old is his equipment? If it's three or more years old, ask if the videographer has plans to upgrade the equipment between now and your wedding? If so, what will change?

➤ Does the videographer own his or her own editing and dubbing machinery? If not, how are the tapes edited and what effect will this have on the date you'll receive your completed tape?

Sue's Suggestions

If the videographer you hire has never worked in your ceremony or reception location before, plan to meet him or her at the site prior to the wedding. Find out where the cameras will be placed and what obstacles may be encountered. There should not be a charge for this meeting, but be sure to ask when you schedule it. Budgets don't take kindly to surprises!

➤ How many cameras are typically used to shoot a wedding? Are all the cameras manned?

➤ Does the videographer use a wireless microphone to capture the best possible audio?

➤ How is the tape edited—in the camera or at the studio later?

➤ What is the charge for the videographer's services? Is this a flat fee or an hourly charge? Does it include the ceremony and reception? Are editing, titles, music, and the addition of still pictures included in the price?

➤ Is there a charge for additional tapes? If so, what is that charge?

➤ Is there an additional charge for mileage between the ceremony and reception sites?

➤ Are there any other additional charges? If so, what are they and how much do they typically run?

➤ Will the videographer be carrying backup equipment or extra batteries in case there's a power failure or other problem?

➤ Will the videographer need any special electrical outlets?

➤ Is the videographer familiar with your ceremony and reception sites? Has he or she ever worked in these locations before?

➤ Does the videographer have copies of any tapes he or she might have shot in your ceremony or reception locations?

In addition, ask to see a video shot by the videographer who will actually be attending your wedding. Sometimes large video companies employ more than one videographer, and you'll want to be sure you see the work of the person who will be taping your wedding. Ask for a contract detailing the exact type of video coverage that you're expecting. This should include the number of cameras, amount and type of editing, name of the camera persons, the date, time, and location of the wedding and reception, and the attire they're expected to wear.

Okay, you've got a list of questions, and that will help you. But in order to be truly helpful, you'll need to know what the answers to those questions mean and what the choices are. That's what I'll give you in this chapter, so read on!

Sue's Suggestions

You may want to ask your videographer if he or she has ever experienced an equipment failure on a job and what he or she did about it. If you're very concerned, ask the videographer to bring an additional camera, just in case the first one doesn't work properly.

What Makes a Good Videotape?

Lighting is a big part of videography, and if you decide to hire a videographer, he or she will need enough light to do the job you're paying for. If you've decided on an evening, totally candlelit ceremony, you might as well save your money and hire a videographer for the reception only. It will be impossible for a videographer to capture the bridesmaids coming down the aisle using only candlelight. Generally, if the videographer is allowed to stand at the altar, we ask him or her to be in place when the first guest arrives at the wedding. If the videographer is dressed in a tuxedo, the guests' eyes will eventually see someone standing there, but by the time the ceremony begins, they won't even notice. If lighting at the altar is necessary, we ask it be lit when the videographer takes his or her position—again, so the guests get used to seeing the setting exactly as it will be for the ceremony. If the videographer turns on the lights when the processional begins, everyone will notice the change and the videographer will become quite obvious.

In a Jewish wedding, the videographer can easily hide behind one of the rear chuppah poles and shine a light up into the top of the chuppah, and no one will notice it at all. Most officiants will allow the videographer to stand at the altar if he or she doesn't move around, which would distract from the solemnity of the service. If the videographer stands very still, focusing the camera down the aisle to capture the bridal party during the processional, and then moves the lens only about an inch to capture the faces of the couple during the ceremony, none of the guests will notice this movement. Naturally, the videographer may not speak during the service! He or she may be wearing a head set, and can be spoken to, either by someone behind the scene who might be editing, or by the other camera person at the back of the church—but the videographer cannot respond.

When you're meeting with a videographer, pay particular attention to his or her equipment. It needs to be up to date and in good condition. Cameras get moved around a lot, and there's a potential for damage if the equipment is not handled with care. These are the tools of the trade and if the videographer doesn't take good care of them, it says something about how he or she does business. Ask to see the editing equipment and dubbing machine. If the videographer's serious about the profession, he or she will not only have this equipment, but will be very anxious to show it off. If the videographer doesn't have this equipment, ask how the editing and *dubbing* are done—it's possible the videographer shares equipment with someone else. If this is the case, be sure to ask how soon after the wedding you can expect to receive your edited tape. It takes a while to complete this, even when the videographer owns the machinery and works on it full time. Sharing the equipment with another videographer will definitely impact the delivery time of your finished video.

Language of Love

Dubbing is adding music or narration to your videotape after it is completed.

Sue's Suggestions

Pay attention to the editing techniques. Is the videotape smooth as it moves from one scene to another? Are you distracted by the scene changes? If so, it may be the equipment used or the skill of the videographer. Try to find out before you hire anyone!

Experienced videographers look for spontaneous and natural reactions while still maintaining a formal approach to the ceremony. You should be able to see this in the finished tapes that you're watching. If things look stiff and perhaps staged, it might be that the people were stiff, or it might be that the videographer didn't capture the natural moments at the wedding.

A good wedding video tells a story. Some videographers start wedding videos with pictures of the bride and groom growing up and dating. Then they lead into the wedding day showing the bride dressing, the groom pacing, and the photographer capturing the before-the-wedding pictures. When you watch such a video you feel transported back in time to that magical day.

One of the most important parts of the video is the smoothness with which the videographer moved the camera to capture the event. This is definitely a learned skill, and not an easy one. Remember, the first time you used a video camera, how choppy the tape looked? It seemed like everyone was running around like a Keystone Cop. That's because you didn't know how to move your body. The videographer has learned to move the camera very slowly, so the subject moves at a normal pace. There should be good, natural color, clear sound, and a sharp picture.

You'll also want to notice how the image fills the screen. Are things cut off, or is everything there that should be? This may not be as big an issue in an action shot. For instance, if the videographer is filming the couple during their first dance, some of the guests who are standing around them will be cut off the screen as they move—but this is to be expected and is certainly not an indication that the videographer is not talented.

How Will the Tape Be Edited?

There are several methods of editing a videotape of an event. One method is to *edit* the tape in the camera while the event is taking place. The videographer just turns off the camera while something uninteresting is happening, or he rewinds the tape and films over the unwanted footage. While this method is the quickest—there's very little *post-production editing* required—it's also the least forgiving. Once something has been erased or shot over, there's no way to retrieve it. So if the videographer considers something uninteresting, he might record over it without you even knowing. If you know there will be ceremonies or toasts that will be meaningful to you, be sure to tell your videographer in advance to capture them on tape in their entirety. Then you can have them edited after the wedding when you've had a chance to preview the tape. You'll probably pay an additional fee for this service, but it will be worth it in the end.

Another method is to edit the tapes after the event. The videographer will review the tape (or tapes, if two or three cameras were used on the event) and edit together the most interesting sequences to tell the story of your wedding. These videographers will be able to add baby pictures, your wedding invitation, special effects, titles, and even special music while working in their studios. The finished video, which will take some time to produce, will have the same high-quality look you see on television.

A few videographers use a combination of these two methods of editing. They hire an extra person to sit behind the scenes to view a screen that shows what every camera in use is seeing. This person acts as a director, speaking into the headset worn by each videographer and giving them directions.

Language of Love

Editing can be done during the event, which is known as "in-camera editing," where the videographer either turns off the camera or films over a sequence he does not want to show. **Post-production editing** is editing done after the event when the videographer trims the scenes, adds music or narration, inserts graphics or titles, or adds special effects.

Wedding Blues

Some churches hire their own videographers to videotape your wedding, and you're obligated to use their services. Be sure you know that before you interview a videographer for your wedding day. You should be able to hire a videographer to record the prewedding activities and the reception for less money, especially if you tell the videographer about your restrictions up front.

For instance, the director might tell camera one to zoom in on the tear coming out of the bride's left eye during the ceremony, then tell camera two to pull back for a long shot of the whole altar, including all the bridesmaids and groomsmen. Camera three might be focused on the expressions of the guests in the audience. Later at the studio the three tapes are edited into one, telling the story of the wedding from several angles. With the work of this very talented director, there are lots of shots filled with emotion that can be edited together to create a meaningful sequence. The equipment to do this is more expensive, so you can expect to pay somewhat more. But there are people who will tell you it's the only way to go!

Wedding Blues

Once the microphone is attached to the groom and turned on, he needs to be careful what he says. These lavaliere microphones are powerful enough to pick up even whispered vows, so they can pick up a lot of other sounds as well!

Language of Love

Betacam refers to the broadcast quality used by some professional videographers to record your wedding because of its superior quality. This format is still widely used in the news media but is not used by consumers. Tape length is limited to 60 minutes.

Capturing the Sound

The majority of videographers today use small wireless microphones to capture the wedding ceremony. These "lavaliere" microphones clip on to the groom's lapel and the minister's robes, and they feed directly into the videography by way of a radio transmitter that's usually clipped to the back of the groom's waist under his jacket. The officiant will have another radio transmitter clipped to his or her waist under the robes. It's important to know that these microphones don't amplify the vows for the guests to hear, only for the videographer. The videographer can't work off the standing microphone used for the guests, because distortion can result from the sound bouncing off the wall in a large church or synagogue.

Master, First Generation, or Second Generation?

Every time a videotape is copied from a copy, the quality is slightly diminished. So you'll want to know which generation tape you'll receive. Generally there is a master tape, which is the completely edited original tape of your wedding, and copies are made off of that. Some videographers produce the master tape on *Betacam* because they believe it to be the very best quality even if this tape cannot be played in your VCR. *VHS (video home system)* is the system you probably have at home to watch your VHS videotapes on.

Each copy ordered from the videographer is then made from the master tape. If all the copies are made from the master, they'll all be first generation and have the same clear quality as the original. But if the copies are made from one another, each one will be slightly less clear than the one it was copied from. Let's say the bride and groom chose a videography package that included just one tape for them. It would be a first generation tape made from the master. Now let's say they want to make a copy to send to the bride's parents. The parents' tape would be the second generation tape. If Mom and Dad wanted to give Grandma and Grandpa a copy as well, they would copy their tape and send the grandparents the third generation of the tape. This could go on and on, but you can quickly see it wouldn't take long for the tape to become very poor quality.

If you do want to make copies of the tape, your best plan is to make each copy from the bride and groom's tape, so each is a second generation. This way the quality remains about the same and everyone can enjoy the tape they're looking at.

Language of Love

VHS (video home system) is the name of the video format used in consumer-quality VCR players. The tape quality is not as fine as beta, but most people do not own beta VCRs. Tape length depends on the speed you're using, but it ranges from two to eight hours. Quality will diminish if you record at the faster speed.

Ask your videographer how many copies of the tape you'll receive in your initial package and what he would charge you to make additional tapes for you. The fee is often quite nominal and this videotape would make a terrific Christmas present for your parents and grandparents.

What Type Video Do You Want?

There are various types of wedding videos and they all vary in quality and price. Your personal preference and budget will most likely dictate the type that is right for you, but before you even begin, check the rules regarding videotaping in your church or synagogue. You'll need to know them when you're speaking to a videographer. Chances are the videographer has worked in your church or synagogue before and is aware of the regulations, but if not, you may need to fill him or her in before you can get an accurate quote for the videographer's services.

The least expensive type of video is shot with only one camera and starts at the beginning of

Sue's Suggestions

If interviews are to be a part of your wedding video, give the videographer a list of the guests who should be interviewed and tell those guests to be prepared. If guests are not prepared, you'll have a lot of "Ummm, what should I say ..." on your tape!

your ceremony and runs straight through to the end of your reception. It has no interruptions and no editing. It may be possible for the videographer to add the couple's names and wedding date at the beginning of the tape. Some videographers will also be able to add music for an additional fee. If you ask a family member to videotape your wedding, this is probably the type of coverage you'll get. It will record everything that happens, or at least everything that happens that the videographer knows about; but other than recording the day, it will not necessarily tell a romantic story of the day.

Tantalizing Trivia

Beta format and VHS format came on the scene at approximately the same time, and it was a race to see which product would be used by the majority of the consumers. It's said that the people who developed Beta assumed that the superior quality would make it the most popular and so did little to promote their product. The VHS manufacturers, however, priced their players quite low, so most consumers purchased the VHS–compatible VCRs and this format "won" the "contest."

Sue's Suggestions

If your professional videographer delivers the master copy of your videotape to you in beta format for safekeeping, store this in your safety deposit box at the bank. Do not put it in a household fire safe because moisture will cause the tape to deteriorate. As long as you have the master in a safe place, a damaged tape can be repaired for a nominal fee.

A slightly more expensive video follows the nostalgic format. It usually begins with baby pictures of the couple, progresses to pictures of their romantic courtship, followed by scenes from the wedding, the reception, and sometimes even the honeymoon. Still pictures are shot with videotape and can be edited into the master tape at any point. This format needs to be edited at the studio and requires more editing time, so it's generally more expensive than the one-camera straight-shot video. You better plan on hiring a professional if this is what you're looking for, unless you actually have a professional videographer in your family.

The most popular type of videography used in weddings today is the documentary style. It will start with shots of the bride dressing and the groom looking at his watch. It will continue throughout the ceremony and reception, capturing spontaneous moments and interviews with family and friends. It will end when the couple leaves their reception in a shower of rose petals, or enjoying their last dance as their guests blow bubbles at them. During editing, baby pictures and pictures from their courtship can be added, as can other special effects. The documentary style can vary in price depending on the quality of the equipment used, the number of cameras used to create it, and the skill of the videographer and editor—not always the same person. Very often this documentary style begins with a brief recap of the event—perhaps a 10-minute overview of the entire wedding—so you can show it to your friends without subjecting them to the entire three- or four-hour videotape!

Tantalizing Trivia

Marla and Bob hired the professional videographer who worked in Marla's father's computer company. Even though he was very familiar with the equipment and videotape, he had never done a wedding before. When Marla came down the aisle, the videographer was standing in the outer aisle and when the guests stood up, he could not see her. During the reception his lights were far too bright and not appropriate for the atmosphere of the wedding. Later, when Marla and Bob went to cut their cake, the videographer was again standing in the wrong place, but by that time it didn't matter, because he was out of batteries, having already used the two he had brought. He may have known about videotape, but he didn't know anything about videotaping *a wedding*!

What If the Videographer Does Not Require a Contract?

There are some talented videographers (and probably other wedding professionals) who have never gotten around to creating a contract and prefer to do business with a handshake. Depending on your comfort level and the reputation of the vendor, you may actually be fine working with such a professional. But if you feel better having something in writing that you and the videographer both sign, you can always create a letter of intent. It would be written by you and would include everything you want in your video.

Letter of Intent

Between

Beth Bride and George Groom
986 Ivy Road
Eden, Illinois 60673
312-555-8824

And

Video Productions, Inc.
5395 Frankfort Avenue
Douglas, Illinois 60660
312-555-2939

It is the intention of Beth Bride and George Groom to secure the services of Video Productions, Inc. to videotape their wedding ceremony on

Sunday, the 11th of July, 1999

at Temple Beth El
1556 Spalding Drive
Douglas, Illinois 60660

at 5:00 o'clock in the afternoon.

The reception and dinner will follow immediately at

Marriott Marquis Hotel
266 Douglas Eden Road
Eden, Illinois 60673

The full-length edited tape of the wedding and reception is to include:

5 Growing-up pictures of the bride
5 Similar pictures of the groom
10 Pictures of the couple together while dating
The wedding invitation
Complete coverage of the wedding and reception
Interviews with immediate family members (a list of names will be provided)
Interviews with the bridal party
Appropriate musical background, including the song that the groom has written and recorded for the bride
A three- to five-minute recap of the wedding day

This videotape will be recorded by three cameras.

We understand that David Smythe, Peter Grady, and Kevin Janus will be working the cameras, and Dianne Grady will be at the controls behind the scenes.

Each videographer will be formally dressed in a black tuxedo.

Edited tapes are to be mastered in <u>VHS format</u>.

We will receive:

>   Two (2) copies of the full-length edited tape
>   Seven (7) copies of the Recap and Photomontage combined
>   One (1) Deluxe Double video-cassette album

The charges for this videotape as stated above will be $2,500.00. Should additional copies be requested by other family members, it is agreed that they will be priced as follows:

Additional full-length, edited tapes available at	$40.00 each
Additional recap and photomontage available at	$25.00 each

Deposit paid on April 21, 1999	<u>$1,000.00</u>
Balance due on completion	**$1,500.00**

_____   _____

Beth Bride/George Groom   David Smythe for Video
                                         Productions, Inc.

Date _____   Date _____

When you've included everything that you discussed with the videographer and that you want to be understood, make two copies of this letter and take them both to the videographer along with your deposit check. Sign both copies and ask the videographer to sign both copies, then leave one with the videographer and file your signed copy in your contract file. This letter will be as binding as a contract, once it's signed by both of you.

Let's be perfectly clear: This letter of intent will not protect you if the videographer doesn't show up at the wedding. Your protection against that is his reputation, which you've already confirmed by talking to former clients. What this letter *will* do is clarify who will be filming the wedding, how they'll be dressed, what type of video you'll receive, and what you'll be paying for it. It will also help ensure that the videographer knows the time and place of the wedding and reception. Of course, you'll be giving details to the videographer during the week before the wedding, but this letter should prevent sleepless nights on your part in the meantime.

Many couples leave the decision about hiring a videographer to the end of their planning to be sure that they have enough money for it. This makes good sense if there are other things you feel more strongly about including in your budget. However, if you are going to hire a videographer at all, make sure you select the most talented professional you can afford. In the years to come, these "moving memories" will become very precious, and you will want to enjoy them. Poor quality should never be tolerated.

The Least You Need to Know

➤ Some photography studios offer videography services as well.

➤ When interviewing a videographer, be sure to watch one wedding tape all the way through, not just cuts from several weddings.

➤ A good video tells the story of the event.

➤ If the professional does not work with a contract, you can use a letter of intent signed by the wedding professional and you.

Your Wedding Cake: A Sweet to Build a Dream On

Cakes have been an important part of the wedding reception since Roman times. Sweet cakes symbolically bestow sweetness and happiness on an event. The grains used to bake cakes were a symbol of abundance and fertility.

Tradition states that when a single woman takes home a piece of wedding cake and places it under her pillow, she will dream of the man she will marry. That certainly speaks to the magical powers of flour, eggs, sugar, and butter! The wedding cake has always been the most magical of confections. No matter how simple your wedding, a wedding cake is one of the absolute requirements. You can be married without photography, a band, or even flowers, but I'm not sure the union is official unless there's a cake!

Finding a Bakery

Chances are that you have had to purchase a birthday cake and found a bakery that you were pleased with at that time. That's a good place to start when it comes to ordering your wedding cake, but it may not be the place that you end up having make your cake. There are several places that you can look for a wedding cake:

➤ Retail bakery

➤ Caterer or reception site

➤ Private bakers

➤ Grocery store bakeries

Retail Bakeries

Retail bakeries may sell sweet rolls, cookies, and loaves of break all week long, but most are proud of their artistry when it comes to making wedding cakes. They have the bakers and designers on hand to turn out cakes rather quickly, and generally have a large variety of cakes for you to choose from. They have books of cake designs from which you can select the look of your cake, and many different flavors to choose from. One of the best advantages of such a facility is that they almost always have cakes for you to taste. It may not be decorated like a wedding cake, but chances are they'll have a carrot cake, or a white cake, or even a pound cake in the display case for you to sample.

Sue's Suggestions

It may sound very basic, but you should make every attempt to taste the cake before ordering it. You'll certainly want your cake to look good, but when it's cut, don't you want it to taste good, too? Don't just choose a picture!

Another advantage of working with a retail bakery is that it's used to producing a lot of cakes quickly. This means your cake will be baked, frosted, and delivered to you in a relatively short time, which ensures its freshness when it's served. Be sure to find out how far in advance the bakery bakes its cakes and if it ever freezes them, so you'll know exactly how fresh your cake will be. There is a possible disadvantage: Since the retail bakery produces so many cakes, it may limit the decorations on each individual cake and may not be as creative as you would like your cake to be.

If you decide to order your cake from a retail bakery, be sure you discuss how the cake will be delivered to your reception site and what time you can expect it to arrive. Some brides believe that they can save money by picking up the cake themselves; however, this is definitely not something that I recommend. Multi-tiered cakes are not easy to transport and many bakeries prefer to transport them in individual layers and assemble them at your reception site. When the bakery does this, it usually sends along a tube of icing, so the delivery person can pipe icing along the line where the two layers meet, giving the cake a finished look.

Caterer or Reception Site

The next most common source for a cake is your caterer or reception site. Very often the site will have a pastry chef who produces cakes for the weddings held in that facility. If this option is available to you, it will usually be the least expensive. Some facilities that offer wedding cakes will charge you a slicing or plating fee if you bring in a cake from another location. Be sure to ask about this extra fee. If your facility has such a policy, you'll be best off financially if you get your wedding cake from there. Again, taste the cake and look at the facility's collection of pictures to make your selection.

Private Bakers

Most communities have bakers that specialize in unique and creative wedding cakes and many delight in the challenge of producing something different. These bakers sell to the consumer, just like any retail bakery, but they differ from other retail bakeries, because they produce wedding and special occasion cakes, only. If you would like to work with one of these wedding cake specialists, the baker will probably have a collection of trade magazines showing all kinds of cakes, and together you'll be able to locate the perfect design for your wedding. I'm sure you'll find that all of these bakers deliver their cakes to your wedding site and will be happy to assemble them on site. If you know in advance what flavor you'll want, tell the baker when you make your initial appointment and you'll be able to taste that flavor. Unfortunately, you'll not be able to sample several different flavors, since these facilities often have only the cakes they've made for a specific wedding on hand on any given day.

In addition to wedding cake specialists, there are bakers who make wedding cakes in their homes by special order. Many of them are licensed and meet health department requirements for producing cakes outside of a commercial kitchen. They'll be less expensive than the wedding cake specialist, the caterer, and the retail bakery, and possibly even less expensive than the grocery store bakery. The reason for their reduced cost is based on the fact that they have almost no overhead, and they do not advertise. The only way you'll be able to find such a baker is to speak to your friends. This is not a bad thing, since you can be sure this baker will not be so

Sue's Suggestions

Begin interviewing bakers three to four months before your wedding, so you have time to taste several before making your decision.

Wedding Blues

If you're *paying* for your cake, be sure the baker is licensed to produce it. You want to be sure you've taken every precaution to protect your guests. If someone *gives* you a cake as a gift, you may not be able to ask if the baker has health board certification.

overwhelmed with cakes on your particular weekend that she'll be unable to complete the cake on time. Usually they deliver and assemble the cake for you.

Grocery Store Bakeries

In addition to the sources I've mentioned, many grocery store bakeries now make wedding cakes to order. In most cities, these bakeries produce the cakes they sell on site so you can meet with the baker and discuss your needs. You'll be able to taste their cakes and even order the flavor you want in a birthday-cake size if they don't have one on display that day. Like the retail baker and the wedding specialist baker, grocery store bakeries will deliver the cake to your wedding site and will be able to show you pictures of cakes that they've created. They also have a large selection of cake toppers.

What Flavor Cake Do You Want?

There was a time when every wedding cake was made of pound cake—some were moister than others, but basically they all tasted the same. Those days are gone! Today wedding cakes come in every flavor imaginable, and probably some we haven't imagined yet. You can even have a cheese cake wedding cake! Some of the popular choices today are …

➤ Banana

➤ Carrot

➤ Chocolate

➤ Chocolate chip

➤ Chocolate mousse

➤ German chocolate

➤ Red velvet

➤ Spice

Of course, you can still choose a white or yellow cake, if you prefer.

The fillings include …

➤ Raspberry

➤ Caramel

➤ Chocolate mousse

➤ Lemon

➤ Mocha

➤ Amaretto

➤ Cream cheese

➤ Vanilla custard

Whatever flavor you choose for the cake and for the filling, the wedding cake is traditionally white, or certainly a light pastel color. Round cakes tend to be the most popular, but wedding cakes can be square, rectangular, or even heart-shaped.

What Does a Wedding Cake Cost?

Wedding cakes are priced by the serving, so you'll want to consider how you're going to serve before you order your cake. For instance, if you're serving a seated dinner with a dessert, you won't need to order cake for everyone in the room, because many people will eat the dessert after dinner and won't be interested in eating wedding cake later. If you're having an elaborate sweet table (sometimes called a Viennese table)—everything from strawberries dipped in chocolate to chocolate mousse—you may want to limit the size of your wedding cake. People may take a small piece, but they will not consume as much cake if there are so many other choices.

Wedding Blues

Don't get carried away and choose a different flavor for each layer of your cake. If you do that, some guests will want a sample of each and you'll actually need more cake than you expected.

Tantalizing Trivia

One bride received her wedding cake as a gift from her next-door neighbor, who just loved to bake. When it arrived, the caterer nearly died. The cake was leaning at a 45-degree angle and he was terrified it would fall over! He suggested that the bride cut the cake immediately after her first dance, so he could roll it away to be sliced and plated and served later in the evening. Fortunately, the bride agreed, so disaster was averted!

If you want a multi-tiered cake, but really don't want to keep all that uneaten cake in your freezer for the next several years, one option is to have the baker use one or even two plastic foam layers. These fake layers give the cake the height you want without having to deal with all that actual cake. The only problem is that this does not really save you money. The baker still has to decorate the fake layers as if they were really cake, and you'll pay for this time.

Language of Love

Royal icing is a sweet, white, meringue-based icing that dries crunchy hard. Royal icing can be used to make cake decorations such as flowers, bows, lattices, string work, and lace. **Rolled fondant** is a sweet, silky smooth icing that has a dough or claylike consistency. It's most often rolled out with a rolling pin, draped over the cake, and then smoothed to conform to the cake shape.

Interestingly, the difference in the price of cakes often has to do with the way the cake is decorated. Most wedding cakes usually have either buttercream frosting or *rolled fondant* icing, and some are decorated with *royal icing*. Buttercream is the most common and the least expensive kind of icing. It's the same frosting you typically see on birthday cakes and is a mixture of butter, sugar, and milk. The decoration on a wedding cake with buttercream frosting could be either buttercream flowers, which are the least expensive, or fresh flowers. The baker can supply the flowers, or the florist can supply flowers to match the decor of the reception.

Rolled fondant icing is a sugar and gelatin mixture. It's rolled out with a rolling pin and placed over the cake. It will seal the cake completely and act as a preservative to the cake inside. It's usually a very smooth icing, and you've probably seen cakes decorated with rolled fondant that look like they have pearls decorating the sides, or like they've been wrapped with a ribbon. The smooth nature of this icing makes many different design choices possible. The fondant can be rolled out and cut into strips to make bows and flowers. A cake iced with rolled fondant icing is more expensive than one iced with buttercream and may be more difficult to locate, because some retail bakers don't offer this option. If your wedding reception is outdoors during the hot days of summer, let your baker guide you to the most appropriate icing for your cake—not every icing will hold up under the sun.

Wedding Blues

If you're having an outdoor reception, let your baker know, so you both can come up with a plan for displaying your cake. Even in the early spring, it's not a good idea to let the cake sit outside for several hours before it's eaten.

The most expensive decorations on a wedding cake are gum-paste flowers. These individually formed, perfect flowers can be painted to look real and take weeks to make. When they're finished, they look like delicate porcelain flowers, and some brides remove them and have them worked into a bouquet to be displayed under a glass dome.

Wedding cakes range in price from about $1.35 per person for a grocery-store-baked wedding cake with buttercream icing and flowers to approximately $10.00 per person for a cake baked by a private baker using royal icing and gum paste flowers. If you have to pay a slicing or plating fee of between $1.50 and $3.00 per slice, you can see that the cake can get very expensive. In most instances, the caterer includes the plating/slicing fee in his or her per person fee for making the cake. It's only when the cake comes from a different source that the fee becomes an issue. That's why it's usually least expensive to have the caterer or pastry chef at your wedding facility provide the cake, if that's an option.

When you've made your final decisions, be sure the baker gives you a contract that outlines everything you've decided on. The type of cake, shape, frosting, decorations, delivery date, time, and place should all be noted on your contract. As with any contract that you sign, the price you've agreed upon should be stated and also the amount of deposit that has been paid. The contract should also tell you when final payment is due.

Displaying the Cake

Your cake is the centerpiece of your reception, but that doesn't mean it should be placed in the center of the room. When you look at the diagram of your reception room, think about the traffic pattern. Where will your guests be for most of the evening? Where is the buffet table going to be placed? The dance floor? Where is the safest place to display your cake?

Pick a Corner

The answer may very well be, off in a corner where it can be viewed, approached, cut by the bride and groom, and eventually served by the catering staff. Don't place it where it can be jostled by dancing celebrants or poked by curious and quick little fingers. That corner will be especially appealing if it's not in direct sunlight. Some food colorings fade in bright light, other decorations run if the sun is beating down on the cake all afternoon. Recessed lighting and spot lighting can make the cake hot enough to melt chocolate or buttercream icing. Consider, too, the filling of the cake. If you've chosen a whipped-cream, custard, or curd filling, remember that your cake needs to be refrigerated to stay fresh. If your room is air-conditioned and the cake is not sitting out for three hours, you're probably going to be fine, but if you encounter a really warm day, you may be much better off having your cake put in place shortly before it's to be sliced. Even a very cool room warms up when it's full of people.

Sue's Suggestions

You want your cake to be the focal point of your reception, but that doesn't mean shining a spotlight on a cake with buttercream frosting. As the frosting gets hot, it will boil, and big blisters can erupt. It's better to have the florist put lights under the cake table than to shine a spotlight directly on the cake.

Don't Move!

Moving a multi-tier cake after it's assembled is every caterer's worst nightmare. Many absolutely refuse to accept responsibility for it, and you really can't blame them. No one is very interested in *who* baked the cake once it hits the floor! So pay close attention to the place in the room where you'll put your cake, and make every effort to have it put in place by the baker when it's delivered.

How High Is the Sky?

While you're considering the placement of your cake in the reception room, take a look at the proportion of the room. How high is the ceiling? If you're hosting your reception in an old mansion, you may be surprised to find the ceilings are slightly less than eight feet high. You may have really wanted a very tall cake—eight or ten layers—but that might look really silly in a room with a low ceiling. If you're faced with a low ceiling, you don't have to have a short cake, just a shorter one. How about a four-tier cake with four individual cakes surrounding the base in a four-leaf clover design? This design can actually be very interesting, and if each of the cakes happens to be a different flavor, your guests will love making their choices! I spent many childhood hours crawling through the grass searching for the lucky four-leaf clovers. Perhaps this is why I believe a wedding cake in that shape would be such a good omen!

On the Level

While looking at the reception site, take a look at the floor. Is it level? Is the carpeting smooth? If not, you may want to select another location for your cake. This may not be a problem in most reception sites, but it can be important in old homes, on terraces and decks, and on grassy lawns where you might not notice the slightly sloping grade and the holes in the lawn. If the catering manager or baker suggests moving the cake to a more level location, listen to that advice. They may not want to share the horrors they've seen, but they do have your best interests at heart!

Wedding Blues

If you're using fresh flowers to decorate your cake, be sure to wrap the stems in cellophane or plastic wrap. Some flowers give off a liquid that spoils the taste of the cake, so if you wrap them, you protect the taste of the cake. Flowers such as bachelor buttons are poisonous to humans—these should never be used to decorate a wedding cake!

Return the Favor

If the layers of your cake are separated with columns, pillars, or fountains, the baker has probably lent these pieces to you and expects them to be returned. The baker will also want any serving pieces returned, too. You may be leaving on your honeymoon shortly after the wedding, and will not want to think about collecting and returning these items. The best way to handle this is to plan ahead. Select a responsible local friend—of several who will ask how they can help—and ask that person to take responsibility for these cake pieces. Be sure to give your friend a list of cake pieces he or she needs to collect, along with the name, address, and phone number of the baker. If the baker expects these items to be returned by a specific date, share that information as well. Now you can forget about the cake. Your friend will make sure that the staff doesn't dispose of the pillars or the plates after the cake is cut.

The Groom's Cake

In the past, there was a second cake baked for the wedding—the *groom's cake*. This cake was usually a two-tiered fruitcake, often iced with chocolate frosting. Frequently it was decorated with marzipan (an edible almond paste), fruits, or fresh fruits dipped in sugar. While the bride's cake was always cut and served as a part of the wedding festivities, the groom's cake was usually not served, but instead, sliced, boxed, and given to the guests to take home as a sweet memory of the day.

The custom has changed recently and more brides are opting to skip the groom's cake for the wedding and serve it at the rehearsal dinner instead. Bakers have begun creating personality cakes for this purpose. For instance, if the groom is a baseball fan, the cake might be shaped like a baseball hat and decorated in the colors of his favorite team. One bride refused to allow cigars to be offered at her wedding reception. Instead, she had the groom's cake formed in the shape of a cigar box with several loose cigars stacked next to it. The groom was delighted to get his cigar, but none of the men left the room to smoke!

Language of Love

The **groom's cake** is a dense cake (frequently a fruit cake), frosted in chocolate, that was originally sliced and given to the guests as they left the wedding reception. This was the cake that single women were supposed to put under their pillows so they could dream of their own true love.

Skipping the groom's cake completely is a good way to save some real money. Shaped cakes can cost as much as $12.50 per person and, even at the rehearsal dinner, that's a lot to spend for dessert.

The Cake Topper

It used to be that every wedding cake was topped with a bride and groom. These little dolls were usually made of plastic, and it was often possible to order them to resemble the bride and groom. For instance, the bride doll might have blonde hair and the groom doll might have red hair, if that was what the couple looked like. Then brides grew tired of these dolls and, wanting something different, began decorating their cakes with flowers on top and around the sides. First it was buttercream-frosting flowers and eventually it became fresh flowers. Gum-paste flowers became available at about the same time. But only very talented bakers have mastered the skill of making them, and even fewer feel they can charge enough to justify the time it takes to create them, so not many bakers offer gum-paste flowers on their cakes.

Wedding Blues

Couples are often disappointed when they defrost the top layer of their wedding cake on their first anniversary. It's usually dried out, freezer-burned, or rotted on the inside from the fresh flowers that had been stuck into it. If you plan to save your cake, wrap it very tightly in plastic wrap, cover it with aluminum foil, and then seal it inside a plastic zipper bag with the air removed.

Sue's Suggestions

Go ahead and serve the top layer of your wedding cake—after all, you paid for it. It's counted in the portions you ordered, so serve it and enjoy it! When you order your wedding cake, order another six-inch cake, same flavor and frosting, to be delivered to your home one year later. You'll taste the same wonderful confection you enjoyed at your wedding reception—fresh and beautiful! What a treat!

Generally the top tier of the wedding cake is not served at the reception, but is instead frozen by the couple to be enjoyed on their first anniversary. Unfortunately, many couples have unwrapped their wedding cake one year later to discover that it is virtually inedible and have thrown it out. For this reason, some bakers now offer couples the option of serving the entire cake at their wedding and picking up a "cake-for-two" on their first anniversary. The baker wants you to enjoy his or her creation, so the price of this cake will either be included in the wedding cake price or be a very nominal additional fee. Some bakers have offered it as a gift to the couple.

A new custom is beginning to emerge. Today bakers are teaming up with photographers and creating a "picture" of the bride and groom for the top of their wedding cake. Some bakers actually use the cut-out photographs that have become so popular. Don't want the groom to see you in your wedding gown before the wedding? That's okay. Have your picture taken together wearing tennis gear or your Rollerblade outfits—helmet and all. You'll create a unique and personal wedding cake top. Something you'll keep for years to come! Prices vary, but these tops are only slightly more expensive than fresh flowers and they certainly last longer.

Another option is to have your likeness created in frosting for the top of your cake. Especially known for her skill in this department is Colette Peters of Colette's Cakes in New York City. Colette can look at a picture of the bride and groom and make a pair of dolls in gum paste to resemble them. These options create a real conversation piece for your wedding, and work equally well for a formal wedding or informal weddings.

Some brides purchase, or receive as gifts, porcelain or crystal figurines of a bride and groom to use on their cakes. Many of these are quite costly. If it's your intention to use such a collector's item on your cake, be sure to discuss it with your baker. The baker will need to reinforce the top of the cake so the figurine won't sink into it. If you want to protect the figurine, you might want to place it next to your cake as a decoration. Something fragile is less likely to fall from on a table than it is from on top of a six-story cake.

Tantalizing Trivia

Two hundred or more years ago in India, it was traditional to prepare the wedding cake with a fake top layer. This top layer was usually made of paper, and inside were sealed two live doves. When it was time to cut the cake at the reception, the bride and groom would climb up ladders and carefully cut through the top of the paper layer, allowing the birds to fly free. If the birds flew many miles away, the couple's marriage would be blessed with happiness and many children.

One more option for the creative bride or her mom: It's possible to purchase needle-point canvases of a bride and groom and have the canvases made into dolls for the top of your cake. The bride doll carries a bouquet and the groom doll wears a top hat. The dolls stand about six inches tall (the groom's hat makes him slightly taller). The bride and groom needlepoint canvases are available from most needlepoint or arts and crafts stores. After the wedding they can be saved under a glass dome. The needlepoint piece isn't costly, but having the two canvases turned into standing dolls will cost approximately $100.

A Cut Above

This is probably a good place to discuss who will cut your cake. You've ordered a cake to feed a certain number of guests. This requires the person slicing the cake to know how to cut a wedding cake, and, specifically, how to cut the shape of wedding cake that you've ordered. If your reception-site catering manager or pastry chef is planning to cut the cake, you're probably safe in assuming they know what they're doing. Nevertheless, it still might be a good idea to ask your baker for a diagram for cutting this cake. Diagrams are available in nearly every bakery trade magazine and it should not be difficult for the baker to make you a copy.

Knowing how to cut the cake will be especially important if you won't have a profes-sional caterer or baker on the scene when the cake is cut and a friend will be doing the honors. In this case, ask your friend to practice on some unfrosted cakes that you and she bake yourselves. Your wedding day is not a good choice for the first attempt. Go to the library and look for books on cakes, and you'll find cutting diagrams, too.

Either copy them on the copy machine, or sketch them so you can practice in advance. If you practice along with your friend, you'll know how to cut her wedding cake at her reception!

Wedding Cakes Around the World

The wedding cake is an important part of the celebration in countries all around the world and each tradition had a slightly different meaning. In England, during medieval times, it was customary for guests to bring small cakes to the wedding. These cakes were piled in the center of the table. The bride was placed on one side of the pile and the groom on the other while everyone waited to see if they could kiss over the pile! Perhaps following this same tradition, French villagers put buns into a pile in preparation for the wedding dinner. One clever baker decided to take some bun-shaped pastries, fill them with whipped cream, form them into a pyramid, and fasten them together with a sticky syrup. This tall caramel-coated cone of cream puffs was called a *croque-en-bouche*. It's still served today, but you don't have to wait for a wedding to enjoy it!

Tantalizing Trivia

Brides and grooms feed each other wedding cake at the reception to honor the tradition that says that friendship is cemented in the breaking of bread together. The shared bite of cake is a symbol of the couple sharing their life together. The act of cutting the cake together is also said to be symbolic of the couple caring for each other through life. In this day of psychologists reading new interpretations into things we have done for years, there is also now commentary about *how* the couple feeds each other. Some believe that smearing the cake into one's beloved's face (at one time considered funny) is now seen as a sign of basic disrespect for the other person and a "predictor" that the marriage will not survive.

In Bermuda the bride and groom have separate wedding cakes. The bride's cake is a tiered fruitcake covered with silver leaf and topped by a small cedar sapling. The sapling is to be replanted after the ceremony, so the couple can watch it grow and blossom as their love grows and deepens. The groom's cake is topped with gold leaf to represent the prosperity it is hoped the couple will enjoy. A Jamaican wedding cake is similar to the Bermuda bride's cake—a dark, rich fruitcake laced with rum. After the ceremony, slices are boxed and mailed to all the relatives and friends who were unable to attend the wedding.

The traditional Irish wedding cake is a fruitcake with almonds, raisins, cherries, and spices, and is laced with brandy and bourbon. Guests generally recite a traditional toast: "May you have warm words on a cold evening, a full moon on a dark night, and the road downhill all the way to your door."

In some countries, bread is used instead of a wedding cake. Ukrainian brides and grooms share a wedding bread called *korovai* which is decorated with designs that represent the joining of two families for eternity. Norwegians serve a bread called *brudlaupskling*. This bread is topped with a mixture of cheese, cream, and syrup. It's folded over and served in squares.

In Asian countries, neither bread nor cake is common. Instead, Korean weddings serve *kuk soo* (noodles) which symbolizes long life. Chinese brides choose food to serve at weddings by a phonetic play on words. A menu of apples, seaweed, and lotus-seed tea denotes the wish that the couple go safely, *fat choy* denotes prosperity, and *liem sun* denotes the wish for many sons.

The wedding cake is an important part of the wedding reception in America. In fact, it is the only item that is *required* at your reception. You may opt to serve cocktails, hors d'eouvres, dinner, or dessert, but if the couple doesn't cut a wedding cake, it's as if they were not married. It's fortunate, then, that we have so many choices today and can find a baker who will prepare the exact flavor of cake, filling, and frosting the bride has been dreaming about!

Sue's Suggestions

Bring a little of your ethnic heritage into your wedding by employing some of the customs of your culture and heritage. A good way to do this is to use the type of cake most popular in the country your ancestors came from. Or, place symbols of marriage from another time and place on the cake table. Some brides decorate their cake tables with their mother's veil or with figurines brought by their grandparents from their country of origin, for example.

The Least You Need to Know

➤ There are many different kinds of places that bake wedding cakes, and many different flavors and fillings to choose from.

➤ Taste should be as important to you as the way your cake looks, so taste in advance the kind of cake you're ordering.

➤ Check out your reception location to find the perfect place in the room to display your wonderful cake.

➤ Cakes are priced as much by the type of frosting and decoration as they are by the number of people they'll serve.

➤ Cake toppers come in lots of varieties; express your creative self with your choice of cake top.

➤ Your cake will feed the number of guests you've planned for only if it's cut by an experienced cake slicer.

➤ The wedding cake is an important part of the celebration in countries around the world.

Part 5

The Honeymoon

The honeymoon is your first trip as a married couple. You really want to enjoy it, so you'll want it to be well planned. The word "honeymoon" really means "sweet month" and should be relaxing and romantic—it's not a time for two worn-out people to collapse in a hotel room. Instead, it's a time for you to concentrate on one another in the afterglow of your beautiful wedding. Whether you're leaving town for two days or two months, taking the time to plan it carefully is the best way to put the "sweet" in your trip.

You didn't work hard budgeting your wedding to overspend on your honeymoon. You will create a separate budget for the honeymoon and plug it into your wedding budget so you know you won't overspend on either one.

Chapter 21

Planning the Perfect Honeymoon

In This Chapter

➤ Do you want to go to the mountains or the seashore?

➤ Planning the honeymoon of your dreams

➤ You don't have to pack the kitchen sink!

➤ When will you go on your honeymoon?

In years past, the honeymoon was always the responsibility of the groom—as were all the expenses thereafter! Today, however, brides and grooms tend to pool their resources to plan a peaceful retreat after the excitement of the wedding. If that's your plan as well, you'll want to include the honeymoon on your original budget.

Everyone wants a wonderful honeymoon. Whether your wedding is big or small, carefully planned or impromptu, you'll definitely need to relax afterward, so be sure to allow yourself this time. That doesn't mean you have to take a trip immediately after your wedding reception—in fact, you probably shouldn't. You should, however, take a day or two away from the rigors of your regular life to come down off the magical cloud that was your wedding.

Those Special Memories

Chances are it will be the odd and unplanned moments of your honeymoon that you'll remember fondly as the years pass. It seems that those are the things that will bond you to one another in a special way. Thirty-four years ago my husband of 48

Sue's Suggestions

Did you know that middle February is the peak travel season? If you're being married around that time of the year, be sure to start your honeymoon planning early so the choices will be yours!

Sue's Suggestions

Cruises can be ideal honeymoons on a budget because everything is included—your meals, room, and entertainment—in the price of the ticket. Some cruise lines also include your airfare to and from the port!

hours and I drank rum punches and sang along as two local guitarists serenaded the tour-boat guests, probably all honeymooners, as it motored around Bermuda. When the tour ended, my husband eagerly purchased the long-playing record album the guitarists were selling. Neither of us realized I had gotten a sunburn on my back during the tour and for the next three days the closest my husband could get to me was to gently pat lotion on my blistered back. I know we rode motorcycles; I know we toured the island; I know we met another couple with whom we corresponded over the next decade; but I don't really remember the details of anything except that tour. We still have that album, even though we no longer own a turntable on which we can play it!

What's Your Perfect Honeymoon?

Just because your honeymoon comes at the end of the wedding doesn't mean you should leave it to the end of the planning. If possible, begin thinking about your honeymoon six months in advance of the wedding weekend. Create a separate budget for your honeymoon and work through it just as you have for your wedding. This budget might include such topics as airfare, hotel, meals, entertainment, and souvenirs.

Next, take a trip to the library and do a little research. What kind of vacation would you find most relaxing? Do you like to lie on the beach? Do you like to hike and climb? Would you prefer to do some sightseeing? Do you want to drive to your destination? Would you consider a cruise? When you have a handle on the kinds of things you'd like to do, you're ready to meet with a travel agent.

Working with a Travel Agent

The next thing you'll need to do is locate a reputable travel agent. If you've worked with a travel agent in the past, start with this person. Your agent already knows where you like to sit in the plane and whether or not you require a special meal. If you've never worked with a travel agent, you'll want to interview several before making your choice.

Travel agents often specialize. Some prefer to plan corporate travel while others specialize in cruises or resorts. Your very first question should be, "Do you specialize in honeymoons?" If your travel agent does not, he or she may be able to refer you to someone in the agency. Meet with this person and see if you relate to one another. Since the agent will be making suggestions for destinations, if the agent doesn't seem to understand what you enjoy, it will be a long and difficult process.

Sue's Suggestions

There are several all-inclusive resorts in the Caribbean. At these locations everything is included in the package—room, meals, entertainment, and gratuity. One company that owns such resorts also owns the airline that takes you there, so airfare may be included in the package or you may need to pay a slight additional fee.

Finding a Travel Agent

If you've never worked with a travel agent, speak to friends or relatives and get their recommendations. Travel agents are important specialists, and they don't cost you a penny! In fact, they're paid a commission by the airlines and resorts for promoting them. You really can't save that commission by doing the work yourself. If you called the airlines and were fortunate enough to actually be given the lowest fare (something that probably will not happen), the commission that would have gone to your travel agent will simply stay with the airlines. It won't be paid to you because you're not a travel agent. So there's really nothing to lose by working with an agent—and a lot to gain!

Resorts, cruises, and vacation hotels invite travel agents to visit their facilities so they'll be knowledgeable about the surroundings and encourage couples to select their facilities. These *Fam (familiarization) trips* are usually quite inexpensive for the facilities to use as encouragement for travel agents to visit them. This can present your first word of caution in selecting a travel agent. When you visit with the travel agent, you're looking for a specialist. You're also looking for someone who knows something about the place you're considering, so be sure to ask whether this particular agent has actually been to the location. If he or she has not been there, and neither has anyone else in the office, this may be a sign that either this travel agent is not for you, or the place is not for you. You are speaking to someone who claims to "specialize in honeymoons" but has not taken advantage of an inexpensive way to visit the places he is

Language of Love

Fam (familiarization) trips are greatly discounted trips to a specific facility offered to travel agents by the facility. This is a working vacation for the travel agents, so they can see a place and be able to tell their clients about its advantages. Fam trips are one of the perks of the travel industry.

recommending. Isn't that kind of strange? You should expect to see brochures and pamphlets about destinations all over the place. The walls might be covered with travel posters, airline promotions, and pictures of cruise ships.

Tantalizing Trivia

Marjorie and Phil were really surprised when they made their first visit to the travel agent they found in the phone book. They decided to visit this particular agent because the address seemed to be just down the street from Phil's office. Marjorie didn't remember ever seeing a travel agency on that block, but they both felt it would be easiest to work with someone close by. They must have driven up and down the street two or three times before Phil walked into the vacuum cleaner store to ask for the address he couldn't locate. The salesman came around the counter and showed Marjorie and Phil to a card table in the back of his store where he ran his travel agency! The "travel agent" may have been more interested in the perks of the business (Fam trips and discounted travel for himself) than in actually being in business. Beware!

Getting a Good Deal

Planning four to six months in advance can often get you special fares on your honeymoon, especially if you want to take a cruise. Sometimes the cruise line will even offer two-for-one discounts (when two people can travel for the full published price of one person) to those who book early. You'll have to pay a deposit at that time, but deposits are frequently refundable up to a certain time.

A word of explanation about two-for-one discounts on cruises. Travel agents are often able to secure discounted passage for their clients on specific cruise ships. Let's say an outside cabin for two books for $1,299.00 ($649.50 for each person), and because you booked several months in advance, your travel agent was able to book your reservation for $1,000, saving you $299. Three months later, the cruise ship is trying to boost its reservations for that particular cruise, so it offers a two-for-one promotion. If your travel agent's on the ball, he or she can amend your ticket so you can be included in that promotion. The original price was $1,299, but now it's two for one, so your rate for two people just dropped to $650.00. That's not two-for-one drop from your $1,000 booking, but it's an additional $350.00 savings to you, and that isn't bad!

In another scenario, the agent may not be able to save you any additional money, but may be able to upgrade your room from an economy cabin to a stateroom on an upper deck.

Travel agents are among the only wedding professionals who stand to benefit from your repeat business. Hopefully, you won't need to hire officiants, reception sites, ceremony musicians, florists, or photographers to produce another wedding until your daughters come of age 20-plus years from now. But you may be able to take wonderful vacations every year, so selecting the right travel agent can be a lifelong decision that's mutually beneficial.

Tantalizing Trivia

Take along a notebook or travel diary and record your experiences during your honeymoon trip. You'll be surprised later at what you'll remember—and how much you'll forget. Make note of the restaurants you enjoyed, the wonderful sights you saw, and the people you met. When friends travel to this same place in the years to come, you'll enjoy looking back at this record and recommending your favorite places. This travel diary is also a great place to record the names and addresses of the people you meet along the way. Some people prefer, instead, to do a brief daily synopsis of their trip on a cassette recorder. If you also record those things you didn't like about your trip, you can avoid these things in your next planning time. For example, if your honeymoon was on a cruise ship and you were assigned the "first seating," you might discover that you actually preferred to be off the boat on the days when it was in port and hated rushing back to be ready for dinner. If you had this in your notes, you might remember to request "second seating" on your next cruise.

Going the Distance

If you decide you want to travel to another country, your travel agent will be able to tell you what visas and vaccinations you'll need. Sometimes the agent can even secure the necessary visas for you. (Sorry, when it comes to vaccinations, you need to appear in person!) If your destination requires a passport, and you don't currently have one, allow at least a month for processing. The bride will not be able to secure a new passport in her new name before the wedding, so she should be careful to book all her travel documents in her maiden name, exactly as it currently appears on her passport. This will not be a major issue in most countries, but might become an issue when you return to the United States. Naturally, if you've decided to take your honeymoon at least a month after the wedding, the bride will be able to secure a new passport and have all her reservations made in her new name.

Keeping the Honey in Your Honeymoon

You and your new spouse may have traveled together before this trip, so how do you make this trip special and romantic? One way is to keep your schedule light. Don't try to see everything in one day. Chances are you'll revisit your honeymoon destination again later in your marriage, so try to concentrate on being together in this beautiful place.

Here are a few tips on ways to make your honeymoon even more memorable:

➤ Pack your lingerie around a bar of your favorite scented soap so a cloud of your special scent will surround you both.

➤ Bring along some romantic cards or little gifts, something that tells your partner how happy you are to be sharing this experience with him.

➤ Even though some honeymoon resorts will welcome newlyweds with a bottle of champagne in the room, you may wish to bring a bottle of your favorite beverage with you. (Be sure to wrap it well, so it doesn't break in your suitcase!) You can call room service for some special snacks to share as you toast each other.

Don't forget your parents while you're on your honeymoon. Take a moment to send them a postcard thanking them for your beautiful wedding, or just sharing a newsy little note about your trip. They'll feel so special that you thought about them during this time, and this will become one of those thoughtful gestures that will mean so much to them in the years to come.

Be a Packing Pro

This will not be the only trip you'll take together, but it may be the most romantic. One groom decided to surprise his bride with a mystery honeymoon. He told her to pack for very cold weather and for very hot, sunny days. He told her she would need both hiking boots and swimwear, but he would not tell her where they were going. During the last few weeks of wedding planning, as her stress level mounted with the details of the wedding, he continued to give her contradictory clues as to their honeymoon destination. She kept packing and packing until finally three large suitcases were full.

The Monday after the wedding, they boarded a plane for Puerto Rico and eventually another smaller plane (where they had to pay a fee for her 15 pounds of overweight luggage) to Beef Island, Tortola, in the British Virgin Islands, where they boarded a private sailboat. They spent the next seven days sailing

Wedding Blues

Save the surprise trip for an anniversary down the road when it can be appreciated. When you're already stressed about wedding details, adding the mystery of what to pack for the honeymoon takes away from the fun!

through the Virgin Islands with only their captain on board. During the honeymoon she wore just three bathing suits, two cover-ups, and one pair of white slacks and a T-shirt! (Two of the three suitcases were not even opened. They contained evening dresses, daytime dresses, high heel shoes, purses, jeans, hiking boots, and rain gear.)

This couple had a terrific time, a relaxing, beautiful honeymoon. But it hadn't been stress-free, and it could have been. If only the groom had told her his plans in advance, she wouldn't have spent so much time packing and guessing. It actually took some of the fun out of this magical trip.

Rain or Shine?

It's a good idea to do at least a little research into the weather at your honeymoon destination, so you'll know the type of clothing to pack. There are several good guide books that will help you, and many countries have boards of tourism (in your community or in New York City), that will be delighted to send you information about the weather and the activities you can enjoy while staying in that country. Take advantage of this information and plan ahead!

If you're traveling to a destination whose weather will be quite different from what you're leaving, it's a good idea to pack the appropriate weight clothing in your carry-on. This will allow you to shed your long-sleeve, wool sweater and wool slacks for shorts and a T-shirt while still on the plane or immediately after landing, and you'll be much more comfortable while getting to your hotel and checking in.

Try Not to Lose It

Unfortunately, it's not uncommon for luggage to be lost or delayed during air travel and it can be a tremendous inconvenience. To lessen the disruption to the beginning of your trip, pack some of your clothes in his bag, and some of his clothes in your bag. Then, if one of your bags is delayed, at least you'll each have a change or two of clothing.

In an effort to keep passengers and their bags together, the airlines require you to label each piece of luggage, both inside and out, with your name and address. Consider using your office address instead of your home address for two reasons:

Sue's Suggestions

Consider packing an empty tote bag (or a small canvas bag that unzips to become a larger duffel bag) to bring home souvenirs. While you're away, this same bag will come in handy as a beach tote or to carry a change of clothing after a long outing.

➤ If a piece of lost luggage is returned to your home when you're not there, no one's there to re-ship it to you or make sure it's secure while you're away. If it's sent to your office, you may be able to ask a

Wedding Blues

Pack your liquids and aerosols in plastic bags to prevent leakage into your luggage.

coworker to put it on the next flight to you. Of course, the coworker will not have a ticket, but if the airlines have lost and found a bag, they may be willing to assist you and your coworker in solving this problem.

➤ Many people handle your bags as they move through the airport. Having your home address on the bags advertises that you're going away and may make your residence a target by the less honest am-ong us. Your office building is far less likely to be in jeopardy.

In addition to your name and address on your bags, you may wish to mark them in another identifying way, since so many pieces of luggage look alike. You can purchase colored cylinders that snap over luggage handles, or tie colored yarn balls to the handles, or mark the sides of your bags with large initials made of colored cloth tape— anything that makes your bags stand out among the hundreds of bags that are unloaded from your flight.

Sue's Suggestions

Airport security recommends removing film from its packaging and carrying it in plastic bags in your carry-on luggage, perhaps even in a lead-lined bag. You can easily remove it and hand it to the security personnel to examine without it being x-rayed. The x-ray used on your carry-on luggage generally won't damage your film; however, the x-ray used on your checked baggage is stronger and could put a white streak across already exposed film. Since it's really easy for you to tell which film has been used and which has not, you can carry all your film together in your carry-on luggage.

Don't Forget the Small Stuff

There are certain items that need to go with you almost wherever you go. In fact, you may want to store them in your suitcase so they will always be available.

➤ Sunscreen

➤ Sunglasses

➤ Umbrella

➤ Extra plastic bags (to hold wet swimsuits and beach towels for the return trip)

➤ Film and camera batteries (though you may have to change these frequently so they don't become outdated)

If you're traveling within the United States, be sure to take along your insurance card in case of a medical emergency. Medical emergencies may be handled differently in other countries; ask your travel agent about purchasing temporary insurance coverage for the trip. If you're going overseas, be sure you have a photocopy of your passport with you. Be sure not to store the copy with your passport, and that you leave another copy of your passport with someone that you'll be able to reach to fax it to you if your passport should be stolen while you're away.

Tantalizing Trivia

An adventuresome woman once told me her husband had purchased an expensive Harley-Davidson motorcycle with saddle bags and two helmets. He told her he would take her anywhere in the world she wanted to go if she could learn to pack for two weeks in one saddle bag! She bought a black skirt, a pair of black slacks, a pair of jeans, three shirts, a silky blouse, and a cardigan sweater. With the addition of two scarves, a pair of black flats and her tennis shoes she had enough outfits to be appropriately dressed for anything except a black-tie event. The last time we spoke, they had traveled through the British Isles, South America, Australia, Asia, and Europe!

Pay particular attention to where you're going and what time it will be when you arrive at your destination. If you'll be changing time zones, think about check-out time where you'll be landing—will your room be available to you, or will you find yourself sitting in a hotel lobby waiting for someone else to check out of the room before you can get in? This isn't much fun, especially if you're jet lagged! Call ahead to your hotel and see what arrangements they can make to assist you.

Wedding Blues

Always pack medications, jewelry, travel documents, and other important items in your carry-on luggage!

Keep It Light

Unless you're going away for a celebration weekend, where you know in advance you'll need several different outfits and lots of accessories, try to get in the habit of packing for your honeymoon in your two allotted carry-on bags. This will save you the frustration of waiting in the baggage claim area to learn that your luggage did not arrive, and speed you through airports. You'll be enjoying your honeymoon that much sooner, and have that much less to unpack when you get back home. The only thing worse than packing for a trip is *unpacking* from it!

Sue's Suggestions

If you're leaving the United States, be sure to check with your travel agent about the type of electrical current available where you're going. You may need to take a small voltage converter in order to use your small appliances (hairdryer, shaver, travel steamer).

Most people do not wear 42 percent of the clothing they take on trips. If you carefully research the weather in your destination you should not need all those "what if it ..." clothes. Always pack all your clothing in plastic, preferably in resealable plastic bags, with all the air squeezed out. This will keep your clothing from moving around in your luggage and getting wrinkled. Plastic bags will also protect your clothing from spills, either from leaking items in your own luggage or from someone else's that leaked into yours!

Give some real thought to what you *need* to pack, and then attempt to take as little as possible. Less is usually more! Aside from the obvious items, such as bathing suits (or skis, as the case may be), other less obvious necessities might include an extra pair of glasses or contact lenses, bandages, nail clippers, a voltage converter (for overseas outlets) and a list of emergency phone numbers including your doctor(s).

If you're planning an adventuresome honeymoon requiring special gear, such as scuba equipment or skis, be sure to ask the airline what you can check and how to pack it. If you need help transporting equipment to a remote locale, the Explorers' Club can help. You can reach them at 212-628-8383.

Time and Place Bargains

There are sales in the travel industry and if you plan ahead, you can take advantage of off-season rates for your honeymoon. For instance, beautiful Vail, Colorado, is an expensive winter vacation spot during ski season; it's also popular in the summer and can be expensive then, too. During "mud" season in mid May, however, rates are greatly reduced. It's true that some things won't be open, because this is the time of the year when ski lifts are repaired and repainted and some restaurants give their staff a break. But there are wonderful hiking trails, beautiful scenic bicycle paths, and lots of places to take romantic, long walks. The restaurants that are open are often not crowded and noisy—perfect for that intimate dinner for two!

Whether you travel in the United States or another country, take along a pocket-sized guidebook. There may be things to see that you don't even know about and you would hate to discover that you've traveled all that way and missed a famous point of interest.

Read the section in your guide book about the culture of the place you're visiting so that you don't accidentally insult the residents by not knowing what's considered proper in their country. For instance, there are places in the world where women are expected to be dressed modestly, where sleeveless blouses and shorts are not appropriate. If you know this in advance, it's quite easy to pack a long skirt to pull on over your shorts and a sweater to cover your exposed arms.

Since it's not necessary to plan a honeymoon to follow immediately after your wedding reception, you may want to decide where you want to go and then set about deciding what's the best time of year to go there. Much of Europe is "on sale" from January through the end of March. This is not the typical tourist season, and airlines, car rental agencies, and hotels are anxious to get your business. So they reduce their rates significantly and hope that you'll bring your topcoat and come! You'll need a travel agent to help you assess the best time to visit some of these locations. Americans tend to travel to warm climates in January and February and so

Sue's Suggestions

If you're traveling in a foreign country, take the time to learn a few key phrases like "good morning," "good night," and "thank you." People will appreciate your attempt to speak their language even if your accent is not perfect. The fact that you have tried is a sign of respect to their culture.

do the Europeans, but the definition of a warm climate might be different depending on where you live. For instance, Scandinavians may consider Spain warm in February, while some Americans would still consider Spain quite cold. Your travel agent will be able to tell the very best time to visit, so allow him or her to guide you.

Most major airlines offer discount travel clubs. These should not be used for a honeymoon, because you can't book a destination more than one week in advance. The travel times won't work, either, if your wedding is held on a weekend, because flights usually depart on Thursday or Friday mornings and return on Sunday or Monday evenings, only. If you love to travel and enjoy spontaneity you may want to consider membership in these clubs and for discounted "escape" weekends later in your marriage.

Sue's Suggestions

Many resort hotels publish their in-season and off-season rates, and this will be a clue as to the most economical time to visit that location. It usually follows that if you're visiting a hotel during its off-season, the air fare will be less expensive as well.

One of the big airfare savings "secrets" are "red-eye" flights. These overnight flights can save you 20 to 50 percent over their prime-time twins. Many do not require advance purchase or even a Saturday-night stay; but if you do know in advance—and you should—you may be able to secure even lower rates by booking the flight in advance. One caution: These flights are frequently crowded because the word has gotten out on this particular secret, so booking early will give you the best opportunity to travel when it's convenient for you. Some red-eye flights are *not* nonstop. That may not bother you; but you should be sure to let your travel agent know your preference.

Shop 'Til You Drop

It's always fun to shop on a trip, even if you have no intention of buying anything. Just looking into store windows can be an interesting way to spend a few hours. If you're planning to make a major purchase while on your honeymoon, do your homework before leaving home. For instance, you may have your heart set on buying a bottle of French perfume while you're in France—but are you really interested in paying more for it than you would for the same bottle in your home town? If it's the souvenir you're after, there are lots of choices; but you'll be very disappointed to discover that you overpaid for something or saved only a few dollars—not enough to make it worth carrying all the way home. Of course, you won't know that's the case unless you've done a little research. Perfume is easy—just check out the brand you wear or would like to wear, and make note of what size it comes in and how much it is. Then, when you see it, be sure to convert to American currency (don't guess on this one, use your calculator) and see if there really is a savings or not.

There was a time when there were bargains all over the world and Americans looked forward to going abroad and shopping until they dropped, but that time is over. There are books on shopping for most major cities. In fact, a great series is *Shop 'Til You Drop—London* (or Paris, or Hong Kong—you get the picture!). This series and others like it will tell you what is unique to purchase in whatever part of the world you're in. Usually it will give you the address of the best merchant for that particular item, so you know you won't be taken advantage of.

Wedding Blues

When making a major credit-card purchase in a foreign currency, before you sign the credit-card chit, write down the currency name or symbol next to the amount. For instance, if you purchase something that's 100 pecos, be sure to write pecos next to the amount, so the credit card company won't think you made a purchase of $100, which might be considerably more money!

Your credit cards will be accepted all around the world and they're the safest way to travel. Because you'll be using credit cards in most places, you won't need large sums of cash in foreign currencies, and you may have difficulty converting foreign money back to dollars when you return.

Take traveler's checks instead of cash, and be sure to purchase them in the most recognizable brand. All traveler's checks tell you they can be replaced if lost or stolen while you're away (if you have the numbers of the checks you've lost); but you'll only be able to do that if you can get to that company's office. Some obscure traveler's checks do not have offices in many places, so if lost or stolen, they can't be replaced until you return home. Write down the numbers of the traveler's checks and credit cards you have with you, and keep that list in a separate location. In fact, it may be wise to keep the list with your airline tickets and passports in the hotel safe. Don't leave your valuables in your room—you'll be so unhappy if they "walk away," because the hotel is not responsible for your losses.

Before you leave home, take extra credit cards, pictures, and business cards out of your wallet, so it will be lighter and less obvious when you travel. You may also want to keep it in a fanny pack in front of you, or in a gentleman's front pocket. Keeping a bulging wallet in a man's back pocket may be a temptation in some places you travel.

Make yourself aware of the customs regulations that govern bringing items back into the United States. Are you limited to a certain dollar amount? Is the limit in some other measurement? There are some things that cannot be brought into the country, and you'll want to be careful not to accidentally make such a purchase. Whatever you do, declare your purchases in the proper way. When the customs officials spot-check bags, they may pass you right through, or they may ask you to

Wedding Blues

On a recent trip, we actually did not make any purchases at all, but we were stopped and our bags searched. Why? Because we answered correctly that we had spent zero money abroad. The officials couldn't believe that I had not purchased a thing!

open your luggage. If you're found with items you haven't declared, it can be very unpleasant. Keep receipts for all your purchases in a special place in your carry-on luggage, so you can retrieve them easily to fill out the forms, and show them to customs if asked.

If you're taking a new camera or other electronic equipment on your trip, you may need to prove that you left the country with it and it was not purchased abroad and subject to duty. Watches pose a similar problem. You can go into your local jeweler or camera store and get a duplicate bill of sale which would tell the customs officials the item was purchased at home before the trip.

You'll remember your honeymoon for the rest of your life, whether it was a magical trip or a monstrous disaster. The key to the magic is in the planning, and it's safe to say that the keys to the disaster are there as well! This should be a happy time, so plan to relax and enjoy it. Most of all, if it should happen that everything is not perfect, look for the humor in the situation and think of the funny stories you'll have to tell your children someday. We can't always fix bad situations, but we can almost always find a way to enjoy even those moments that are out of our control.

The Least You Need to Know

➤ If you're leaving the country for your honeymoon directly after the wedding, make sure your travel documents are in your maiden name.

➤ If you plan to leave the country for a honeymoon later, be sure to have your passport changed to your new name.

➤ Not every merchant you meet will be honorable, so protect yourself and your money while traveling.

➤ Take most of your cash in traveler's checks and convert only small amounts into local currency.

➤ Be sure to put your valuables into the hotel's main safe or the safe in your room. Hotels are not responsible for your missing valuables.

Honeymoon Bits and Pieces

The wedding was perfect, and the reception was everything you planned it would be, but now you are off to begin your life together. You can use the same planning and budgeting skills you have learned as you move through your life together—thinking ahead, asking questions whose answers will give you the information that you need to make the next decision and the next.

The Wedding Night

There was a time when brides and grooms always changed into their going-away out-fits before they left the reception, went to some hotel near their departure, and then left on their honeymoon the next morning. Over the years couples gradually got away from purchasing *another* outfit, and began leaving the reception in their wedding attire. It's great fun to enter a hotel lobby in your wedding gown. Other hotel guests make a fuss over you and it can be very charming. Besides, if you didn't tell the front desk this was your wedding night when you made the reservation, they'll be able to figure it out and many will send up a complimentary bottle of champagne for you!

It's important to remember two things if you leave your reception in your bridal attire:

1. Make sure someone drops off your overnight bag at the hotel so you'll have both your sexy nightie and a change of clothes for the next morning.

2. Make arrangements for someone to pick up your wedding attire and take it home the next day before you leave the hotel.

Brides don't often think about these two details, but whether you're leaving on your honeymoon or just going home, you won't want to wear your wedding gown the next day! Naturally, if you're not leaving on your honeymoon immediately, you can take your bridal gown and accessories back to your home yourself, and if necessary, return the groom's tuxedo to the rental facility.

Be a Smart Traveler

A good travel agent can get you the best deals on flights, hotels, and package deals. (See Chapter 21, "Planning the Perfect Honeymoon.") If you don't have a travel agent, you can find one in your area by contacting the Institute of Certified Travel Agents at 1-800-542-4282 or the American Society of Travel Agents at 703-739-2782.

The travel industry, like every other industry, has its own lingo. You may see phrases like "all-inclusive," "fly/drive," and "wedding/honeymoon" and not know what they mean. Here's the scoop on these terms:

Wedding Blues

The travel industry has its own abbreviated vocabulary. The words may be familiar, but the meanings may not be what you think. Don't guess. If you are unsure of a phrase on a brochure, be sure to ask. You will be wise to ask even if you think you know what it means!

➤ *All-inclusive.* Pay one price for everything including accommodations, meals, sports activities, and entertainment. Many times these all-inclusive packages also include airfare. Be sure to ask!

➤ *Fly/drive.* Airfare, car rental, and many times hotel accommodations are included in one price.

➤ *Wedding/honeymoon.* Many hotels and resorts offer newlyweds special amenities that can include flowers, breakfast in bed, and a bottle of champagne as a special honeymoon package. In addition, these same establishments also offer wedding packages that include the ceremony, minister, and reception for those couples who want a destination wedding.

A smart traveler is someone who has read the whole brochure, including the fine print, before making a deposit. There are a few more points to consider, whether you're doing this on your own or working with a travel agent:

➤ When a package quotes land costs, it's a safe bet that airfare is *not* included. The brochure may offer to arrange it for you, but that doesn't mean you won't be paying for it, or that you'll get the best available price.

➤ Count on discount fares and even discount airlines. You'll need to check with the airlines for restrictions as to travel. There may also be blackout days—days on which you cannot use your frequent-flyer bonus points.

➤ A direct flight means no change of planes, although there may be one or more scheduled stops; a connecting flight means you'll need to change planes between departure and destination; a nonstop flight means no change of planes and no scheduled stops.

➤ Check out the hotel location. You'll want to know in advance if you'll have a long bus ride before you reach your final destination. Some wonderful locations are too remote to be near an airport, and that's the idea, but you don't want to be surprised to discover this.

➤ Always check whether taxes, tips, and transfers (transportation from the airport to the hotel) are covered in the agreement. These items can add up quickly and you don't want to come up short.

> **Wedding Blues**
>
> To stop thieves from using stolen cards, many credit card companies automatically cut off credit if a card is used more than six times a day. If your credit is cut off, it can be difficult to reinstate it, and this could spoil your entire trip. Protect yourself from this policy by calling your credit card company and explaining your plans before leaving on your honeymoon.

Cruisin' on a Sunday Afternoon

The romance of the sea, the freedom to do as much or as little as you want, and the all-inclusive pricing structure are just a few of the reasons that make cruises such popular honeymoons. Cruise vacations can be among the most romantic you can take, so they make wonderful honeymoons. Most of the major charges (room, meals, and entertainment) are covered in the fare, and they can be very reasonable. But you'll pay an additional fee for shore excursions, onboard alcohol, wine with your dinner, and any purchases you may make while on the ship. Most cruise lines ask you to open an onboard account upon arrival and issue a cruise card which is used in lieu of money while you're on the ship. You'll want to be careful about this since the cruise card takes on the feeling of "free money," and you may find that you've run up quite a bill by the time you leave the ship.

311

When booking cruises keep in mind that the prices vary according to your cabin size and location. Inside rooms are always least expensive. The middle of the ship is always smoothest. If you request a double, king-size, or queen-size room, be sure your travel agent checks to make sure you've been assigned what you've requested.

The Cost of Getting to the Ship

Many cruise lines quote their prices with and without airfare and it's wise to do a little research before determining which is most beneficial to you. If you book your airfare through the cruise line, the cruise line assumes the responsibility for getting you on the ship. If the airline is late, causing you to miss the ship departure time, the cruise line will make arrangements to get you on the ship. If you book your own airline to the departure port, you're responsible for arriving before the ship departs. Since airline delays are always a possibility, you'll want to make sure you allow yourself plenty of time. Of course, if that means arriving at the departure port the day before departure, add the cost of your hotel room and meals into the equation to determine if what you're saving by booking your own airfare is really the savings you think it will be.

Wedding Blues

If you're prone to seasickness, purchase a pair of wristbands with little metal buttons that put pressure on the inside of your wrist. These offer a natural way to avoid seasickness, similar to acupressure. Or try "the patch"—a little circular bandage that dispenses a drug, which you put behind your ear. Discuss your options and possible side affects with your prescribing physician.

Getting More for Your Money

There are cruises to fit just about any budget. It's important to book early so you'll be able to coordinate the ship, ports, and dollars that are most important to you. An interesting point about a cruise is that the cabins are priced based on location and view. On the same ship you may have guests paying $800 per person for an inside cabin and $4,500 per person for a multiple room outside suite with a balcony. Once you're on the ship, everything else is the same whether you're sleeping in a penthouse cabin with a balcony or in a cabin on one of the least popular decks. Everyone uses the same facilities, and everyone eats the same meals! If you won't be spending much time in your cabin, then book the least expensive cabin.

Once you know what's most important to you, you'll be able to decide which of your travel agent's suggestions you can pass up and which you can accept to save money on your cruise. For instance, you may decide to book your cruise on a slightly older ship and save money by making only that one change. If you can be very flexible and allow the cruise line to select the location and size of your room, you'll save money. (You may find yourself in a nicer cabin than you would have otherwise been able to afford.) You would simply instruct your travel agent to book you into an outside cabin (the least expensive location) and let the cruise line do the rest. You would be guaranteed the outside room but might be surprised with its location.

The Right Time to Sail

If you can time it correctly, you can take a *repositioning cruise*. That's a cruise that moves a ship from one series of ports to the next. For instance, in the spring, cruise lines move their ships from the Caribbean to Alaska to begin a series of cruises in the inland waterways. If you pick up the ship in the Caribbean and sail to Seattle or Vancouver, you can have a very interesting cruise. There are unique ports and the company generally charges less for these cruises, since the ships have to make the trip anyway. The ships make the reverse route in the fall, so you may want to consider booking the ship from Vancouver or Seattle back to the Caribbean.

Keep in mind that you're *beginning* your life of travel together. There will be other opportunities to take another cruise down the road—perhaps on a bigger ship or for a longer time. If you really want to take a cruise vacation, but can't swing seven or 10 days right now, consider a four-day cruise. You'll have all the entertainment, meals, and romance of the seven- or ten-day cruises, but at a lower rate.

If you're definitely booking a cruise vacation, be sure to consider the departure dates with your wedding in mind. Many cruise ships begin their travel on a Saturday or Sunday, so if your wedding is on a weekend, you won't be able to get married and set sail on the same day. Some of the four-day cruises actually leave during the week, so this may be another option for you to consider.

Renting a Car

If you've decided to go to an exciting city for your honeymoon, you may need to rent a car. Again, your travel agent will be able to help you get the best price during your stay.

Sue's Suggestions

If seasickness might be a problem, select a short cruise that puts you in ports every day. This way, if you do run into rough waters (which is rare in the Caribbean), you'll be getting off the ship frequently.

Language of Love

Most cruise ship companies have their ships in warm locations in the winter months and in colder locations in the summer months. For example, one ship may cruise the Eastern Caribbean from October to May and then to go Alaska from May to October. Thus, the ship would travel between Alaska and the Caribbean twice a year. The cruise company would love to have passengers onboard for these **repositioning cruises** to keep their onboard crew busy and to help defray the cost of the cruise. These cruises may be very economical and, depending on your timing, something to look into.

Hidden Charges

Be especially careful about hidden charges. Some of these might be a drop-off charge if you're returning your vehicle to a location other than the one where you picked it up. For instance, if you rented a car in Los Angeles and wanted to return it in San Francisco, you would pay a fee for the rental company to get the car back to Los Angeles. Another hidden charge might be gasoline. If the rental car company wants the car returned with a full tank of gas and you forget, they'll do it for you. But they always seem to charge you the highest possible price for gasoline, so make it a point to stop for gas on your own somewhere near the airport and fill it up.

Some companies offer a flat fee for refilling the tank, which is often lower than what you would pay for the actual refill by the company. But it's still more than you'd pay if you filled the tank yourself. The best policy is for you to fill the tank yourself before returning the car.

Check out the company's policy on the age of renters. Many companies do not rent vehicles to drivers under the age of 25. Some do, but with a daily surcharge or a higher deposit. All companies will expect you to answer the questions about insurance and will attempt to charge you a daily insurance fee for the automobile. Many credit cards provide insurance coverage for you while you're driving a rented vehicle. It's important to check with your credit card company to understand any coverage and to check with your regular automobile insurance company, as well, on this issue. You may already be covered and won't need to be concerned about insurance at all.

Tantalizing Trivia

Be sure to inform your automobile insurance company when you get married. You will want to be sure your husband or wife is insured on the vehicle that you have been driving and may also want to list his or hers on your policy. If you and your spouse have been using different insurance companies prior to your marriage, you will probably want to begin using either one or the other. Most companies offer lower rates if you insure more than one vehicle (some even discount further if your home is also insured through them) and for married couples than they do for single young men. Surprisingly, if a young couple gets divorced, the man's insurance rate stays low, but the woman's increases!

Watch Your Mileage

Be sure to keep track of your mileage while in the rental car. Many companies offer free, unlimited miles but others limit your mileage to 100 miles a day. If you exceed this limit, the per-mile charge can be quite expensive. You'll also want to be sure you understand what the company considers a "day." Your first day may end at midnight if the company is calculating calendar days, or your day may run for 24 hours from the time you picked up the car. Be sure to ask how the day is calculated and what the penalty will be if you return the car more than one hour after the time it's due back. Some companies charge you for a whole new day one minute after the time due back. Other companies offer a break-down fee. In other words, if the car is due back at 1:00 P.M. but you return it at 2:30 P.M., you pay an additional quarter day for that extra period of time. If you're renting the car from the airport and plan to return it to that same airport, try to negotiate the return time to coordinate with the departure time of your flight.

Sue's Suggestions

To save on car rentals, check the newspaper and the Internet for advertised specials. (Try www.travel-zoo.com for discounts online or www.vacationweb.com for direct links to the automobile rental agencies.) Write down the detail of the promotion including the discount code (in small print). Try for weekend rates that frequently start on Thursday at noon and extend until noon on Monday. If you'll be returning your vehicle on Sunday, ask for further discounts.

Odds and Ends

The name on your rental agreement and the name on your driver's license and credit card all must match. Don't use your new name when you make the reservation if you don't have any identification in that name. Better still, make the reservation in your husband's name and make him the primary driver. Be sure to understand the company's policy on "primary driver" versus another driver. You want to be sure you can relieve your husband when he's tired of driving, without breaking any important rules.

Car rental companies sometimes put an advance hold on the entire estimated amount of your car rental. If they do this, you may not be able to use your credit card for other things without going over your limit. You can avoid this problem by calling the credit-card company and having your limit increased before the wedding weekend. You

Sue's Suggestions

Car rental companies often need to reposition their vehicles from one part of the country to another to be ready for seasonal business. If you can plan the time correctly, you may be able to drive to your destination at a reduced rate. But you'll have to pay the regular price on the way back home (or you may decide to fly), so research this before making your decision.

may also want to have a second card for restaurants, activities, and souvenirs, and use your regular card for the car rental and hotel, only.

You may be entitled to car rental discounts that you didn't think of. Automobile Association of America (AAA) offers discounts on car rentals to their members and does the American Medical Association (AMA). Some corporations will get discounted rates on car rentals as well. Check these out before renting your vehicle.

A Few Tips About Tipping

Most people have no difficulty determining how much to tip the waiter at their favorite restaurant, but don't travel enough to know how to tip the people they'll come in contact with on their honeymoon. Here are some easy guidelines:

Wedding Blues

When you pick up your traveler's checks at the bank, be sure to get several one dollar bills for tips. It's fine to give a cab driver a five-dollar bill and ask for change, but one does not do that to a skycap.

Sue's Suggestions

Keep your tip money in one section of your wallet and your larger bills somewhere else in the wallet so you don't accidentally pull out a bigger bill than you intended.

➤ *Porters and skycaps* should be tipped $1.00 per bag; if extra service is provided, such as leading you to the head of the check-in line, plan on tipping more.

➤ *Taxi or limousine drivers* should be tipped 15 to 20 percent of the fare, depending on the service you receive, and more if the driver loads and unloads your bags. Sometimes gratuities are included in your limousine contract, so be sure to ask when you book the limousine.

➤ *Tour bus drivers and tour guides* should be tipped 10 percent of the cost of the tour per person.

➤ *Hotel bellhops* should be tipped $1.00 per bag (more if extra services are provided).

➤ *Hotel housekeepers* should be tipped $2.00 per day per guest. Leave this money in the room either with a note or in an envelope that says "For Housekeeping."

➤ *Hotel concierges* should be tipped if they provide a special service, such as obtaining theater tickets for you. The amount varies, but 10 percent of the value of the item procured is standard.

➤ *Room service delivery people* should be tipped 10 to 15 percent of the bill, with a minimum of $2.00. If you receive extra special or particularly speedy service, you'll probably want to tip more than is recommended.

➤ *Waiters and waitresses* generally receive an extremely small salary and depend on their tips. If you're in a situation where all meals are included, you should tip at the end of your stay. If gratuities are included, but you feel that you've received exceptional service, leave an additional 5 to 10 percent—it will certainly be appreciated. If you're going to a restaurant, tip as you would in your own home town.

➤ *The maitre d'* should be tipped $5.00 to $10.00 when you enter the restaurant—you'll be assured a first-rate table and seating on a busy night. If you will be eating most or all your meals in this restaurant during your honeymoon, tipping the maitre d' at the beginning of the honeymoon will help him remember you, and if you should have special needs, he will want to assist you with them.

Cruises present a slightly different tipping situation. On a cruise everything is included in your cruise fee, except your on-ship alcohol, shore excursions, any gambling you might choose to do, and any purchases you make. You'll be served three meals a day and as many additional meals as you wish. When you're served drinks anywhere on the ship, the tip is already added into the cost of the drink. In the dining room, if you decide to order wine with your dinner, either by the bottle or the drink, you should tip the wine steward for each order.

At the end of the cruise you'll be provided with labeled envelopes to make it easy for you to tip the people who have assisted you throughout the cruise. The suggested tips are $3.50 per person per day for your waiter, and $2.00 per person per day for your assistant waiter. Your head waiter (this is usually the person who tosses your special salad and makes the flaming desserts) may be tipped an amount you believe to be appropriate, but it's suggested that this amount be between the amount given to the assistant waiter and the waiter. It's suggested that your room steward receive $3.50 per person per day. Of course, you certainly may tip each of these people more than the suggested amount. The cruise ships pay their employees very little money and the staff depends on their tips for their salary. These amounts are printed in the materials you receive from the cruise line. You will see them in the information packets you will be sent in advance of the cruise and again in the next-to-the-last daily "newspaper" that will be delivered to your room. The purser's office on the ship will supply you with envelopes labeled for each of the staff members you are expected to tip.

Planning Ahead to Use Your Frequent-Traveler Programs

If you've decided to use a credit card to pay for a portion of your wedding expenses, be sure you select one that offers premiums. Naturally, low interest is the most important consideration, but if you're planning to pay your bill in full each month, the perks can be very beneficial. Some cards offer points per dollars purchased that can be transferred to a variety of airlines and hotels to earn free tickets or complimentary nights.

By planning ahead and purchasing everything you possibly can on your credit card, you can earn a lot of miles in a relatively short time. Use the card at the grocery store, at your hair salon, at gas station, and even the bridal shop where you buy your wedding gown. Of course, you'll want to exercise enough restraint to charge only as much as you can afford to pay off each month in full. Never lose sight of the fact that you're trying to save money, not put yourself deeply in debt.

If you've been planning your wedding for a while and using the same credit card all that time, you may actually have accumulated enough points for free airfare on your honeymoon. But getting frequent-flyer points is sometimes easier than using them, because airlines allow only a certain number of seats to be booked by frequent travelers. Call well in advance and reserve the seats on the flight you want. Awards programs vary, but in many, you have just a month to get your tickets, so you make sure your plans are definite before you ask for the tickets. The airlines expect you to "convert" your award into a ticket within one month of requesting the reward. But if you have the points, you can convert them as much as 12 months before you travel.

Have a Safe Trip

I've always found it curious that when we leave on a vacation, friends and family wish us a "safe trip." We're going away for fun, romance, and adventure, relaxation, and sightseeing, so why the caution to be safe? Exactly for that reason—so many of us concentrate on the romance, fun, and excitement of the trip that we may neglect the common-sense cautions we normally apply to our daily lives. When we're someplace not familiar to us, we can be unaware of the dangers we face. For instance, there are areas in my hometown where I would never consider walking alone after dark, but wherever I may travel I frequently walk around in the neighborhood of my hotel without giving my safety a second thought. Even though most honeymooners spend their time together, and not alone, you'll still need to think about your safety as a couple.

Wedding Blues

If either you or your spouse like to run or jog, be sure to ask the concierge to recommend a safe and scenic route for you to take. You may also want to ask if the route is the same if you exercise early in the morning and late in the evening. It may not be.

Choosing the Right Hotel

Being safe on your honeymoon starts with selecting the right hotel. When you're speaking to your travel agent or to the hotel directly, ask if the hotel is located in an area with shops and restaurants nearby. If it is, you'll know that it's on a well-trafficked street. This generally means you'll be safer when you walk back to the hotel after dark. If the hotel is located in an office park or even a residential area, the streets will likely be deserted after dark, and you should plan to travel by cab when returning to the hotel after dinner. Once you've arrived at the hotel, ask the concierge about areas where it may be safe to walk or jog. Even if you're not in the habit of jogging, knowing that it's considered safe to do so in the area will put your mind at ease.

Keep Those Numbers Secret

The hotel should have provisions to make your check-in process private. No other guest should be able to overhear your name or room number. The room number actually should be written on the key envelope, not spoken out loud or inscribed on the key. This way, anyone finding your key will not have access to your room. Once you're in the room, leave the key envelope there and carry only the key with you. If the key card has a magnetic strip on it, find out how to handle it so you don't inadvertently erase the code. If you've driven to the city, or rented a car, you'll want to know if the hotel has its own parking garage that is well lit. If you've decided to use the valet parking option, check on the hours that it's available.

You have the right to inspect your room before accepting it. Rooms nearest the elevator will be the noisiest, because other guests congregate there while they wait for the elevator. If there's an ice machine on your floor you can expect that area to be somewhat noisy also. Although you'll want to be aware of the location of emergency exits, you don't necessarily need to be near them—uninvited guests might be able to gain access to your floor through them. The door in your room should have double locks (one should be a dead bolt) and a peephole. For extra security, bring along a rubber doorstop so you can prevent anyone from entering your room once you're in it.

Come on In!

When you leave your hotel room, don't put out the sign asking the housekeeper to make up the room. This is notice to everyone on the floor that you're not in your room. If you want the room cleaned early, it's much wiser to call housekeeping and ask for the room to be cleaned by a specific time. However, using the "Do Not Disturb" sign and leaving the television on can make the room seem occupied and can discourage intrusion. It should go without saying that jewelry, tickets, extra money, and passports should always be placed in the hotel safe—the one in your room or at the front desk.

Hang expensive clothing under other clothing (bathrobes, raincoats), since thieves "shop" what they can see. If your bag is taken from your room, enlist the management to search for it. Most hotel robberies are committed by the staff and for this

Sue's Suggestions

If the hotel doesn't have individual safety deposit boxes for guests, place your valuables in a manila envelope, seal it, and write your name diagonally across the sealed envelope flap. Then cover your signature with a piece of clear tape and ask the clerk to place it in the main hotel safe. It will be impossible for anyone to open your envelope without destroying the signature.

reason, many properties do not allow employees to leave with packages; the thieves take the money and dump the rest.

Don't Be an Easy Mark

While you may love being a tourist, looking like one on the street can make you easy prey to the unscrupulous among us. Study your maps before going out and try to avoid standing on a street corner checking the map. If you can't find what you're looking for, you'll be safer asking directions of a shopkeeper than you will be asking someone on the street.

Wedding Blues

Carry only one credit card in your wallet at a time. Make sure you have a photocopy of this credit card with your travel documents so you'll be able to report the number if the card is stolen.

Wear little or no jewelry. A new bride may even want to consider wearing a plain gold wedding band instead of her beautiful diamond engagement ring and wedding band set. Jewelry calls attention to you, and it may not be the type of attention you want. Men should carry their wallets in their front pockets or in fanny packs and be especially careful getting on and off buses or trains where pickpockets tend to strike. Traveler's checks in small denominations are the best money to carry; make sure you record the numbers and keep them in a safe place (separate from the checks).

You may also want to keep a separate stash of small bills (ones, fives, and tens), so you can easily pull tips and cab fare out of your wallet without exposing a wad of money. And speaking of taxis, it's a good idea to stay inside the taxi until you're certain you've been delivered to the right address. Then, while still inside the vehicle, pay the driver and collect your change. This will protect you from the driver pulling away without giving you the appropriate change.

Make yourself comfortable with the currency in the location that you'll be traveling to and with its approximate exchange value. These values can fluctuate almost daily, so you won't always get the same amount of local currency when you exchange a specific amount of money. Most experienced travelers recommend that you exchange only enough money to cover one day's travel at a time. You'll also want to be sure that you're not left with a large amount of foreign currency when your trip is over. Some people spend half a day trying to find the most favorable exchange; but generally the difference between the best rate and the worst rate is less than two dollars per one hundred dollars exchanged. This may be a factor to you but is it worth half a day on your honeymoon? To get the best exchange rate, experienced travelers recommend using your credit card for purchases and ATM cards for cash—it's safer, too.

If you rent a car in your honeymoon destination, use the same cautious behavior you employ at home. Naturally, you'll familiarize yourself with the basic rules of the road in this location, especially in a foreign country, and pay close attention to these regulations. Keep maps, guide books, and luggage out of sight. This may mean not renting a hatchback vehicle where suitcases may be visible in the trunk. If someone bumps your vehicle or tries to get your attention, don't stop until you're in a well-lit, busy area, or stay in the car and honk the horn until someone comes to your aid. Even police do not expect you to stop for them unless they're in a well-marked vehicle. They expect you to drive within the speed limit and find a lighted area before you stop. It's always a good idea to carry a cell phone with you, so bring your own from home or rent a vehicle that comes with one and put the local police department on your speed dial.

These simple techniques will help you enjoy your honeymoon, and all the other wonderful trips you'll take in your married life. So pack up and have a safe trip!

Sue's Suggestions

Keep an eye on the exchange rate while you're out of the country. This fluctuates almost daily. Sometimes it's in your favor, and your dollars will have more buying power; other times it's not in your favor. On those days, don't go shopping!

The Least You Need to Know

➤ Make arrangements for someone to come by your hotel and pick up your wedding gown if you plan to leave your wedding reception wearing it.

➤ Reading the whole travel brochure will give you the best picture of what you can expect of your honeymoon destination.

➤ Once you have decided on a specific cruise itinerary and ship, the pricing is based on the size and location of your cabin. Everything else on the ship is available to everyone.

➤ You will need a credit card in your own name to rent a car.

➤ Many of the people who assist you during your honeymoon will depend on your tips for their income.

➤ Be safe to enjoy your honeymoon to the fullest.

Glossary of Wedding Attire

Alencon lace   Named for a city in France, this is needlepoint lace with a delicate floral or leaf design. Patterns are outlined in a heavy **cordonnet.**

A-line skirt   A skirt that fits close at the waist and tapers to a flared hem.

ankle length   A skirt length that graces the ankle.

antebellum waist   A natural waist that dips approximately two inches to a point in the center front. This style of waist was originally seen in ladies attire after the Civil War.

appliqué   An embellished fabric or lace applied to the dress.

apron   A fabric overskirt joined to the dress at the back of the waist.

ascot   A broad scarf that is looped under the chin, named for the racetrack in Ascot, England, where it was originally worn.

asymmetrical waist   An angled-waist design that falls to one side of the natural waist.

ballerina length   A full skirt that ends above the ankle. Ballerina length is shorter than ankle length.

banana clip veil   A curved hair ornament with a spring grip decorated with silk flowers, beading, and tulle.

Basque waist   A waistline that drops approximately 2 inches below the natural waist and dips to a point in the center front of the skirt.

bateau neckline   A neckline forming a straight line across the collarbone to the tip of the shoulders. Sometimes called a boat neck.

batiste   A soft, delicate summer fabric made of cotton or a cotton-linen blend. Its texture is fine and sheer.

bell sleeve   A long sleeve that flares gently from the shoulder to the wrist.

Bertha collar   A cape of fabric or lace attached to the neckline for a shawl effect.

bishop sleeve   A full sleeve that ends in a gathered band at the wrist.

black tie   Referring to formal attire, generally the black bow tie that is worn with a tuxedo.

blouson   The drooping fullness in fabric from the bodice to the waist, gathered at or below the waist.

blusher veil   The short veil that covers the bride's face during the processional.

bodice   The part of the gown covering the body above the waistline.

bolero   A short jacket that ends above the waist, usually worn open at the front.

bouffant skirt   A full, puffed-out, flaring skirt.

bow sleeve   A short sleeve constructed of looped fabric formed in the shape of a bow.

bow veil   A looped ribbon of elegant fabric and tulle worn at the nape of the neck or crown.

branches   Decorative bead extensions used on headpieces.

brocade   A heavy woven fabric with a raised design.

brush train   A very short train that just sweeps (or brushes) the floor.

Brussels lace   Named for the town in Belgium where it originated, this is a light, delicate lace with a subtle floral pattern.

bubble skirt   A full skirt with the hem attached to the lining, which creates a rounded, airy edge.

bugle beads   Long, tubelike beads.

bustle back   An exaggerated fullness in the rear of the skirt, built with a pad or frame. The train of the gown can be lifted into a bustle for ease of movement at the reception.

butterfly   The design the gathered fabric or train creates as it is folded into a bustle at the back waist of a wedding or formal gown.

cameo neckline   A decorative circular motif in the center front of the bodice of the gown.

cap sleeve   A short sleeve that barely covers the top of the arm.

capelet sleeve   A sleeve that falls several inches below the elbow in a soft flare.

capelet train   A train that flows from the back of the shoulders. Capelet trains may be cathedral length, chapel length, or court length, but their measurements start at the shoulder instead of at the waist.

cathedral train   A train that extends three yards from the waist.

Chantilly lace   A soft, weblike pattern of lace named for Chantilly, France, where the pattern originated. The pattern is characterized by scrolls, branches, and flowers. Generally, the edge is scalloped on bridal gowns.

chapel train   A train that extends a yard and a half from the waist.

charmeuse   A soft, flexible fabric, usually shiny. It can be satin, silk, or synthetic.

chintz   Printed cotton fabric with a polished finish.

chuppah   The covering under which Jewish brides and grooms are married. It is symbolic of the home the couple will create.

circular skirt   A very full skirt that is attached smoothly at the waist and forms a complete circle at the hem.

Cluny lace   Lace made of linen thread, named for Cluny, France, where it was first seen.

cordonnet   A thread, cord, or yarn used to outline a lace motif.

court train   A train that extends one yard from the waist.

crepe   A fluid, thin fabric often displaying a crinkled or ridged pattern.

crepe de chine   A soft, light, thin fabric of silk, cotton, polyester, or rayon.

crinoline   The underskirt used to add fullness to a skirt.

crown   A traditional half-circle headpiece reminiscent of the headpieces worn by royalty.

cummerbund   A broad waistband usually worn by men in formal attire instead of a vest. When it is pleated, the pleats are worn open side up to catch any "crumbs" that might fall into the gentleman's lap. An adapted version of this waistband is also seen in women's attire.

cutaway/morning coat   A style of tuxedo worn before noon. This longer style jacket tapers from the front waist to the back.

cut-outs   The see-through effect created by cutting out the fabric from behind lace appliques.

décolletage   A plunging neckline that reveals cleavage.

detachable train   Fabric that is attached to the gown with hooks and eyes during the wedding ceremony, but is removed for the reception.

details A general term for decorations on a gown.

dolman sleeve A sleeve that is very wide at the armhole and tight at the wrist. It's usually a continuation of the fabric of the bodice.

drop waist A waistline that falls is several inches below the natural waist.

embroidery A pattern sewn onto fabric usually with colored thread.

empire waist A waistline that begins two inches above the natural waist, just below the bustline.

English net Fine, sheer, cotton netting. Often the base of embroidered lace.

eyelet Cotton fabric decorated by small round holes finished around the edges with embroidery.

faille Stiff textured fabric with a slightly riblike weave.

fitted bodice A body-hugging **bodice.**

fitted sleeve A narrow, usually long, sleeve.

floor length A hemline $1\frac{1}{2}$ to 2 inches from the floor.

forehead band veil A decorated strip of fabric worked across the forehead with veiling attached.

four-in-hand tie A necktie tied in a slip knot with long tails overlapping vertically in the front. It is the style most men wear with business suits today.

full skirt A gathered skirt, usually less full than **bouffant** style.

garden hat A hat with a large round crown and wide brim, with or without veiling attached to the back of the crown.

gauntlet The lace or fabric that covers the hands and arms but not the fingers; usually has a loop that the second finger goes through.

Georgette Silk or synthetic crepe with a dull texture and soft drape.

Gibson sleeve A sleeve that is full at the shoulder and fitted at the wrist.

gusset A triangular piece of fabric inserted into seam of a garment to create fullness. Also called a godet.

half-hat veil Slightly larger than a Juliet cap, the half hat fits snugly on the head, mid-crown.

hair-comb veil A hair comb decorated with silk flowers, beading, and tulle. It can be inserted into a French twist hairdo so that the attached veil comes from the bottom of the hair comb.

headband veil The veiling attached to the decorated strip of fabric covering the headband.

hoopskirt   Circular stays in the underskirt which keep the skirt full.

illusion   A silk tulle fabric used primarily for veils.

jersey   A soft, fluid fabric with a matte finish.

jewel neckline   A round neckline that fits closely to the natural neckline where a short necklace would naturally fall.

Juliet cap   A headpiece that fits snugly over the crown of the head like a skull cap.

keyhole   A teardrop-shaped opening, usually at the neckline or back of the bodice.

leg o' mutton   A full sleeve, puffed at shoulder, that fits tightly on forearm.

Lyon lace   Named for Lyon, France, where it originated, this is a bobbin lace with predominately dainty floral patterns outlined in a cordonnet. This is the most expensive lace used on wedding gowns.

mantilla veil   A veil trimmed with heavy lace and often worn over a small cap to add height.

mermaid skirt   A skirt that fits tight over the hips and flares below the knee. Sometimes called a **trumpet skirt.**

midriff   The middle of the bodice, between the chest and waist.

moiré   A watery or wavelike effect in a silk or synthetic fabric.

natural waistline   The line where the bodice and skirt join at the normal waist position.

net   An open-thread weave fabric often used in veils.

organdy   A stiff, semi-sheer cotton fabric with a crisp finish.

organza   A silk version of **organdy.**

panniers   Exaggerated gathers, usually supported by a cage, worn on the hips.

peau de soie   A blended fabric with a light, silky texture and a dull satinlike finish.

peek-a-boo   The effect created when a different fabric shows through a sheer fabric on top.

peplum   A short overskirt or flounce attached at the waist.

petal sleeve   Layered panels that create a short sleeve.

pillbox hat   A small, round, brimless hat with a flat crown. It is worn straight on the head, not tipped in any direction.

poet sleeve   A sleeve that is pleated at shoulder with fullness through to the cuff.

point d'espirit   Net fabric with an overall pattern of either ovals or square dots.

pointed sleeve   A long sleeve that ends in a point on the top of the hand.

polyester   a synthetic fabric that does not wrinkle easily. When blended with other fabrics, it adds durability and reduces wrinkles.

poly-organza   A summer-weight fabric of double-layer construction.

poly-silk chiffon   A sheer, summery fabric often used in dresses with multi-layered skirts. It is more durable than silk-chiffon.

poly-silk organza   A sheer, crisp, blended summer-weight fabric.

portrait neckline   A neckline that is created by wrapping a piece of fabric around the shoulders and bust line to "frame" the top of the dress.

pouf   A fabric overskirt gathered up with lace, ribbons, or beading.

princess line   A skirt that is slightly flared, skimming the body and emphasizing the waist. Usually no seam joins the bodice with the skirt.

puff sleeve   A very full, short sleeve that can be worn on or off the shoulder.

Queen Anne neck   A sculptured design, high on the back and sides of the neck.

Queen Elizabeth neckline   A high portrait neckline that stands up in the back and closes in a V at the front neckline.

raised waist   A waistline that hits about 1 inch above waist.

raw silk   Silk fabric characterized by random raised slugs (thickening in the fabric).

rayon satin   A heavy, blended shiny fabric. If not properly reinforced, this fabric will unravel.

redingote   A dress or coat, often belted, worn open in the front to reveal a dress or petticoat beneath.

rhinestone   A shiny, artificial gem used to decorate gowns.

royal train   The longest train available at more than three yards from waist.

ruche   A piece of pleated fabric used to trim the gown.

ruffle   A strip of fabric or lace gathered along one edge.

Sabrina neckline   A straight neckline that begins two inches inside the shoulder line.

satin   A smooth–surfaced, heavy fabric with either a shiny or matte finish.

Schiffli embroidery   Machine-made lace in fine, delicate patterns. It is most effective when made of cotton.

scoop neckline   A rounded, low neckline.

sequin   A small, shiny disc or spangle used for decoration.

sheath   A straight, fitted gown, often with a detachable train.

shirred waistline   Gathered fabric that creates a horizontal panel at waist.

silk chiffon   A sheer tissuelike fabric, usually used in dresses with multi-layered skirts. It's most effective when worn in spring and summer.

silk organza   A sheer, crisp material used in summer gowns. It wrinkles easily.

silk-faced satin   Traditionally a winter fabric due to its heavy weight and sheen.

snood   A delicate netting that covers the hair, sometimes fronted with a headband and decorated with silk flowers, pearls, and bows. It can be worn as an alternative to a veil.

suttee   Appliqués of ribbons or cords that are applied to a garment to create a curved design.

strapless gown   A gown designed to reveal the shoulders with no support from straps.

stroller/walking coat   A style of tuxedo jacket that is longer than a suit coat but shorter than a morning coat.

sweep train   A train that sweeps the ground as you walk. It is slightly longer than a **brush train.**

sweetheart neckline   An open neckline that starts 2 inches inside the shoulder and is shaped like a heart.

taffeta   A light or medium fabric in silk or synthetic, characterized by a smooth, crisp plain weave.

tailcoat   A style of men's formalwear in which the jacket front and sides are cut to the waist but two pieces of fabric extend down the center back approximately to the knees.

tea length   Describes a hemline that falls between the knee and ankle.

tiara   A jeweled, crownlike headpiece.

tiered skirt   A series of layered panels that fall from the waist in graduated lengths.

train   Gown fabric that trails behind the bride as she walks.

trumpet skirt   A skirt flared below the knee. It is sometimes called a **mermaid skirt.**

Tudor hat veil   A veil attached to a headpiece with a peaked crown and a narrow brim in front.

tulle   A sheer, stiff material used both in veils and skirts.

tuxedo   A generic term applied to male formal wear.

V neck   A neckline that is V-shaped in the front.

velvet   A cold-weather fabric made of silk, cotton, or a silk and cotton blend. It has a thick, soft pile with a matte finish. Velvet can be taken in if the dress is too large but it can never be let out without leaving a line.

Venice lace   A heavy needlepoint lace with a floral design put in high relief with embroidery or buttonhole stitching. It is sometimes called Venetian point lace.

Victorian style   Describes the typical style of gowns worn in the latter half of the nineteenth century during the Victorian era.

voile   A light, open-weave fabric commonly used for informal gowns.

waistline   The point at which the bodice and skirt come together.

Watteau   Describes the loose, full back of a gown formed by wide box pleats extending from the shoulder to the hem in an unbroken line.

wedding band collar   The traditional, upright collar, encircling the base of the neck.

white tie and tails   Refers to men's formal attire and is a "commandment" that the guest wear a tailcoat, white pique tie, and vest.

wreath   A circular headband of either fresh or silk flowers worn by brides with veiling and by flower girls without.

yoke   A fitted piece of fabric fitted at the neckline, shoulder, or hips, from which the rest of the garment hangs.

Looking for More Information?

Books

There are many books in the library and bookstores on weddings that will be very helpful to you in your planning. Here are just a very few you may want to examine:

Altman, Don. *151 Unique Ways to Make Your Wedding Special.* Los Angeles, CA: Moon Lake Media, 1994.

Editors of *Bride's Magazine. Bride's Wedding Planner.* New York: Fawcett Columbine, 1997.

Dream Weddings. Kansas City, MO: Hallmark Cards, 1989.

Lalli, Cele. *Modern Bride Wedding Celebration.* New York: John Wiley & Sons, 1992.

Lenderman, Teddy. *The Complete Idiot's Guide to the Perfect Wedding,* 2nd ed. New York: Alpha Books, 1997.

Post, Elizabeth. *Emily Post's Complete Book of Wedding Etiquette.* New York: Harper & Row, 1982.

Roney, Carley. *Knot's Complete Guide to Weddings in the Real World.* New York: Broadway Books, 1998.

Ingram, Leah. *Portable Wedding Consultant.* Chicago: Contemporary Books, 1997.

Shaw, David. *Cheapskate's Guide to Weddings and Honeymoons.* Secaucas, NJ: Citadel Press Books, 1996.

The Internet

The Internet is becoming a wonderful source for all kinds of wedding information. The sites listed here are those I especially recommend. They represent just the tip of the iceberg for wedding research:

www.abride.com: This site boasts a one-stop shop for all your wedding needs. Here you can even contact wedding professionals in your state.

www.modernbride.com/: Includes a dress finder and an interactive calendar that allows you to create your own reference and reminder calendar. You can order wedding accessories online at this site, too.

www.theknot.com: Here you'll find ideas for gowns, honeymoons, and planning tips. You can also register for gifts as well.

www.weddingchannel.com: This site shows pictures of wedding gowns and bridesmaid dresses and provides a look at weddings that made the news throughout the century. Also included is a humorous look at etiquette in the nineteenth century.

www.wedding411.com/: This site includes a budget tracker, guest manager, and photo album, as well as tips on planning.

www.women.com/weddings/: At this site you'll find beauty tips and ideas on dealing with a joint checking account, plus a gown finder and other planning tips.

Magazines

National bridal magazines are a tremendous help in planning your wedding and honeymoon, so be sure not to overlook them. Here is a list of magazines available at your local bookstore or newsstand:

Bridal Guide. Published six times a year. Call 1-800-834-9998 for subscription information.

Bride's Magazine. Published six times a year. Each new issue is available on the first day of the previous month. (For example, the June/July issue is on the stands May 1.) For subscription information, call 1-800-456-6162.

Elegant Bride. Published four times each year. Subscriptions are available from Pace Communications at 336-378-6065.

For The Bride. Published quarterly. This magazine features the gowns manufactured by the Ilissa, Watters & Watters, New Image, Champagne Formals and Bill Levkoff companies. For subscription information, call 212-967-5222.

Modern Bride. Published six times a year. Subscriptions are available at 1-800-777-5786.

Wedding Insurance

No couple expects anything to go wrong at their wedding or to find that they'll become responsible for damages they had nothing to do with. When circumstances beyond their control arise, the host and hostess of an event can find unique protection through wedding insurance.

Weddinginsurance is the name of an insurance policy offered by only one insurance retailer in the United States, R.V. Nuccio Agency. There are nine different levels of insurance coverage that you can select to customize your policy. I've included a brief summary of each here. If you're interested in this insurance or would like more information, contact R.V. Nuccio directly at 1-800-ENGAGED.

Coverage 1, Cancellation or Postponement: This coverage will pay up to the policy limit you select, subject to a $250 deductible, for the nonrefundable expenses incurred if the rehearsal, rehearsal dinner, wedding, reception, or honeymoon must be canceled or postponed for certain reasons beyond your control. (Change of heart is *not* covered.)

Coverage 2, Additional Expenses: This coverage will pay up to 25 percent of the limit that you select in Coverage 1 for any additional expenses necessary to arrange alternate services to avoid cancellation or postponement of services covered in Coverage 1.

Coverage 3, Photographs and Video (optional): The policy will pay up to the coverage limit you select, subject to a $250 deductible, to retake photographs if the photographer fails to appear for any reason, or if the original negatives are lost, damaged, stolen, or not properly developed. If the covered loss or damage is to a videotape which was produced by a professional videographer, the policy will pay up to $500 to have a video montage or video compilation made of the photographs and other wedding memorabilia.

Coverage 4, Gifts (optional): Gift coverage will pay to repair or replace nonmonetary gifts that are lost, stolen, or damaged anyplace within the policy territory of the United States.

Coverage 5, Rented Property (optional): This coverage will pay to repair or replace rented property for which you are responsible and which you used to facilitate the production of the wedding (including tents) if lost, stolen, or damaged anywhere within the policy territory of the United States.

Coverage 6, Special Attire (optional): This coverage will pay to repair or replace the bridal gown or other special attire if it is lost, stolen, or damaged (including financial failure of the bridal store).

Coverage 7, Jewelry (optional): This coverage will pay to repair or replace owned, borrowed, or rented jewelry for which you are responsible if it is lost, stolen, or damaged.

Coverage 8, Personal Liability (optional): This coverage (including supplemental defense) will pay up to the coverage limit that you select toward the sums for which you become legally responsible as a result of bodily injury, personal injury, or property damage caused by a covered accident that occurs during the course of a covered event. Host liquor liability is included.

Coverage 9, Medical Payments: This coverage will pay up to $1,000 of reasonable medical expenses for each person who, during the covered event, is injured in an accident covered by the Personal Liability coverage. Medical Payments coverage is included with the Personal Liability coverage.

A Southern Charm Wedding for 150 Guests

The average wedding in the United States today includes 150 people and costs $17,300. With that in mind, the April/May 1999 issue of *Bridal Guide Magazine* asked bridal consultants around the country to plan a complete wedding for $16,000. I was one of those consultants asked to plan such a wedding, and here is an account of it, including the names of the Atlanta wedding professionals who came together to produce this event. At the end, I've included a total budget. As you read about this event, you will find each budgeted item shown in italic.

The wedding was to be held on a Sunday afternoon in May with the ceremony and reception in one of Roswell, Georgia's loveliest historic homes—Naylor Hall. The original part of this home was built in the 1840s by Barrington King for Mr. H. W. Proudfoot and his wife. Mr. King was the son of Roswell's founder, and Mr. Proudfoot was the bookkeeper in his newly constructed Roswell Mill. (This same mill became quite famous later during the "War of Northern Aggression" because it produced the Roswell gray cloth used in Confederate uniforms. It is also reported that in anticipation of Sherman's March to the Sea, huge quantities of Confederate uniforms were taken from the mill and stored at Naylor Hall.) The home was heavily damaged by the Federal troops, but after the war Mr. Proudfoot rebuilt the house and remained there, and in the employ of the mill until his death in 1871. In the late 1930s Colonel Harrison Broadwell purchased the property, naming it Naylor Hall. He is credited with adding the columns, the hand-crafted woodwork, and the portico encompassing the original structure.

Imagine our bride wearing her organza *designer gown and coordinating veil,* both purchased from Discount Bridal Service, Inc. Her hair is styled in a flattering *chignon* by Dennis Barrett of <u>Barrett & Moore Salon</u>. Our bride met Dennis at his shop early on Sunday morning. By opening the salon, Dennis was able to save her money and do a better job on her hair since he had all his equipment handy. (Note: A stylist charges more to meet the bride at her wedding site and less to meet her at the salon, even if the stylist has to open the salon especially for her.)

When Dennis finished her hair, the bride traveled directly to Naylor Hall where Robin Appelbaum of <u>Optimage</u> met her and applied her *make-up* flawlessly. As her make-up was being completed, her *bridal consultant*, Sue Winner from <u>Sue Winner & Associates, Ltd.</u> steamed the gowns and helped the bridesmaids dress. Everyone was ready on time for the photographer.

At exactly 1:00 P.M. the bride descended majestically on her father's arm from a *carriage* provided by the <u>Yellow Rose Carriage Company</u> and drawn by a white horse. They walk across the beautifully landscaped lawn of Naylor Hall in the shade of 100-year-old magnolia and oak trees. As she and her father walked between the rows of guests seated on the lawn, they are accompanied by the music of *harp, flute, and cello* provided by <u>Nancy Enslin Trio</u>. As the bride walks, she is breathless from the beauty of the scene around her. There, standing at the top of the steps is the man of her dreams, her groom. He looks particularly dapper in his *black tuxedo, white vest and bow tie, and black patent shoes* all rented from <u>Formal America Atlanta</u>. She feels a sense of nostalgia as she proudly stands on the porch of this historic home, knowing other brides have stood in this very spot for over 100 years. Behind her she hears the whispers of her 150 guests commenting on the beauty of this facility and a smile of satisfaction crosses her face knowing how economically she planned her wedding. She hears the *minister's* words and realizes that in a few short moments the man of her dreams will be her husband for life.

The bride carries a rounded, hand-tied *bouquet* of open roses, freesia, lilies, and dahlias. The agapanthus ranunculus and spray roses are integrated for a more unique summer feeling. They offer a palette of soft and vibrant colors, creating the best of both worlds. Blush and hot pink, springtime lavender and deep purple, along with a touch of traditional white and a bold splash of yellow! Loops of sheer ribbon integrate the design for a touch of softness and romantic style. The maid of honor and four bridesmaids each carry a small cluster of three dahlias tied with organza ribbons. This great look complements both the bride's bouquet and their lavender *dresses* purchased at discount from <u>Discount Bridal Service</u> and delivered to each bridesmaids home in time for alterations before the wedding. Both mothers and the bride's grandmother are honored with a petite *corsage* of roses and freesia tied with soft, sheer ribbons and pinned to their shoulders.

The groom's *boutonniere* is two blooms of white freesia and a single lavender rose—a perfect complement to the bride's bouquet. The best man and four groomsmen wear single, fragrant freesia blooms, and the two fathers are honored with single roses. All the flowers were provided by <u>Eventscapes, Inc.</u>, who also charges *tax* and a *delivery fee*.

Immediately after being pronounced husband and wife, the bride and groom walk back up the "aisle" sidewalk where they are met by the *horse and carriage* for a short ride around Roswell as the guests move through the front door of the house and into the foyer. Here they get the true sense of the Old South. The parlor rooms are tastefully furnished with antiques and are beautifully decorated. They all lead into the main ballroom. The ballroom is the perfect size for this standup reception, leaving plenty of room for cocktail tables and chairs to be scattered around the dance floor, all draped with the lovely cream damask linen and magnolia blossom centerpieces included in the *facility rental fee.*

As the guests enter the ballroom, they are greeted by white-gloved staff offering *champagne and strawberries* from silver trays. The *hosted bar* in the room offers champagne-based drinks, mimosas, magnolias, and soft drinks appropriate for a warm summer afternoon. (Magnolias are the signature drink of Naylor Hall—a tasty, secret recipe served in tall flutes and garnished with fresh kiwi.)

When the bride and groom return from their ride around Roswell, they are met on the front porch steps by their *photographer* from <u>Wittmayer Studios</u>. Before the ceremony the photographer had photographed the bride with her family and bridesmaids, and the groom with his family and groomsmen, so now he finishes the posed pictures of the bride and groom together. The couple has selected Wittmayer's documentary/candid style of photography which includes seven hours of photography, up to 400 proofs, and two photographers at the wedding. The package further includes a large portrait and 65 photographs in the finest album. For an additional fee, the couple added the *black and white package,* which is photographs taken with black and white equipment for the sharpest images. Naturally, the couple can expand their album, and both sets of parents can order either individual photographs or smaller albums for an additional fee.

While the couple completes their pictures outside, inside the general feeling in the room is one of a lovely afternoon tea, which is enhanced by the serenity of a gracious sun-filled garden setting, complete with topiaries, ivy, classical urns, and garden cherubs. Elegant silver and porcelain add a formal touch to this genteel *buffet,* accented with cloths of pastel brocade and floral prints. The guests are being treated to hors d'oeuvres provided by caterer <u>Affairs to Remember</u>, including:

> Roast filet of beef canapès offered with barissa sauce
>
> Smoked salmon carpaccio with Creole ginger sauce
>
> Plump blush shrimp offered with red seafood sauce
>
> Mascarpone-filled baguettes studded with apricots and almonds
>
> Chilled crab fingers offered with red seafood sauce

The room is filled with music, provided by the <u>Nancy Enslin Trio</u> who have moved their *harp, flute, and cello* inside the house. The music provides a beautiful background for dancing or easy listening music.

On the buffet table are small champagne buckets filled with berries and presented with whipped chocolate cream and lemon crème for dipping. In addition, guests are

337

experiencing absolute bliss as they embark on this new twist to an old favorite—the Sweet Brushetta Bar, which offers an array of bite-sized breads along with a variety of sweet delectable toppings to include:

> Spreadable chocolate ganache
> Rum-spiked whipped cream
> Expresso cannoli cream
> Raspberry jam
> Orange marmalade
> Peanut butter
> Pomegranate syrup
> Honey with walnut pieces
> Dried berries
> Fresh kiwi slices
> Star fruit slices
> Dried apricot halves
> Grilled pineapple quarters
> Coarse grated white chocolate

Battenberg lace napkins and white-glove service are included, naturally! Also available is a beverage presentation of assorted gourmet teas presented from a polished wooden chest, offered with lemon wedges, milk, and appropriate condiments. A cold beverage selection of peach- or raspberry-flavored teas or fresh lemonade is also available.

The *wedding cake* is featured in a special alcove of the room, highlighted with soft lighting installed specifically to show off a wedding cake. After the ceremony, the bridesmaids arranged their bouquets around the cake to decorate the table. The bride ordered her cake from Publix grocery store bakery, and they delivered the cake directly to Naylor Hall. For the 150 guests, she choose a three-tiered chocolate cake with raspberry filling and a butter cream frosting.

At the rehearsal dinner the bride and groom presented their *gifts* to their attendants. They had gone to the Atlanta Apparel Mart and purchased their gifts from The Atlanta Connection, a wholesale jewelry distributor. The bride chose *silver-plated purse mirrors* that were engraved with each bridesmaid's first name. The groom selected *silver-plated pocketknives* and had these engraved with each groomsman's initials. While shopping, the couple decided on *silver-plated bottle stoppers* as favors for all their guests. The Atlanta Connection would have engraved the stoppers at no additional charge, but the couple could not decide what to engrave on them, so they decided to present them to their guests without engraving. The 82 favors (68 couples and 14 of their single guests had responded that they would be at the wedding) were wrapped into *a bundle with white almonds tied with a lavender ribbon printed with the couple's names and wedding date.*

Four months before the wedding the bride selected a lovely *ivory invitation* with an embossed design from local stationer Sincerely, Sue Winner who offers a 20 percent discount on invitations. She ordered 100 invitations (enough to invite the 73 couples and 22 single guests that were on the guest list—a total of 168 people). She did not order reception cards, since the ceremony and reception were both in the same location, but she did order *response cards, card envelopes,* and *100 thank-you notes.* When the bride purchased the *stamps* for her invitations and response cards, she remembered to also purchase stamps for her thank-you notes. On the morning of the wedding she was glad she had acknowledged all the gifts that had arrived before the wedding because, after her honeymoon, she would need to thank only those guests who brought gifts to the wedding.

The bride and groom were delighted when they totaled their expenditures two months before the wedding and realized that they would be able to afford to record their wedding day with a professional *videographer.* After conferring with their bridal consultant and interviewing several videographers, the couple selected Tracey Misner of <u>Videotimes, Inc.</u> They decided on one camera for the ceremony and reception with all the editing and music included.

Guests gathered around the bottom of the front steps of Naylor Hall and showered the couple with handfuls of *birdseed* as they ran from the house to the car parked at the curb. The best man acted as chauffeur and delivered the couple to their apartment to change clothes before they started out on their honeymoon—a driving trip to north Georgia.

As they pulled away, the bride looked over her shoulder and thought, this was perfect—exactly as I dreamed!

The Budget

Item	Retail	Paid	Total
Designer gown	880.00	635.00	
Shipping		26.25	
Tax		42.29	703.50
Veil	166.50	125.13	
Shipping		15.25	
Tax		9.83	150.21
Hairstylist		100.00	
Tip		20.00	120.00
Make-up		85.00	
Tip		17.00	102.00
Bridal consultant		2,200.00	2,200.00
Bridesmaids' gowns	140.00	103.60	
Shipping		15.25	

continues

The Budget   (continued)

Item	Retail	Paid	Total
Tax	0*	0*	
Naylor Hall rental		1,300.00	1,300.00
Carriage		250.00	250.00
Ceremony music		400.00	400.00
Tuxedo		92.50	
Tax		6.48	98.98
Groomsmen's tuxedos		98.98	0*
Minister		300.00	300.00
Bridal bouquet		170.00	
Bridesmaids' bouquet		100.00	
Corsages		45.00	
Boutonnieres		59.00	
Tax & delivery		79.68	453.68
Bar (unlimited for 3 hours, includes tax. tip)		1,500.00	1,500.00
Photographer		2,336.55	
Tax		163.45	2,500.00
Reception Music		600.00	600.00
Food (includes some decor)		2,550.00	
Tip/service		440.60	
Tax		209.40	3,200.00
Cake		210.00	
Tax		14.70	224.70
Bridesmaids' gifts		44.78	
Tax		3.13	47.91
Groomsmen gifts		49.75	
Tax		3.48	53.23
Favors (wine stoppers)		325.20	
Tax		22.75	347.95
Net & almonds		177.46	
Ribbons		208.32	385.78
Invitations	183.60	146.88	
Tax		10.28	157.16
Postage		119.00	119.00
Videographer		1,400.00	1,400.00
Total wedding			**$16,614.10**

* *Not paid for by the couple.*

Master Bridal Consultants

To become a Master bridal consultant, a candidate must first complete the Professional Development Program of the Association of Bridal Consultants and pass the tests to become a professional bridal consultant. Then, three years later when that designation expires, the consultant must continue his or her education to become an accredited bridal consultant. When this designation expires three years later, the consultant then completes the extensive requirements necessary to become a Master bridal consultant. This designation does not expire, and those who go on to achieve this level of certification are viewed as experts in the wedding industry.

To date there are 18 Master bridal consultants in the world. They are …

Frank J. Andonoplas
Bridal Consulting by Frank
Chicago, IL
Phone: 773-275-6804
E-mail: FrankAndon@AOL.com

Beverly Ann Bonner
The Wedding Beautiful
Norwood, MA
Phone: 781-255-1996
E-mail:
wedding@weddingbeautiful.com

Karen DeKay
K D Productions
Daphne, AL
Phone: 334-626-3506
E-mail: KDPROD33@aol.com

Mimi Doke
The Wedding Specialist
Lake Havasu City, AZ
Phone: 520-453-6000
E-mail: wedd@craz.com

Lu Ann Dunn
Artful Parties & Events
Salina, KS
Phone: 913-827-8448

Joyce Edelen
Joyce "A Floral Specialist"
Port Tobacco, MD
Phone: 301-934-9056
E-mail: Joycekeech@olg.com

Renee Grannis
Reston, VA
Phone: 703-4571-1850
E-mail: grannis@erols.com

JoAnn Gregoli
Elegant Occasions, Inc.
New York, NY
Phone: 212-704-0048
E-mail: Elegwed204@aol.com

Mary E. Kelley
Parker, CO
Phone: 303-805-5825
E-mail: mkelley@rmi.net

Gayle Lebanow
Event Design & Management
Palm Beach, FL
Phone: 561-630-0049
E-mail: PartyDiva@aol.com

Teddy Lenderman
Bearable Weddings by Teddy
Terre Haute, IN
Phone: 812-242-2051
E-mail: sdevlende@amber.indstate.edu

Helen F. Louie
Mother of the Bride
Orangevale, CA
Phone: 916-989-1787
E-mail: Wedng4u@aol.com

Lois A. Pearce
Beautiful Occasions
Hamden, CT
Phone: 203-248-2661
E-mail: BeauOccsn@aol.com

Mary A. Rahall
Waldorf Engraving & Printing
Waldorf, MA
Phone: 301-645-0320

JoAnn Swofford
That Special Touch
Berryville, AR
Phone: 870-423-2861
E-mail:
Joann@eurekaphotography.com

Priscilla Vasicek
Forever Yours Weddings
Ypsilanti, MI
Phone: 734-481-8093
E-mail: Foreveryours@ameritech

Sue Winner
Sue Winner & Associates
Atlanta, GA
Phone: 404-255-3804
E-mail: winwed@mindspring.com

Christine M. Young
The Wedding Directory
Rockland, MA
Phone: 781-878-5931
E-mail: WeddingDir@aol.com

Need help with your wedding? Call one of the bridal consultants listed here, or contact The Association of Bridal Consultants at 860-355-0464 (or online at BridalAssn@aol.com) for a referral to a consultant in your area.

Index

Q-R